The Fall of the Turkish Model

The Fall of the Turkish Model

How the Arab Uprisings Brought Down Islamic Liberalism

BY

CIHAN TUĞAL

VERSO

London • New York

First published by Verso 2016

1 3 5 7 9 10 8 6 4 2

Verso
UK: 6 Meard Street, London W1F 0EG
US: 20 Jay Street, Suite 1010, Brooklyn, NY 11201
versobooks.com

Verso is the imprint of New Left Books

ISBN-13: 978-1-78478-332-7 (PB)
ISBN-13: 978-1-78478-331-0 (HB)
eISBN-13: 978-1-78478-334-1 (US)
eISBN-13: 978-1-78478-333-4 (UK)

British Library Cataloguing in Publication Data
A catalogue record for this book is available from the British Library

Library of Congress Cataloging-in-Publication Data
A catalog record for this book is available from the Library of Congress

Typeset in Sabon MT by Hewer Text UK Ltd, Edinburgh
Printed and bound by CPI Group (UK) Ltd, Croydon, CR0 4YY

Contents

ACKNOWLEDGEMENTS

This book was the result of a collective effort, even if all of its faults belong to the author. Michael Burawoy's feedback on the first part of the book, Peter Evans' help with issues of development, and the comments of both over the years on political and social theory, as well as the Egypt–Turkey–Iran comparison, were central to the maturation of my arguments. Kevan Harris and Charles Kurzman read the entire manuscript and offered detailed reviews. Salwa Ismail weighed in with instructive criticism of the Egyptian parts of the book. I also benefited from their suggestions starting with the earlier stages of this comparative project.

Joel Beinin, Vicky Bonnell, Beshara Doumani, Marion Fourcade, Samuel Lucas, Raka Ray, Dylan Riley, Nezar AlSayyad, Berna Turam, Kim Voss, Susan Watkins, Margaret Weir and Tony Wood have all helped sharpen the comparative analysis as my study evolved. Especially helpful in fine-tuning the comparison were Asef Bayat's, Ann Swidler's, Loïc Wacquant's, and Erik Wright's advice. I spent a semester at UCSD, where Richard Biernacki, John H. Evans, David Fitzgerald, Kwai Ng, Akos Rona-Tas, Gershon Shafir and Carlos Waisman contributed to my study of Iran, Egypt and Turkey. The audience's responses at two UCLA presentations (especially remarks by Perry Anderson, Robert Brenner, Rogers Brubaker, Hazem Kandil and Michael Mann) aided some of the conceptualization and comparison. As we worked on a comparative volume together, Cedric de Leon's and Manali Desai's interventions led to the further calibration of my Egypt–Turkey comparison.

Finding my way in Egypt's political and religious mazes wouldn't be possible without Momen el-Husseiny's research assistance. Ghaleb Attrache provided last-minute assistance as I revised the manuscript. Funding from the Hellman Family Faculty Fund (University of California, Berkeley) facilitated some of the research in Egypt.

I wouldn't know how to interpret the 'maelstrom of change' in Turkey if it were not for my daily debates with Aynur Sadet and Özgur Sadet. My discussions of Turkish political economy with Çağlar Keyder and Ayşe Buğra were also immensely stimulating, and thanks to Zafer Yenal I could situate that economy within global capitalist dynamics.

INTRODUCTION

The Charm of the Turkish Model

If American neoconservatives and liberals disagreed on a range of burning issues, they united in their embrace of what they called the 'Turkish model'. Around the turn of the millennium, the celebration of the Turkish model also brought together divided American and European elites: investment in the Turkish model could perhaps suture the wounds of a disintegrating global order. When US President George W. Bush gave a public speech at the end of the 2004 NATO summit in Istanbul, he stood on the grounds of a public university, further buttressing this rare concurrence. The TV cameras captured the magnificent Bosporus Bridge linking Europe and Asia and a beautiful Turkish mosque behind him. Thirty American and Turkish experts had worked on the choice of location and the specific setup.[1] The bridge, as metaphor, informed his speech:

> Your country, with 150 years of democratic and social reform, stands as a model to others, and as Europe's bridge to the wider world. Your success is vital to a future of progress and peace in Europe and in the broader Middle East . . . America believes that as a European power, Turkey belongs in the European Union. Your membership would also be a crucial advance in relations between the Muslim world and the West, because you are part of both. Including Turkey in the EU would prove that Europe is not the exclusive club of a single religion; it would expose the 'clash of civilizations' as a passing myth of history . . . Democratic societies should welcome, not fear, the participation of the faithful.[2]

1 'Tarihi fotoğrafın öyküsü', *Milliyet*, 1 July 2004.
2 'George Bush Addresses the NATO Summit in Turkey', 29 June 2014, theguardian.com.

This inclusive message embraced Tayyip Erdoğan's pious regime, established in 2002. It took dozens of experts to combine these messages and images, but ordinary Turkish citizens had, in their own ways, already become virtuosos of such bricolage. When veiled women first started to drive SUVs in the 1990s, old-style secularists reacted furiously: how could the marvels of technology be polluted by signs of backwardness? By the 2000s, the practice had become so widespread that the reaction lost its meaning. Indeed, businesses capitalized on this articulation of dissimilar signs. In 2014, a booming conservative clothes company decorated the billboards of Istanbul with the image of two young women, fashionably clothed but veiled, driving a chic red convertible and looking around with coy smiles (rather than watching the road). Ultimately, even the anti-Islamists came to understand that pious people were wholeheartedly embracing many aspects of Western modernity, though they were still disturbed by the political implications of this convergence: Would the Islamists do away with democracy and personal freedoms once fully entrenched in power? Such doubts were sidelined in global public discourse, enchanted as it was by the bridge metaphor.

In the summer of 2013, however, new images started to populate the media: the tear gas used against peaceful Turkish protesters, gas masks that became everyday accessories and the prime minister's frequent posturing with the Rabia sign (a four-fingered salute). Erdoğan's government mercilessly repressed the protests in Istanbul's Gezi Park; the police even killed protestors elsewhere in June. Soon afterwards, Erdoğan and his followers adopted the Rabia sign in solidarity with the uprising against the recent coup in Egypt, during which Islamists were massacred in Rabia Square (to which the four-fingered sign refers).[3] While aggressively undermining liberties at home, Erdoğan thus fashioned himself as supporting the slain Egyptian protestors, suggesting that his party defended civil liberties only for practising Muslims.

---

3 *Rabia* means fourth in Arabic. For the global war over this symbol and what it implies for the Turkish leadership of Muslims, see 'What This Hand Gesture Means for Egypt's Future', *Atlantic*, 17 September 2013; and 'Rabaa Sign Becomes the Symbol of Massacre in Egypt', aa.com.tr, 16 August 2013.

Since the violent suppression of the protests during the summer of 2013, global circles have been perturbed by the following questions: what happened to Erdoğan's liberalizing political party, which had brought so many freedoms to the country? Are liberal Muslims becoming more conservative? Will Erdoğan become the leader of a regional, Islamic uprising, as presaged by his flashing the Rabia sign? These worries are perhaps justified, but the questions are not asked in the right way. This book advances the argument that the successful liberalization in Turkey during the last three decades itself paved the way for Islam's later authoritarian and conservative incarnations. Moreover, the proper answer has to integrate an analysis of not only Turkey's own trajectory, but of the rise of authoritarianism and conservatism on a global scale, as captured by the spread of police state techniques and the 'smell of tear gas' across much of the globe.[4] Although not a comprehensive account of that global scene, this book puts the liberalization of Islam within the context of Middle Eastern (and secondarily global) developments, to which revolts are central.

The last thirty-five years of the Middle East are full of revolutionary and pseudo-revolutionary dramas. Counter-revolts follow revolts. Inept leaders and organizations claim the pedestal of revolution only to carry out restoration. Their attempts at containment are clumsy and sooner or later give rise to new revolts.

The first major manoeuvre to absorb the Middle Eastern revolution came with the Islamic Republic of Iran, which erected a highly contradictory and explosive Islamic state (initially and temporarily) based on clerical-merchant containment of the urban revolts of 1978–79. In the decades that followed, the surrounding regimes scrambled for bits and pieces of 'Islam', democratization and populism to absorb the wave of revolution spreading from Iran – all under diverse pressures from Washington and the IMF.

The death throes of the old order ultimately gave way to the Turkish model: an Islamic Americanism with a revolutionary rhetoric, backed by liberals and some leftists in its half-hearted fight against

4 Egyptian activists summarized this historical environment in a digital leaflet they circulated throughout the globe: 'From Taksim and Rio to Tahrir, the Smell of Teargas', roarmag.org.

the remnants of authoritarian secularism. Islamic neoliberalism in Turkey brought about an uneven (but still real) cultural, political and economic inclusion of disadvantaged strata into established institutions without the need for revolutionary mobilization. It seemed, for a while, that the Turkish Islamists had found a formula that could absorb the shock of the Iranian revolution.

The Arab revolts of 2011–13, however, pulled the rug from under the feet of the Turkish regime. Mainstream hopes that Egypt would follow the Turkish model with a much more Arab and Islamic (and therefore regionally acceptable) face crumbled with the July 2013 coup. With the region enmeshed in sustained 'revolt without revolution', neither Turkey (with its increasingly authoritarian liberalism) nor Iran (which has itself turned away from revolutionary promises to occasional liberalization) can show the way forward.

Under these circumstances, it is no surprise that the Sunni Gulf states are flexing their muscles and spreading the seeds of not only restoration but outright reaction. This might well lead to years of counter-revolution in the region. This book will explore the multiple dynamics that have thrown the region into such turmoil and prepared the ground for a refurbished conservatism. It will, however, also emphasize that the recent wave of revolt introduced new dynamics and fired new hopes that are likely to sink in roots across the region.

The Rise of the Turkish Model

What was the Turkish model? In two words, it was 'Islamic liberalism': marriage of formal democracy, free market capitalism and (a toned down) conservative Islam. Global business circles trumpeted it. International media celebrated it. And regional and national elites embraced it. This, in a nutshell, was how these circles perceived the Turkey of the 2000s: It was not only a successful, growing free market economy, but also (unlike the similar free market success Malaysia, for instance) a liberalizing democracy. This success, moreover, was based on incorporating the challenge of political Islam, rather than repressing it. Following a series of party closures and other acts of repression, the liberal-conservative Justice and Development Party (Adalet ve Kalkınma Partisi, henceforth AKP) came to power in Turkey in 2002. The perception of the Islamic threat explains the warm reception of the AKP. Pondering, right after the party's 2002 electoral victory, the counterweight that the AKP brought to the table, the Pulitzer Prize–winning journalist David Remnick stated: 'Since the Iranian revolution in 1979, and with particular energy since 11 September 2001, many analysts have pointed to Turkey as an exemplar of regional enlightenment, a model of moderate secularism and democratic ambition.'[5]

From the beginning, then, the Turkish model was imagined as a weapon against the Iranian model and, if there ever was one, the al-Qaeda model. The Turkish model was promoted not only by national and international journalists and think tanks, but also by academics, many of whom simply elaborated the media portrait of the model rather than taking a critical distance to the global hype.

According to the predominant academic narrative of the 2000s,[6] the late Ottomans and the early Turkish Republic (founded in 1923) had taken important steps to modernize Turkey, but they had done so by severing the country from its roots. That modernization programme consequently did not become popular. The modernizers had achieved a lot, including a multiparty democracy, a more or less functioning economy and state, NATO membership and a peaceful relationship with Israel. Yet the price of top-down modernization was the lack of popular élan and the modernizing military's persistent 'tutelage', as a result of which democracy was occasionally interrupted and market reforms stalled. The political 'centre' came to be excessively secularist and alienated from the pro-Islamic, but quite dynamic and flexible, 'periphery' (in fact, the majority of society).

In the 1980s, however, there were attempts at coming to terms with the country's Islamic identity, sometimes resulting in fundamentalist movements (there were similar tendencies the 1950s, as well, under

---

5 David Remnick, 'The Experiment: Will Turkey Be the Model for Islamic Democracy?' *New Yorker*, 18 November 2002. Remnick also raises questions about the AKP in this report.

6 The theoretical basis for this framework was first developed by Mardin ('Centre-Periphery Relations: A Key to Turkish Politics', *Daedalus* 102:1 [1972]: 169–90) and then expanded by Göle and M. Hakan Yavuz (*Islamic Political Identity in Turkey*, Oxford: Oxford University Press, 2003; and 'Introduction: The Role of the New Bourgeoisie in the Transformation of the Turkish Islamic Movement', in M. H. Yavuz, ed., *The Emergence of a New Turkey: Islam, Democracy and the AK Party*, Salt Lake City: University of Utah Press, 2006) among others.

the leadership of the liberal-conservative Prime Minister Adnan Menderes). Fortunately, a splinter Islamist group (led by Erdoğan, Gül and Arınç) moderated itself and combined forces with the more conservative of the modernizers to establish a 'liberal' Islamic platform, the AKP.[7] Ultimately, the less staunchly secularist of the liberals also came to support the AKP, as did the secular business community and broad popular strata, given its success in local government (where Islamists had already proved themselves throughout the course of the 1990s) and macroeconomic policy. The AKP represented 'the transformation of political Islam into a moderate conservative democratic party, reconciled to the secular principles of the constitution'.[8] The AKP seemed to be 'normalizing' Turkish democracy.[9] 'Ironically', one could argue, 'the egalitarianism and republican legacies' of the earlier ('Kemalist') elite had provided the groundwork upon which the new Islamic activists expanded and established a (relatively) more pluralistic republic.[10]

The AKP's economic and democratic advances also resulted in a new confidence, allowing Turkey to embark on a quite active (but not expansionist) foreign policy. Unshackled from its earlier ultra-Western obsession, the country was also now benefiting from trade with the Middle East, and enriching its neighbours in this process.[11] Only radical Islamists, the military and its hard-line secularist sympathizers (as well as some groups who benefited from the statist economy the 'Kemalists' had built over the decades) opposed Turkey's new direction. The Islamic actors turned out to be much more in tune with the values promoted by globalization, at least when compared to

7 Ergun Özbudun and William Hale, *Islamism, Democracy and Liberalism in Turkey: The Case of the AKP*, London: Routledge, 2010.

8 Ergun Özbudun, 'From Political Islam to Conservative Democracy: The Case of the Justice and Development Party in Turkey', *South European Society and Politics* 11:3/4 (2006): 547.

9 Ahmet Insel, 'The AKP and Normalizing Democracy in Turkey', *South Atlantic Quarterly* 102:2/3 (2003): 300 and passim.

10 Seyla Benhabib, 'Turkey's Constitutional Zigzags', *Dissent* 56:1 (2009): 26–7.

11 The Turkish political scientist Kemal Kirişçi embraces most of this narrative, but uses the term *demonstrative effect*, rather than *model*. Kirişçi, 'Turkey's 'Demonstrative Effect' and the Transformation of the Middle East', *Insight Turkey* 13:2, (2011): 33-55. Also see Bülent Aras and Sevgi Akarçeşme, 'Turkey and the Arab Spring', *International Journal* 67:1 (Winter 2012): 39–51.

the defensive Kemalists.[12] Actually, their success consisted precisely in converting even the (erstwhile defensive-nationalist) less skilled workers and small merchants to the cause of free markets and globalization.[13]

By mobilizing Turkey's latent energy, the AKP put its signature on a decade of rapid development: to the amazement of many observers, the country's annual GDP growth hovered around 7 to 8 per cent for years. Most important of all, the former Islamists accomplished this without trampling on individual freedoms and the core secular reforms of the early Republic (such as a larger public role for women).[14] They even expanded some of these freedoms and put an end to military tutelage. After a constitutional referendum in 2010, Turks finally sidelined the military and moved one step closer to establishing the rule of law,[15] which they probably couldn't have done under secularist rule. Why shouldn't this story of religiously supported growth and liberty be replicated elsewhere? Wouldn't such a successful programme be the best antidote against the Islamic extremism that worries so much of the international community?

Robert Kaplan, a prominent journalist and US military consultant, provides a cogent account of what Turkey stood for in the

---

12 See Gokhan Bacik, 'The Separation of Islam and Nationalism in Turkey', *Nationalism and Ethnic Politics* 17:2 (2011): 140–60; Menderes Cinar, 'Turkey's Transformation under the AKP Rule', *Muslim World* 96 (2006): 469–86; Ziya Öniş, 'Turgut Özal and His Economic Legacy: Turkish Neo-Liberalism in Critical Perspective', *Middle Eastern Studies* 40:4 (2007): 251; Özbudun and Hale, *Islamism, Democracy and Liberalism in Turkey*; Jenny White, *Muslim Nationalism and the New Turks*, Princeton, NJ: Princeton University Press, 2013; M. Yeğenoğlu, 'The Sacralization of Secularism in Turkey', *Radical Philosophy* 145 (2007): 2–6.

13 Soli Ozel, 'After the Tsunamı: Turkey at the Polls', *Journal of Democracy* 14:2 (2003): 84.

14 The party was thus an actor of Islamic democracy, even if it avoided this label and preferred 'conservative democrat'. The party's academic sympathizers diverged on whether this made it more comparable to European Christian democracy (Yeğenoğlu, *Sacralization of Secularism in Turkey*) or American popular conservatism (Insel, 'The AKP and Normalizing Democracy in Turkey'). Özbudun and Hale problematized both comparisons in *Islamism, Democracy and Liberalism in Turkey*, since they found the AKP much more opposed to the status quo than either counterpart.

15 Ahmet Kuru and Alfred Stepan, 'Introduction' in Kuru and Stepan, eds, *Democracy, Islam, and Secularism in Turkey*, New York: Columbia University Press, 2012.

imagination of the Western elite. The cheerleading part of his story starts with Turgut Özal, the conservative liberalizer of the 1980s, and culminates in Tayyip Erdoğan, the AKP's prime minister from 2003 to 2014:

> Ozal was a wily politician from the heartland of Asia Minor who shared the deep religiosity and crass nouveau riche tastes of many Turks. He loved to read the Koran and watch soap operas, to bang his head against the carpet in a Sufi mosque and go to Texas barbecues. He restored religion to Turkey's political space without threatening the country's pro-Western orientation or its tendency toward tolerance . . . Erdoğan's moderate, reformist Islam now offers the single best hope for reconciling Muslims – from Morocco to Indonesia – with twenty-first-century social and political realities . . . Never before has the West been so lucky in Turkey as now. The re-Islamization of Turkey through the rejuvenation of the country's Ottoman roots was going to happen anyway; Atatürk's republican-minded secularization had simply gone too far. The only question was whether this retrenchment from Kemalism would take a radical or a moderate path. Erdoğan's political leanings suggest the latter. Europe should seize the opportunity.[16]

Turkey, then, was the global system's best bet for rendering Islam governable. Turkey's (and by implication, the whole Muslim world's) return to its Islamic roots was unavoidable – and Turkey promised to channel this energy not in any dangerous, unpredictable direction, but along the path paved by soap operas, Texas barbecues . . . and Calvinism.

An influential report published by the European Stability Initiative provided ample data from the Anatolian backwaters to prove that the AKP regime's success was an outcome of bottom-up entrepreneurial activity.[17] Thanks to engagement with politics-free business, entrepreneurs with small and medium-sized businesses had spontaneously

---

16 Robert D. Kaplan, 'At the Gates of Brussels', *Atlantic*, December 2004.

17 European Stability Initiative, *Islamic Calvinists: Change and Conservatism in Central Anatolia*, Berlin: European Stability Initiative, 2005.

developed Calvinist predispositions towards religion and economics. Islam, then, was traveling along the road of universal wisdom. Money was bringing down age-old barriers between civilizations through a newly devised 'Muslim Calvinist' ethics: Turks were both returning to their Muslim roots and also becoming more Western at the same time – a veritable win-win situation indeed.

It was in this environment that Western politicians, right and left, wholeheartedly embraced Turkey and pointed to it as a model, with George W. Bush underlining the country's role as a model during his 2004 visit to Istanbul. Within the same year, British foreign secretary Jack Straw declared that the AKP's reforms 'put Turkey on a path of no return' (towards the European Union, democratization and higher standards of living). As Straw emphasized, within the context of the Big Middle East Project, Turkey could now 'share with the region its experience in the field of the management of change' given 'its historical ties' (by implication, much better than Britain could).[18] These endorsements at the highest level of global power emphasized Turkey's capacity to act as a bridge between Western projects and the Middle East. Some voices in the Arab media echoed the bridge metaphor:

> Turkey's entry into the [European] union would also serve the interests of the entire Middle East. What country can explain the pains, sufferings and woes of the Middle East region better than Turkey? Turkey can be the bridge between the Middle East and Brussels, where decision [sic] with far-reaching consequences are taken.[19]

Such statements were common in the Arab press. Fieldwork also uncovered interest in the Turkish model among the broader Arab intelligentsia.[20]

The enthusiasm was not restricted to elites and opinion makers: over a decade, it spread like wildfire throughout the world. In 2012,

---

18 'Türkiye AKP ile değişti', *Hürriyet*, 3 March 2004.

19 Walid M. Sadi, 'Revisiting Turkey's EU membership', *Jordan Times*, 16 October 2005.

20 Sadik J. al-Azm, 'The "Turkish Model": A View from Damascus', *Turkish Studies* 12:4 (2011): 633–41.

the American media reported the musings of a Tunisian small merchant: 'We want Tunisia to become a modern country, not extremist . . . A place like Turkey. People work hard there and also practice Islam. They are modest and modern at the same time.'[21] An opinion poll conducted by the Brookings Institute found that, in 2011, 'Egyptians want[ed] their country to look more like Turkey than any of the other Muslim, Arab and other choices provided.'[22] Turkey's claims to leadership were widely accepted among the broader Arab public, as another report published in 2011 showed: 66 per cent of survey respondents thought that Turkey could 'be a model for Middle Eastern countries'.[23]

The Marketing of the Turkish Model

Major Western media outlets insisted throughout the 2000s that the Muslims should follow the Turkish model,[24] with excitement about the Turkish model peaking during the Arab revolts of 2011. While there was more balanced discussion in some of the months preceding and following the climax of the Arab revolts, the mainstream remained positive overall. The *Economist*, for example, had been fascinated by Turkey for a decade and became a militant promoter of the Turkish model's virtues after the rise of the AKP regime, and even more so after the Tunisian and Egyptian revolts. The magazine frequently blended propaganda with criticism, warning the AKP not to become too self-confident.[25] Occasionally, however, all caution was brushed aside:

21 See Peter Kenyon, 'The Turkish Model: Can It Be Replicated?', 6 January 2012, npr.org.

22 Shibley Telhami, 'The 2011 Arab Public Opinion Poll', 21 November 2011, brookings.edu.

23 Paul Salem, 'Turkey's Image in the Arab World', TESEV, May 2011, tesev.org.

24 There were, however, major exceptions. The pro-neocon think tank Washington Institute, while supportive in the AKP's initial years, gradually adapted a bitter tone after the mid-2000s. Its staff also contributed to major outlets such as *Newsweek*, the *Wall Street Journal* and *Washington Post* along these lines; see washingtoninstitute.org. The liberal press also fluctuated on its support circa 2006–07.

25 'Turkey's Islamists: Erbakan's Legacy', *Economist*, 3 March 2011.

> From North Africa to the Gulf, the region seems to be going through a Turkish moment. . . . The Turkish case . . . showed that Islam did not pose an insuperable barrier to multiparty democracy. But nothing much flowed from that observation – until the Arab spring. Turkey is now being studied by Arabs as a unique phenomenon . . . Whatever the flaws of the Turkish experiment, it is clearly true that Turkey under the AK party presents a more benign picture than many other versions – real and hypothetical – of Islamist rule . . . For Western observers of the Middle East, an evolution in a Turkish direction – towards relative political and economic freedom – would be a happier outcome than many others.[26]

Turkey was offered as the path to follow not in abstract terms, but in subtle contradistinction to Iran.

Some actors were more explicit regarding the economic desirability of the Turkish model than others. For instance, a policy paper published by the Carnegie Endowment pointed out that the distinctiveness of Turkish Islamism was its exceptionally pro-business attitude. Even the more liberal of the Islamist movements (those in Tunisia, Jordan and Egypt) paled in comparison with the AKP in terms of their acceptance of big business and international economic institutions as partners. They remained too wedded to small and medium-sized businesses, while the way forward for the Islamists of the Arab Spring, the paper concluded, was development of an economic liberalism as deep, consistent and sincere as the AKP's.[27]

These were the hegemonic Western hopes for the region as a whole. But how did the potential receivers of these messages respond? The Egyptian press was full of praise for the AKP experience. Even some liberals (distancing themselves from their own Muslim Brotherhood) looked to Turkey as a possible model for integrating Islamists into democratic institutions. For its part, the Egyptian Muslim Brotherhood publicly declared that it took Turkey as its economic model, especially in terms of the expansion of investments (*tatwir*

26 'The Turkish Model: A Hard Act to Follow', *Economist*, 6 August 2011.

27 Ibrahim Saif and Muhammad Abu Rumman, 'The Economic Agenda of the Islamist Parties', 29 May 2012, carnegieendowment.org.

al-istithmarat), increasing growth rates, human development (*tanmiyya bashariyya*) and the promotion of education.[28] The most prominent Tunisian Islamist leader also declared Turkish free market Islamism as his economic model.[29] Elsewhere in the Muslim world, locals pointed to Turkey as the nontextualist, flexible interpreter of Islam, in contrast to their own reduction of Islam to its classical texts.[30]

For some, the positive attributes of the Turkish model were condensed in Prime Minister Tayyip Erdoğan. Many Arabs approvingly called the Turkish prime minister ''Anid Qasimbasha' (a son of Kasımpaşa, a downtrodden, tough Istanbul neighborhood) and 'qabadayi' (tough guy).[31] These descriptors referred to his tenacity and strictness, especially regarding the Israel–Palestine issue: he was widely seen by Arabs as the world's most resolute leader against Israel.[32]

Egyptian-born and globally published journalist Tarek Osman also offered Turkey as the model for the Arab Spring countries, especially Egypt:

> In Turkey, the AK Party, under Recep Tayyib Erdoğan, has been meticulously bridging the gap between Turkish society's increasing religiosity and the establishment's (and the army's) strict secularism. The [Mubarak] regime did not take note . . . Leading wings within the Islamic movement believe that the Islamists, plagued by the experience of militant Islamism from the 1970s to the 1990s, should move towards a more liberal framework. Influenced by the seemingly successful Turkish experience under

28 'Al-Ikhwan wa al-Hurriyya wa al-'adala yukallifan Khayrat al-Shatir bi i'dad mashru' li al-nahda', *al-Masry al-Yawm*, 12 December 2012.

29 'Ghannouchi: State Does Not Have Right to Monopolize Islam', *Today's Zaman*, 23 September 2011.

30 Husnul Amin, 'Our Textual Religiosity', 2 April 2013, thenews.com.

31 *Kabadayı* (or *qabadayi*), literally 'tough uncle', is a Turkish word for ultra-masculine neighborhood leaders, roughly comparable to gang leaders in the Western context. However, unlike the word *gang leader*, kabadayı invokes patriarchal, paternalistic, protectionist, moralistic and other traditional values. The word is widely used in the Arab world.

32 Sameer Saliha, 'Limadha Yatamassak Erdoghan bi Ziyara Ghazza?', *al-Sharq al-Awsat*, 1 May 2013.

the AK Party in the 2000s, these wings advocate a return to the thinking of the liberal Islamists of the early decades of the twentieth century.[33]

Despite the overall positive atmosphere, some Arab thinkers continued to question the Turkish model. They raised doubts not only about the Turkish regime's handling of the Kurdish issue, but of sectarian issues as well. When Yalçın Akdoğan (a top advisor of Erdoğan) attacked the (heterodox Muslim) Alevis and the (Kurdish guerrilla) PKK as the real reasons behind terrorism and the lack of peace in Turkey, the Arab press did not miss the opportunity to point out the entrenchment of sectarian hatred in Turkey.[34] Still others questioned Turkey's intentions in its dealings with the Arab Spring and warned of a revived Ottoman control over the Arab world, a worry shared by both the supporters of the recently overthrown dictators and some Arab revolutionaries themselves.[35]

Scholars were no less enthusiastic regarding the possibilities that the AKP presented to the region and the Muslim world,[36] but some also modified certain aspects of that framing. Anthropologist Jenny White, for instance, suggested the term 'Muslimhood model' rather than the 'Turkish model', because the amorphousness of the latter allowed even Egyptian coup-mongers to draw inspiration from the authoritarian military example set by Turkey. White defined Muslimhood as 'a model developed by the AKP and modernist theologians in Ankara that replaced Islamism'.[37] The element of personal choice (enabled by commercialization), this cornerstone of liberalism, promised a model beyond Islamism. White saw this specific

---

33 Tarek Osman, *Egypt on the Brink: From the Rise of Nasser to the Fall of Mubarak*, New Haven, CT: Yale University Press, 2011, 210, 251.

34 Muhammad Noureddin, '`Andama yandhur Turkiyya ila al-Akrad `ala annahum mushkila `alawiyya', *al-Arabiya*, 16 April 2013.

35 See, for example, http://weekly.ahram.org.eg/News/2540/21/Poor-harvest-of-Arab-revolutions.aspx.

36 Nader Hashemi, *Islam, Secularism, and Liberal Democracy: Toward a Democratic Theory for Muslim Societies*, Oxford: Oxford University Press, 2009; Stathis N. Kalyvas, 'The "Turkish Model" in the Matrix of Political Catholicism' in Ahmet Kuru and Alfred Stepan, eds, *Democracy, Islam, and Secularism in Turkey*, New York: Columbia University Press, 2012.

37 White, *Muslim Nationalism and the New Turks*, 182, 189.

experience as the contribution of the AKP and as the basis of its potential to serve as a model:

> The Muslimhood model posits that Islam is a personal attribute that may be carried into the public arena, for instance, in the form of personal ethics, but does not define what a person does there . . . Ennahda explicitly models itself on the AKP and has stated its commitment to democracy and women's rights . . . Young, modern Muslims seeking justice and material well-being would be more likely to find their mirror image in Turkey's Muslimhood model, not in a politically amorphous 'Turkish model'.[38]

The Crisis and Its Liberal Resolution: Personalize and Culturalize the Issue!

The June 2013 revolt threw Western and Arab coverage of Turkey into disarray. Even Reuters sometimes turned against its beloved Turkey in the months following the Gezi uprising. Yet most of the hegemonic Western press had come up with a more consistent narrative by 2014, whereas the Arab press was slower to do so. Despite fluctuations, Arab opinion remained in fact divided. There were those who spoke, with excitement, about the return of the Ottoman Empire; but there were those who lamented it. Some jihadis saw in Turkey an ally in coming regional sectarian wars; others thought Turkey would side with the 'infidels' in a coming *global* war. A columnist mocked those who had a dream vision of Erdoğan riding on horseback from Ankara to conquer Quds.[39] In this effervescent environment, Turkish and Arab intellectuals appeared on al-Jazeera (and wrote opinion pieces on its website) to present the Gezi revolt as a reactionary, Kemalist insurgency on the part of the elite.[40]

Neoconservative pundits' attacks on the Turkish intelligence services strengthened the perception that only Turkey could counterbalance Israel. The major pan-Arabic outlets kept on publishing

38 Ibid., 189–90.

39 Jamil Matar, 'Min al-sanduq ila al-istibdad . . . al-tajraba al-Turkiyya', *al-Arabiya*, 13 June 2013.

40 For example, Ali Murat Yel and Alparslan Nas, 'Taksim Square Is Not Tahrir Square', aljazeera.com, 12 June 2013.

pieces (by both Turks and Arabs) that came to the defence of Turkey against the neocons. These ideologues argued that the neocons did not want any strong state and economy in the region except Israel.[41] They still upheld not only the political and religious, but also the economic model, of Turkey as the best way to go.

Nevertheless, at the end of 2013, there was a growing criticism of the Turkish model in the Arab press. Many columnists took it as fact that the imposition of the Turkish model and moderate Islam had failed, given the experiences in Tunisia, Egypt and Syria, as well as the inability of Washington and Ankara to push their agenda in these countries.[42] There were also sharper responses to Turkey. Egyptian columnists reacted to Erdoğan's tears for the daughter of a top Brotherhood leader, Mohammed Baltagi (she was slain after the July 2013 coup in Egypt). These were not tears of sorrow and empathy, they argued, but of frustrated ambition: Erdoğan was grieving his loss of imperial control over Egypt. His dreams of a new Ottoman Empire were dead. The tears were allegedly also from 'hysteria' due to his failures in internal politics. One Egyptian newspaper accused Turkish authorities of provoking Turks against non–Muslim Brotherhood Egyptians.[43] The same paper had been full of 'Turkish model' articles during 2011, which had hoped that democracy would come slowly and gradually through imitation of the AKP. Opinion polls also demonstrated how the Arab public was in flux: survey respondents who perceived Turkey as a model declined throughout the period – yet even in 2013 a significant 51 per cent still thought Turkey could be a model.[44]

The hegemonic Western press responded in a much more united and 'performative' way, in the sense that the main storyline harboured a semi-covert prescription. The title of an editorial from the *Financial Times* summarized the liberal analysis of Turkey's dilemma:

---

41 Aylin Kocaman, 'Limadha Turkiyya', *al-Sharq al-Awsat*, 23 October 2013.

42 Raja Talab, 'al-Sharq al-Awsat yaghraq bi al-fawda wa lakin bi al-hudu'!', *Al-Rai*, 24 October 2013.

43 ʿAmru ʿAbd al-Hamid, 'Manadil Erdoghan', *al-Masry al-Youm*, 30 August 2013.

44 See Mensür Akgun and Sabiha Senyücel Gündoğar, 'The Perception of Turkey in the Middle East 2012' and 'The Perception of Turkey in the Middle East 2013', Turkish Economic and Social Studies Foundation, tesev.org.tr.

'Arrogance undoes the Turkish model'. The piece was echoed by other once-unquestioning supporters of the AKP model in Turkey: 'At the heart of Turkey's problems is the authoritarian style Mr Erdoğan has adopted since the AK party won its third election in 2011'.[45] The *New York Times* and others now emphasized Erdoğan's authoritarian style: everything else about the Turkish model was good, the implication went. Turks and Kurds had been enjoying a liberal-conservative heaven up until 2011. The Western personal attack on Erdoğan was coupled with cultural reductionism, as some writers rediscovered the Turkic–Ottoman roots of his authoritarianism.

In response to the ever more obvious failings and weaknesses of the Turkish model, its erstwhile backers channelled their rage against Erdoğan and his Islamist roots. They also occasionally discussed the structural issues they had been sidelining (though not completely neglecting) over the previous ten years (such as Turkey's dependence on hot money flows). *Foreign Affairs*, perhaps the most influential think tank–based foreign policy magazine in the US, still exalted, in early 2014, the economic success of the Turkish model (while emphasizing Erdoğan as the reason why this successful path was being forsaken):

> A boom in infrastructure development and construction added to the good times. Since the outset of Erdoğan's tenure, the country's highway network has been expanded by more than 10,000 miles. The number of airports has doubled, to 50, and Turkish Airlines now flies to more than 100 countries, more than any other carrier in the world. New, upscale housing complexes and shopping malls seem to flank every major city.[46]

Foreign Affairs forgot to add that millions of citizens had revolted against these very construction and road projects, setting off global talk of Erdoğan's replacement. In line with this perspective, many

45 'Arrogance Undoes the Turkish Model: Erdoğan's High-Handedness Threatens Country's Prosperity', *Financial Times*, 8 January 2014.

46 Daniel Dombey, 'Turkey: How Erdoğan Did It – and Could Blow It', *Foreign Affairs*, January/February 2014.

mainstream accounts promoted the more aggressively pro-Western faction of the Turkish regime (led by the global cleric Fethullah Gülen) as the antidote to Erdoğan's authoritarianism, ignoring how the Gülen wing of the regime had participated in the making of Erdoğan's authoritarian marginalization of all opponents for ten years.[47]

What happened, in this context, to the more refined defences of the AKP experience? Today, scholarship on the AKP is in disarray. As of now, there isn't one predominant way of dealing with how Islamic liberalism ended in Turkey (and consequently, no consistent explanation of how scholarship mishandled the situation and served to consolidate an emergent authoritarian regime during the AKP's first ten years). Keeping in mind how long the academy took to construct a consensus on Islamic liberalism (taking Şerif Mardin's centre-periphery piece as the beginning point, about three decades), it might take a long time before a strong mainstream explanation can establish itself.[48]

One of the interesting current analyses comes again from Mardin, who bases his explanation on 'neighborhood pressure', a concept that sidelines the constitutive power of politics and traces the main dynamics back to society. In a series of interviews, Mardin explained the increasing authoritarianism and conservatism in Turkey by referring to suspicion of the outsider and other similar traits of Turkish neighborhood culture. Mardin thus accounted for increasing authoritarianism based not on the AKP's policies, vision or global connections, but on its growing submission to its own social base. Even though some of his earlier pieces foreshadow this analysis, Mardin has never fully theorized the concept, a gap which other scholars are now trying to fill.[49] It is not clear today whether this view can form the foundation of a fully developed scholarly analysis.

---

47 For an editorial defense of Gülen against Erdoğan's assault, see 'Turkey's Wrong Turn', *New York Times*, 27 January 2014. *Foreign Affairs* also published, soon after the cited essay, another one that upheld Gülen as the 'Martin Luther' of Islam and called for global action on his behalf.

48 Şerif Mardin, 'Centre–Periphery Relations: A Key to Turkish Politics', *Daedalus* 102:1 (1973): 169–90.

49 See, for example, B. Toprak, İ. Bozan, T. Morgül and N. Şener, *Türkiye'de farklı olmak: din ve muhafazakârlık ekseninde ötekileştirilenler (mahalle baskısı raporu)*, İstanbul: Metis, 2009.

Jenny White provided a much more elaborate explanation (though drawing on similar themes). She explained the decline of liberty under AKP rule based on the specificities of Turkish culture. According to White, the problem is not the 'Muslimhood model', but its hybridization with the collectivism of the Turks:

> In a society characterized by powerful group identities and norms, belief in the desirability of individual liberty almost inevitably collides with collective norms . . . Turks have *always* pursued their personal choices and motivations within powerful collective frameworks provided by family, community, nation . . . The coexistence of subjective freedom and the demands of the collectivity lead to sometimes *surprising* and contradictory discourses and practices that cross social divisions. For example, it is not uncommon for people to claim to be simultaneously liberal and conservative. [Emphases mine][50]

Following this logic, White traced AKP authoritarianism regarding issues such as alcohol and the place of women in society to Turkish culture. Her resolution of the problem, therefore, called for 'denationalization', which would presumably open up more space for Muslimhood and cut back on the poison of collectivism.[51]

What is most telling about this account is how it presents the marriage of liberalism and conservatism as a Turkish curiosity, thereby obscuring how the couple have entrenched roots in Western modernity. Based on the fascination with de Tocqueville today, one could even argue that liberal-conservatism is the most mainstream of all discourses, and not least in the United States. As much as liberals have fought against collectivism throughout the centuries, they have frequently smuggled in less nefarious communities (religious, familial, sometimes even national) to fight more subversive collectivities (such as class). The contradictoriness of Turkish liberalization is by no means exceptional.

These new analyses, as represented by Mardin and White, certainly reinforce the public trend of culturalizing the AKP's democratic

50 White, *Muslim Nationalism and the New Turks*, 15–17.
51 Ibid., 190–3.

failures. We should never lose sight of this fact: just as the binary opposition (Islamic) society versus (secular) state was not only an analysis, but also a performative intervention in the social, so is culturalization (including the concept of 'neighborhood pressure', which has come in handy for Kemalist and elitist criticisms of the AKP's social base). By contrast, I show throughout this book how the neoliberal-liberal democratic model (rather than Erdoğan the villain – or, for that matter, 'Turkish culture') was the cause of Turkey's crisis. That model was in reality what allowed Erdoğan's authoritarianism to pass as democratic during the last ten years.

Before jumping on the bandwagon of Erdoğan-bashing (or 'neighborhood'-bashing), we need to pause and ask: what was at stake in this fascination with the Turkish model? Why was the Turkish model being pushed so aggressively, lately with modifications (The Real Turkish Model = The Apparent Turkish Model minus Erdoğan; or Muslimhood = The AKP minus Nationalism)? Which dynamics does the culturalization of the model's limits obscure?

The Downfall of Islamic Liberalism: A Political Society–Based Explanation

This book goes beyond the personalistic and culturalist analyses of Turkey's recent authoritarian turn by pointing out the structural and conjunctural (as well as cultural) dynamics behind it. The (national and regional) spread and development of Islamic liberalism ran against strong limits, which the existing literature is ill-equipped to appreciate:

1. The Turkish model (*the marriage of neoliberalization and democratization through Islam*) was contextually specific and could not be exported to other countries in the region. The religious and political balances in Egypt, more specifically, made even half-hearted emulation impossible. Moreover, the Turkish model not only relied on unique national underpinnings, but was also *relationally* tied to its opposite in the region. Turkey needed Iran's antisystemic orientation (with the subsequent militarization of the Gulf) and the Egyptian garrison state in order to present itself as *the* safe haven for global investment in the region. Turkey held this structural advantage relationally; by definition, then, the Turkish model could *not* have been universalized across the region.

2. The Turkish model was internationally bolstered (and internally created) partly to counter the Iranian model, *the marriage of corporatism and revolution through Islam*. 'Corporatism', a non-individualist model based on the *top-down* integration of interest groups, characterized many Middle Eastern regimes in the post-war era.[52] Whereas neoliberal reforms in Turkey, Egypt and Tunisia attacked its collectivistic spirit, the Iranian revolution further bolstered corporatism by mobilizing subaltern strata (previously marginalized by the more exclusive corporatism of the Shah era). The Iranian model, even though still a perceived threat for Turkey and other Muslim countries, turned out to be highly unstable and unsustainable (as revolutionary *and* corporatist *and* Islamic at the same time). The convulsions the Iranian model produced both boosted and chipped away at the relevance of the Turkish model.

3. The stabilization of neoliberalization through democratization had run up against limits even in Turkey, and new limits were introduced by the Arab revolts. Interaction with Arab (and Iranian) dynamics wrecked the already shaky connections between democratization and neoliberalization. The already sectarian regime in Turkey further intensified its sectarianism, undermining not only democratization at home, but its claim to stand above the Saudi–Iranian rift in the region as well.

4. The focus on the question of Islam and democracy leads to a shallow debate. If the overall dynamics of a country take it in a democratic direction, Islamic forces might develop their own practices and discourses of democracy. *The question, then, should be whether democratization is sustainable under conditions of neoliberalization*. Two terms are of key importance here: in the current era, *liberalism*, the apotheosis of individual property and freedom, frequently goes hand in hand with *neoliberalization* (privatization of property, restructuring of the welfare state to render individuals self-sufficient, and financialization).[53] This book demonstrates that

52 Nazih N. M. Ayubi, *Over-Stating the Arab State: Politics and Society in the Middle East*, London: I. B. Tauris, 1995.

53 For an expanded definition of liberalism, see chapter 2. The discussion of neoliberalization in this book draws on two literatures: The 'variegated' neoliberalization and subjectivity debates: see Neil Brenner, Jamie Peck and Nik Theodore, 'Variegated Neoliberalization: Geographies, Modalities, Pathways',

neoliberalization and democratization can proceed together only for a certain time (through the aid of religious forces). When they start to undermine each other, Islamic actors take up more and more nondemocratic and non-neoliberal practices (as in Turkey). When they don't ally together from the beginning (as in Egypt), Islamic actors never become strong leaders of liberalism and neoliberalization.

5. So where did the Turkish model go wrong? What are the limits of the marriage of democracy and economic liberalism? From the beginning, the Turkish model was *exclusionary* (it was ethnically and religiously hierarchical). One trouble with the Turkish model was the sustained, armed insubordination of an ethnic minority. But this element, the Kurdish question, is context-specific and does not directly translate into a theoretical point on the internal contradictions of neoliberalization. The more generalizable trouble came when one of the key social groups *included in* and enriched by neoliberalization (the new middle class) revolted against the neoliberal regime (even if not simply and only against neoliberalization). The revolt pushed the regime to intensify its authoritarianism and conservatism. The Gezi revolt of summer 2013 thus draws our attention to the contradictions at the heart of neoliberalism: it leads to a socially stifling world even for the groups it enriches. The Turkish model was at least temporarily successful in appeasing large sections of the urban poor; but the dissatisfaction of the new middle classes is fatal beyond the boundaries of Turkey, since their boring life is what the model holds in store for the imagined future of these strata across the region.

The misreading of the Turkish case is not an isolated fallacy. It is solidly based in the intellectual and scholarly fashions of the last decades, which eulogize civil society against politics and the state and thereby miss most of these dynamics. The root of the problem in many Muslim societies, it is held, is the structure of the state, which

---

Global Networks 10:2 (2010): 182–222; Cihan Tuğal, *Passive Revolution: Absorbing the Islamic Challenge to Capitalism*, Stanford, CA: Stanford University Press, 2012; Tuğal, 'Serbest Meslek Sahibi': Neoliberal Subjectivity among Istanbul's Popular Sectors', *New Perspectives on Turkey* 46 (2012): 65–93; and Tuğal, 'Contesting Benevolence: Market Orientations among Muslim Aid Providers in Egypt', *Qualitative Sociology* 36:2 (2013): 141–59.

is secular rather than Islamic. Actually, as many Muslims (for example, in Indonesia) become more pious, they also come to embrace democratic values, even if this development is not yet completely reflected at the level of the state. Similarly, most Muslims in Bangladesh and Malaysia reconcile a deep piety and a sincere regard for political rights and pluralism, even if their governments cannot accommodate these aspirations.[54] The implicit or explicit suggestion is therefore as follows: provide the right set of opportunities to the nascent pious civil societies and they will take their countries in democratic directions.[55] This sanguine take on civil society ignores the structure and effects of political projects.

The extant scholarship thus overemphasizes distinctions between the centre and the periphery, state and society, the elite and the people. The 'moderation' of peripheral forces,[56] therefore, becomes the panacea for comprehensive political visions (which are deemed to be totalitarian in our post-Enlightenment world). State and politics come to be perceived as impediments that just need to move out of the way of the moderating actors in civil society.

This intellectual distrust of politics is counterproductive for two reasons. The first is simple: the so-called moderating actors often have comprehensive visions of their own, and those comprehensive visions frequently encourage further centralization of the state. We need to develop a conceptual distinction between civic actors who pursue sectional interests or specific issues and those who seek to regulate the totality of social life (even if this regulation is in a more liberal direction, as in the case of the early AKP): the former

---

54 See, for example, chapters 2, 4 and 5, in John Esposito and John Voll, eds, *Makers of Contemporary Islam*, Oxford: Oxford University Press, 2001; and Hashemi, *Islam, Secularism, and Liberal Democracy*, 158–65.

55 See Robert Hefner, 'Public Islam and the Problem of Democratization', *Sociology of Religion* 62 (2001): 491–514; Masoud Kamali, 'Civil Society and Islam: A Sociological Perspective', *Archives Europeennes de Sociologie* 42 (2001): 457–82; John Kelsay, 'Civil Society and Government in Islam', in S. H. Hashmi, ed., *Islamic Political Ethics: Civil Society, Pluralism, and Conflict*, Princeton, NJ: Princeton University Press, 2002; A. Norton, ed., *Civil Society in the Middle East*, 2 vols, New York: Brill, 1995, 1996; Denis J. Sullivan and Sana Adeb-Kotob, *Islam in Contemporary Egypt: Civil Society vs. the State*, Boulder, CO: Lynne Rienner Publishers, 1999.

56 Raymond W. Baker, *Islam without Fear: Egypt and the New Islamists*, Cambridge, MA: Harvard University Press, 2003.

constitute civil society, and the latter political society. The second, theoretical, reason is that the distinctions some scholars take for granted are actually constructed through the activities of these actors (and others). The lines between state and society, the elite and the people, are drawn and redrawn continuously.[57]

This book studies the making of these distinctions. At the centre of this 'making' is political society: a field of actors and organizations that have comprehensive social visions. In developed and settled democracies, parties usually predominate in political society, but in more dynamic situations, the field is populated by sociopolitical organizations and groups that are difficult to classify and label. Political society frequently remakes the boundaries between the power bloc and the people.

The interaction of political society with state and civic structures determines whether a country takes a sustainable revolutionary, 'passive revolutionary', or counter-revolutionary path. In a revolution, the political and economic structures of a society are overturned through bottom-up mobilization. In a passive revolution, by contrast, an inchoate bottom-up mobilization is 'absorbed' into existing political and economic structures. Absorption is not simply incorporation: it entails a thorough remaking of certain policies and dispositions, even if the overall structures remain the same.

The Italian thinker Antonio Gramsci has summed up this process by calling the passive revolution a 'restoration–revolution'. Passive revolutions involve innovative combinations of mobilization and demobilization. In inter-war Italy, ex-socialists, former officers and middle strata were mobilized to hunt down the working classes and communists, with some disastrous consequences for those who initially welcomed fascism. The Italian passive revolution first united the fragmented dominant classes and put a stagnant Italian capitalism on an efficient path (its restorative dimension); it then wrecked the whole country by dragging it into military conflict.

The Turkish passive revolution restored the post-1980 neoliberal–conservative regime through the absorption of Islamic revolutionary

57 For a full exposition and genealogy of this second argument, see Cedric de Leon, Manali Desai and Cihan Tuğal, *Building Blocs: How Parties Organize Society*, Stanford, CA: Stanford University Press, 2015.

cadres, discourses, and policies. The economic liberalism, cultural conservatism, and political authoritarianism that the 1980 coup initiated were first 'democratized' by the Özal regime. Despite an initial decade of popular enthusiasm, liberal conservatism stagnated and alienated broad strata in the 1990s. The neoliberal actors could save Turkey's post-1980 direction only through merging with their former enemies. The Islamists inherited their overall package (the 'restorative' dimension of the passive revolution) and modified it through radical policies and discourses (its 'revolutionary' face). The results are gradually turning out to be almost as fatal as Italian fascism for their erstwhile benefactors.

As chapters 4 and 5 examine in more detail, what the concept of political society allows us to understand is not the moment and location of revolutionary outbreaks, but whether revolutionary and/or passive revolutionary routes are sustainable once taken. Islamic actors outside of Turkey have also attempted passive revolution, to no avail. The successful Turkish passive revolution, in this light, turns out to be unique due to the *political* characteristics that set Turkey apart from Egypt, Iran and Tunisia.

Chapter 5 also includes three final sections on the scholarly study of revolutions. Here the main argument is that political society and political blocs are central to the making and unmaking of revolutions. However, these concepts allow us to analyze revolutionary and passive revolutionary processes, rather than the exact place and timing of massive revolts. Political economic, social psychological and institutionalist generations of revolutionary theory have unfortunately downplayed the role of political activity. Sociologists, political scientists and other analysts of revolution may want to read that section before the empirical chapters, since the scholarly debates discussed there (as well as a preliminary theoretical discussion at the end of chapter 2) have shaped much of the analytical narrative in the chapters to follow.

The Historical Making and Unmaking of the Turkish Model

The picture of the Turkish model, then, needs to be emended through an examination of how the politics of mobilization and absorption reconfigured state and society at every turn. The Turkish model didn't just exist. It was (intentionally and unintentionally) brought into being to combat specific evils. What is today known as the Turkish model was perhaps finalized by the AKP regime, but its foundations were laid by a coup and its civilian extension in the 1980s, which in turn had come as responses to the turbulence of the 1970s.

The mobilizations, hopes and fears introduced by (the global) 1968 and 1979 were too rich and intense to be appeased by already existing Middle Eastern toolkits. Something innovative had to be done. The Turkish military regime of 1980 (of General Kenan Evren) and its slightly Islamized version of Turkish conservatism (led by Turgut Özal) opened a new horizon. The only way to demobilize the threats was to mobilize. In the 1980s, the Turkish regime promised to empower subaltern strata against the secular elites, the organized working classes and the minorities. The regime had before it huge tasks of restoration. It had to put down workers' resistance. This it did successfully between 1989 and 1995. It had to put down the armed Kurdish uprising. The uprising was the result of a regional monstrosity (the failed forced assimilation of the Kurdish population), but the Kurdish question became a challenge only as part of a local refashioning of global 1968: the Kurdish/Turkish reinterpretation of Maoism and the 'people's war' strategy. Here, the Evren–Özal regime and its successors failed miserably.

The third challenge that had to be contained (rather than completely put down) was 1979 – the (real or imagined) threat of Islamic revolution. Yet neither repression nor containment worked here. The last hopeless move (the 'soft coup' in 1997) ended up further strengthening the Islamic challenge and even pushing some conservative Muslims into the Islamist camp. But due to the global and the national context, this new Islamism resembled the Iranian challenge very little. Once Turkish 'Islamism' came to power in 2002, the global and national mainstream hope was that it would become the perfect tool to deal with all three challenges.

This was the solution the Turks reached (with some global probing): mobilize a part of the threat to put down all the other threats (plus that threat itself). At first the strategy seemed to work. Not only did Turkey join the post-1968 'global restoration' with staggering growth rates, but it did so with little resistance, even though the growth-restoration caused a lot of displacement, dispossession and inequality.

However, this mixture of mobilization, demobilization and counter-mobilization ultimately backfired. The mobilized subaltern strata became too confident – an overconfidence that was further boosted in 2011 by a misreading of the events across the region. Actually, these (pious) strata were no longer the subaltern by the end of the 2000s. They boasted a powerful business class, appropriated huge chunks of the bureaucracy and had built many civic institutions that surrounded the core of Turkish power. Circa 2010 they started to attack their erstwhile benefactors (the liberals and liberalized leftists of Turkey and the relatively more liberal wing of the old power bloc). Just as in the case of a classical passive revolution, interwar Italy, the absorption of mobilization worked only for a while. Now it is time for us to watch the disasters the passive revolution will produce.

Even though there is a growing literature on passive revolutions, there has been little discussion of how passive revolutions end. Some passive revolutions combine force and consent successfully for a while, but then drag the whole nation into global bloodshed. This was the case with Italian fascism. Turkey might now be heading into a similar, self-destructive phase of the passive revolution. In my previous book, I admittedly underemphasized the self-destructive potential of the Turkish passive revolution, [58] even though I drew attention to its authoritarian, 'soft-totalitarian',[59] and Islamizing aspects in other pieces.[60] I hope this book will contribute to a deeper understanding of the collapse of passive revolutions, though a full theorization of how they end requires further comparative research.

This alternative account of the Turkish model thus underlines that political society was the key to the making of Islamic liberalism (and the overcoming of secular corporatism and the problems stemming from it). Secular corporatism could be transcended only through passive mobilization of potentially subversive groups through political society. If attempts at liberalization and revolution occur via a zigzag process, or if a middling route is the imposed outcome from above, then corporatism will persist, as my analysis of Iran will show.

---

58 But see Tuğal, *Passive Revolution*, 8–10, 162–71.

59 'Party of One', *The National*, 29 August 2008.

60 Tuğal, 'Transforming Everyday Life: Islamism and Social Movement Theory', *Theory and Society* 38:5 (2009): 423–58.

The analysis of the Egyptian and Iranian cases, along with the Turkish one, also raises doubt on the independence of 'opportunities' or 'institutional structures' as isolated variables. These cases demonstrate that opportunities are influenced by movement within political society. Whereas celebration of civil society has been the predominant trend in the scholarship on Turkey, many scholars who focus on Islamic movements elsewhere place much more emphasis on how opportunities and institutional structures shape Islamism.[61] Despite this serious theoretical difference, most institutionalist scholars have reached the same policy conclusions as those working within the civil society tradition: if Islamists are included in the political process, both the institutions and the Islamists will become more democratic.[62] The political society approach, by contrast, highlights the constitutive power of politics itself: the political platforms and organizations of Islamists have shaped institutional structures in contradictory ways, while at the same time being shaped by them. Moreover, from the political society perspective, unlike institutionalist approaches, a state's relations to global capitalism and to revolutionary upheavals constitute much more than a background motive.

It would thus be disingenuous to look at the Turkish model as simply the marriage of Islam and democracy. Versions of Islam and democracy were already combined throughout the world. Most important for the region was the combination of the Cold War version of democracy (liberal authoritarianism with elections) with several versions of official Islam. What the Turkish model contributed to this existing combination was its sociopolitical genius: put activists with revolutionary rhetoric at the helm of a counterrevolutionary state, and mobilize parts of the population in order to demobilize the rest. This was the Turkish solution to the crises generated by 1968, the Iranian revolution of 1979 and the challenge of radical Islam. And it was this solution that had failed by 2013. Its

---

61 For a prominent example of this approach, see Nathan J. Brown, *When Victory Is Not an Option: Islamist Movements in Arab Politics*, Ithaca, NY: Cornell University Press, 2012.

62 For a thorough criticism of this conclusion from within the institutionalist perspective, see Güneş Murat Tezcür, *Muslim Reformers in Iran and Turkey: The Paradox of Moderation*, Austin: University of Texas Press, 2010.

failure was due not only to internal tensions within the model, but also to unexpected (and unpredictable) interactions with the Middle East. Last but not least, the roller-coaster dynamics of global capitalist processes also helped undermine Islamic liberalism.

The Global Crisis of Capitalism

Twenty-first-century capitalism faces many difficulties, including environmental limits, skyrocketing levels of inequality, a chaotic financial system and growing youth unemployment, but I focus on only one element in this book: capitalism has not found a way to socially and politically satisfy the new middle classes. The Turkish model has failed not simply because of the frictions between Islamic positions and democracy, but also because capitalism has generated hopes, joys and fears the management of which is beyond its capacities. A full understanding of the Turkish model, which fell out of Western favour as a result of the Gezi revolt, would be therefore incomplete without an exploration of the global crisis of capital.

Capital is not just the name of an economic reality. It is also a project implemented by intellectuals, experts, militants and ideologues. The regional consent built around that reality-project (the Turkish model) has foundered on the shoals of the new petty bourgeoisie – and *not* on its 'rising expectations', as is often held, but on its *contradictory aspirations*. The new petty bourgeoisie aspires for wealth, success, luxury and hierarchy. It also craves social justice, equality (of opportunity, at least), and the joys and the beauty of the commons. It easily falls under the spell of 'career' and 'growth'; yet as easily it gets drawn into revolt.

The Turkish model was built by first winning the petty bourgeoisie to the side of business in the 1980s, then the subproletariat. It simultaneously waged a war on (some of) the proletariat and certain sectors of the new petty bourgeoisie who were too dependent on corporatism. But in the meantime, it built its own gravediggers – gravediggers who were, however, without the potential to build a new world.

The global questions now become: can the revolt of the Turkish new petty bourgeoisie give us insights into middle-class revolts elsewhere, or is its significance restricted to the erosion of regional hegemony? How does this revolt compare with other recent middle-class revolts and their relationship to capital and to state(s)? I start to answer these questions in the last two chapters, but a fuller answer must wait for another book.

A Note on Sources and Methodology

The research for this book is based on mixed sources, mostly qualitative though some quantitative. Throughout the course of the Arab revolts, I have studied the major pan-Arabic and Egyptian media outlets (newspapers, magazines, television and radio channels). The developmental and welfare policies of four Middle Eastern regimes were studied based on an analytical survey of secondary sources, as well as a study of the databases of the World Bank, the IMF and the United Nations. I consulted nationally or regionally focused statistical sources (such as the Arab Barometer and Konda) for the study of the revolts. I have also personally participated in demonstrations and revolts in Turkey, and also in Egypt. I conducted informal interviews with participants in and leaders of the demonstrations and revolts in both countries.

My ongoing fieldwork in Egypt and Turkey forms the background of much of the analysis here. Having ethnographically studied the neighbourhood dynamics and popular participation in Turkish Islamic movements ever since 2000, in 2009 I extended my fieldwork to Egypt with slightly different lenses: I now compare the business and upper middle class participation in Islamic circles in Egypt and Turkey, with specific emphasis on charitable networks and organizations.[63] I integrate little of this fieldwork in this book, which is mostly a comparative historical text. Due to space considerations, I focus mostly on the broad historical trajectories of the movements under scrutiny and resort to field notes only when necessary.

The discussion of politics, religion, economic transformation and social movements in three major nation states (Iran, Turkey and Egypt) constitute the core of the book, and another, smaller nation state (Tunisia) is also integrated into the discussion. However, the

63 See, for example, 'Contesting Benevolence: Market Orientations among Muslim Aid Providers in Egypt', *Qualitative Sociology* 36:2 (2013): 141–59.

methodology followed is not one of tightly controlled comparison,[64] though it owes certain insights to this genre of scholarship. The book rather follows these cases in their connections with each other. The ways the four countries interacted, attempted leadership of one another, became half-hearted or enthusiastic followers, and staged resistances to each other's influence are central to the story. Since many of the political, religious and economic steps taken in each country were responses to movements and regimes in the other countries (as well as to broader regional and global balances), there is no way to isolate the cases and control the dependent and independent factors under scrutiny.

Nevertheless, certain sections of the book approximate the received model of comparative analysis for multiple purposes. For instance, to evaluate the global and regional claims of Turkish economic success, one of the chapters takes a close look at how Turkey compares to the other countries based on various economic indices. The goal of such comparisons, however, is not to test hypotheses but to evaluate the potentials for and limits of Islamic liberalization in the region. The question is one of leadership and consent.

Why these specific four cases? The questions of Islamic consent and liberalization (as well as comparability) have shaped this choice. First, Turkey, Egypt and Tunisia were the main neoliberalizing republics in the region. Iran also displayed signs of neoliberalization. Second, all four cases were integrated territorial states, with strong national identities, which makes them more comparable. Third, Tunisia, Egypt and Iran were, partly for the first two reasons, more likely followers of the Turkish model. As will be discussed, the other countries in the region are much less likely homes to Islamic liberalism.[65] While comparisons between them and the countries at hand

---

64 See Peter Evans, *Dependent Development: The Alliance of Multinational, State, and Local Capital in Brazil*. Princeton, NJ: Princeton University Press, 1979; and Theda Skocpol, *States and Social Revolutions*, Cambridge: Cambridge University Press, 1979.

65 Jordan, Morocco and secondarily Kuwait have also witnessed some Islamic liberalization, but they are much less comparable to the nation states covered here. Moreover, they are not likely to be trendsetters. Another reason why they are not included in the discussion is their marginal role in the Arab uprisings, which is central to this book.

might be meaningful on other levels, a book on Islamic liberalization does not require bringing them in as full-blown cases. Finally, Turkey, Egypt and Iran have been trendsetters in Islamic currents. It is important to follow the twists and turns of their Islamic movements, since these have had serious ripple effects throughout the Islamic world.

Outline of the Book

The first part of the book (chapters 1–3) studies the old regimes, class balances, religious movements and territorial and imperial balances in the region, paying special attention to the crises of secular dictatorships, neoliberal development programmes and Islamic movements. The bulk of this part focuses on Islamic neoliberalizations in Turkey, Egypt and Iran before 2011. It also brings in a study of the weaker signs of such (Islamic neoliberal) developments in the rest of the region. It argues that 'bloc formation' (and the social and political processes that underlie it) account for the divergent paths of liberalization.

The second part (chapters 4–6) explores why not only the Arab dictatorships but also Turkish democratic-authoritarianism plunged into crisis after 2011. It begins with a scrutiny of the harbingers of the Arab uprisings (workers' and liberal movements), and is followed by an overall analysis of the 2011–13 revolts and Turkey's and the West's role in them (with a shorter look at the Iranian protests of 2009). It especially focuses on the gradual receding of the social question throughout 2011 and the declining prospects for the resolution of the political question. The impact of Islamisms on the revolt is also central to this part of the book.

This part also situates the limits of the 2011–13 revolt within an analytical history of Arab and Turkish radicalism. It discusses whether the rise of the new middle classes provides a more popular base for Middle Eastern radicalism when compared to the movements of the twentieth century. This topic leads to a broader question on the role of the new middle classes in late capitalism, which is only introduced in this book: what are the strengths and limits of middle-class revolt?

The book concludes with a discussion of how the aftermath of the Arab Spring might disturb (or reinforce) global capitalism and imperial balances. The discussion is built on a suggestive rereading of regional (and secondarily, world) history. I argue that responses to revolutions connect the dots between disparate events, social groups and institutions. What unites and divides the Middle East are its relations to 1789, 1968, 1979 and 2011. The interpretation of Middle Eastern history as a history of integration into capitalism can be salvaged only if it incorporates as a counterpoint the role of these explosive events in world history.

CHAPTER 1

Regime Crises: No (Secular) Way Out

What was the Turkish model a response to? Why did world and regional leaders and intellectuals feel that they had to support Islamic liberalism? What disease was the Turkish model a medicine for, or perhaps, what poison was it an antidote to? The crises of secular dictatorships and neoliberal development programmes (with corporatist vestiges) constituted the disease, while radical Islamic movements and regimes represented more threatening poison. A region mired in financial and real estate speculation and other semi- or nonproductive gain invited massive popular upheaval, though the leftist opposition that could organize such a resistance was absent.

Islamist opposition emerged throughout the Middle East as a criticism of secularism and conservatism, as well as their contested economic and political implications. But lacking the tools to distinguish itself sufficiently from either secularism or conservatism, it came to share the stagnation and crisis of the existing regimes and societies by the end of the 1990s. Ultimately, instead of presenting a real alternative to the system, Islamism would provide the organization and spirit for the revival of the decaying structures.

The perpetual stagnation and crises were partially due to the political disorganization that afflicted many Middle Eastern nations. The specific combination of socio-economic, political and cultural paths a nation takes is sustainable only when it rests on a well-organized power bloc. A power bloc is not simply a passing political coalition of groups, but an 'articulation' of the interests, dispositions and outlooks of various dominant strata.[1] A hegemonic power bloc is further defined by its ability to mobilize broader

1 Articulation is a contingent combination of interests and sectors that nevertheless has long-lasting effects, especially in the way it recasts the combined interests and sectors. For a fuller discussion, see Cedric de Leon, Manali Desai and Cihan Tuğal, *Building Blocs: How Parties Organize Society*, Stanford: Stanford University Press, 2015.

subordinate strata for the execution and reproduction of its rule and policies.[2]

The power bloc is itself in turn organized by interactions between state agencies, political society and civil society. While parties are frequently essential elements of political society, the latter is best defined as a field of actors and organizations that have comprehensive social visions. As we will see, these are not necessarily parties. 'Professionalization' (the extent to which politicians have become autonomous experts) is one of the core features that determine a political society's capacity to generate solid blocs. Professionalization also entails the development of programmes, platforms and visions. Professional cadres are separated by clear programmatic boundaries from their competitors. Programmes determine what actions are taken more than do personal whim or morality.

With help from these concepts, this chapter will examine the regimes, political societies and blocs in the Middle East to decipher the dynamics behind the unending crises.

Secularist Corporatism

The Kemalist 'revolution' in Turkey was the first major republican transformation in the region. Its secularism and corporatism set the agenda for many progressives in the decades to come. These secular republicanisms (and their stepbrother, Iran's modernizing monarchism) were influenced in one way or another by Kemalism and created the suffocating political, cultural and economic structures that led to the crystallization, over the span of a century, of a new kind of oppositional vocabulary based on a critique of authoritarianism and militarism.

From the standpoint of the secularist regimes, their path was the only way out of the backwardness caused by Islam (and later reinforced by colonialism). Saudi Arabia, the Gulf monarchies and the

---

2 Hence, the classical question 'what is the class basis of *x* movement, policy, regime, etc.' should be appended by another question: 'what bloc can sustain it'? Blocs, more than classes, can be taken as the (decentred) subjects of history. This definition draws on, but revises, Nikos Poulantzas's definition; see *Fascism and Dictatorship*, London: New Left Books, 1974 [1970], 72; and *Classes in Contemporary Capitalism*, London: New Left Books, 1975 [1974], 24.

other kingdoms in the region (with the exception of Iran) followed a different path. Not only secularism, but most aspects of the centralizing revolution from above were anathema to them. They based their authority on existing tribal structures, as well as a strict interpretation of classical Islam. In the Saudi case, the historical leader of the regional conservative bloc, authority was also based on oil wealth and a particular, literalist version of Islam (Wahhabism). These regimes' perceived reproduction of tribalism, women's subordination, international dependency, shallow religiosity and unproductive wealth came to constitute an absolute 'other' for the secularists, through which they further consolidated their identity.

Turkish 'Secularism'

To understand the conservative reaction to the Kemalist elite and the later Islamist challenges, it is necessary to consider the peculiar meaning that 'secularism' (*laiklik*) had for the Turkish Republic and to understand the actors who organized, revised and contested this Turkish version of secularism. Religious homogenization was an important constituent element of national unity. *Turk* came to mean 'Muslim' as well: the implicit definition of the nation was from the beginning quasi-religious.[3] Mustafa Kemal held the Muslim title of *gazi*, warrior for the faith. The question was not simply one of having less or more Islam in social life, but of the relation between religion and the state.

Secularization – as an expansion of state control over religion, rather than the simple removal of religion from public life – had become an official project starting with the Ottoman Tanzimat reforms of 1839. However, there were serious conservative revisions of this tendency, most notably under Sultan Hamid (the Second), who reigned between 1876 and 1909. With the twentieth century, secularism became an explicitly stated basic element of official ideology. In 1924, the founding constitution of the Republic retained Islam as the state religion, even as the caliphate, religious courts and schools and other institutions were swept away and the Latin alphabet and

3 Such centrality of religion in national identity is not restricted to Islamic contexts. Varieties of Christianity have been central in the formation of secular nationalisms in America, Poland, etc.

Western legal codes were introduced; the clause was removed in 1928. Secularization was formally enunciated as one of the six principles of the programme of the Kemalist Republican People's Party (CHP) in 1931 and was finally incorporated into the constitution in 1937.

Subsequent Turkish secularization can best be seen as an ongoing struggle over the nature and development of an 'official Islam', characterized by the public use of religion to promote national cohesion and capitalist development. The secularization project was continually remade, its (partially unintended) outcomes the result of a series of interventions by different social forces. This process has involved conflicts both within the power bloc constituted by the reforms of the late Ottoman period and the early years of the Republic and with social layers excluded from it. Since the 1930s, the dominant sectors within this bloc – the military leadership, the modernizing layers of the civil bureaucracy, an officially protected industrial bourgeoisie and a Western-oriented intelligentsia – favoured a more or less complete exclusion of religion from the public sphere.

The bloc's subordinate sectors – conservative elements of the bureaucracy and professional middle class, the export-oriented bourgeoisie,[4] merchants and provincial notables – tended to advocate a larger space for Islam, albeit still under 'secular' control. They occasionally mobilized broader popular layers – workers, peasants, artisans, the unemployed, small provincial entrepreneurs, clerics – against the dominant sectors and often succeeded in extracting concessions from them. The Kemalist Republican People's Party was the political vehicle (and maker) of the dominant, statist sectors of this bloc, while the more traditionalist-religious layers have been represented (and made) by a variety of different parties since the end of single-party rule in 1950: Adnan Menderes's Democrat Party in the 1950s, and Süleyman Demirel's Justice Party in the 1960s and the 1970s.

In other words, old regime secularism was much more dynamic and flexible (and very much intertwined with class and bloc balances)

4 Differences between the more locally and internationally oriented bourgeois fractions, however, should not be exaggerated. The proto-liberal bourgeoisie also benefited hugely from import-substitution, which persisted even in the 1950s, though in loosened and unplanned fashion. Ayşe Buğra and Osman Savaşkan, *New Capitalism in Turkey: The Relationship between Politics, Religion and Business*, Cheltenham, UK: Edward Elgar, 2014.

than its critics could admit. Yet such a simplified account was necessary to sustain mobilization against the old regime and bring it down.

The Turkish Route to Corporatism

Mustafa Kemal Atatürk's revolution from above left a legacy of authoritarian corporatism in Turkey, which gradually liberalized, with zigzags, after 1950. Class struggle was denied and social groups were incorporated into the state based on occupation and employment status. Although the general orientation of the Egyptian regime was similar, it was also less democratic. Corporatist incorporation,[5] much deeper than in Turkey, was organized through state-run unions and workers' quotas in parliament and other elected bodies. Creation of a state-guided, import-substituting industrial capitalism was a key policy in both countries. Tunisia followed a very similar pattern of political and social change.

The underdevelopment of the bourgeoisie was both the precondition and the result of Turkish corporatism. The overwhelmingly Greek and Armenian merchant bourgeoisie of the Ottoman period had been virtually liquidated through war, population exchange and massacre. The vast majority of Turks – over 70 per cent – were peasant smallholders, scattered in innumerable relatively self-contained villages. This left the military and civil bureaucracy (now organized as a party) as the only effective forces capable of undertaking the social-engineering tasks of the new nation. They tried to ensure that the import-substitution industries they created served, first and foremost, the national interest. To this end, both industrialists and factory workers were offered different forms of state protection,[6] which for the latter included social security, collective bargaining, unionization and the right to strike.

The manufacturing bourgeoisie, itself protected by heavy state subsidy against both internal and external competitors, tolerated these concessions because they bolstered the development of a domestic market.[7] But by the late 1960s an increasingly self-organized

5 Nazih N. M. Ayubi, *Over-Stating the Arab State: Politics and Society in the Middle East*, London: I. B. Tauris, 1995.

6 Ayşe Buğra, *State and Business in Modern Turkey: A Comparative Study*, Albany: State University of New York, 1994.

7 Çağlar Keyder, *State and Class in Turkey: A Study in Capitalist Development*, London: Verso, 1987.

working class soon threatened to break loose from state tutelage. The Turkish Workers' Party took fifteen seats in parliament in 1965,[8] and large-scale metalworkers' strikes led to a split in the state-sponsored union Türk-İş, culminating in the formation of the militant Confederation of Revolutionary Worker Unions, DİSK. As the left's power grew in the 1970s, the state backed both hard-right nationalist vigilantes and Islamists against them. Finally, in 1980 a military coup d'état put paid to the militant left with three years of state terror during which executions, torture and imprisonment effected a permanent alteration in the political landscape.

On the welfare front, the old Turkish regime resembled the southern European cases of family-based corporatism. Social policies were based on a conservative, family-oriented corporatism, which assumed that the primary beneficiaries of welfare are people whose families cannot take care of them.[9] In addition, social benefits (not only health care and pensions, but even holiday camps and social clubs) were organized on the basis of sectors. This meant that formal employees in the public and private sectors were disproportionately privileged when compared to informal workers and peddlers, layers which would later be mobilized during the antisecularist upheaval.

Though ultimately an unviable and oppressive path, republican corporatism was also far from being the monolithically top-down statism that its liberal critics held it to be. The CHP gradually moved away from its authoritarian state capitalism towards a more popular and democratic version of left-wing populism in the 1970s, but this came to an end with the 1980 military coup.

Egypt and Tunisia

Though the Kemalist experiment reverberated throughout the region, Egypt and Tunisia were its closest followers. Reza Shah's more explicit interest in and sympathy with Kemal's reforms did not put Iran on a more comparable path with Turkey, due to certain structural barriers (of which more below). These three countries leaders' and

8 Dankwart Rustow, 'Turkish Democracy in Historical and Comparative Perspective', in Metin Heper and Ahmet Evin, eds., *Politics in the Third Turkish Republic*, Boulder, CO: Westview, 1994, 3–12.

9 Ayşe Bugra and Çaglar Keyder, 'The Turkish Welfare Regime in Transformation', *Journal of European Social Policy* 16:3 (2006): 211–28.

intellectuals' attention to this Turkish model, however, was not as focused as it became in the 2000s. Similarities, to the degree they existed, can therefore be also traced back to the global spirit of the times and these countries' structural positions in world capitalism as a whole (for example, the appeal of national developmentalism as a way to catch up with the West, first put into practice in the region by Kemalism, then replicated elsewhere). Moreover, the historical context intervened in the application of Kemalism's lessons in Arab lands: the post-war era led to a pattern of secular corporatisms with socialistic overtones.

The 1920s and 1930s witnessed lively debate among Egyptian politicians, intellectuals and clerics regarding the role of established Islamic institutions. The public controversy certainly had indigenous roots, but the historian Panayiotis Vatikiotis points out that these institutions 'came into focus in part as a result of the shock served on the Islamic community everywhere by Mustafa Kemal's attack on Islam in Turkey in 1924–6'.[10] Reformists of all colours (including some liberals and clerics) drew inspiration from Kemalism in their campaign against certain aspects of Islamic law. Pious foundations or endowments (*waqf*, pl. *awqaf*), regulated by Islamic law rather than the market (and partially autonomous from the government), were among the main targets. For more than a century reformers had sought to rationalize them, but now 'Turkey's action was held up as a model by the abolitionists'.[11] This Kemalism-infused intellectual climate ultimately led to the abolishment of private endowments in 1952. Given such deep influence of Kemalism earlier on, it is not surprising that even a top-down Islamizer such as Anwar Sadat nevertheless expressed his love and admiration for Mustafa Kemal.[12]

The British-backed monarchy was overthrown in 1952. In the following years, President Gamal Nasser (the towering figure of pan-Arab nationalism) brought Islam under control. Nasser's nationalization of pious endowments undercut one source of religious autonomy. He also further disciplined al-Azhar, an institution which

10 Panayiotis J. Vatikiotis, *The History of Modern Egypt: From Muhammad Ali to Mubarak*. London: Weidenfeld and Nicolson, 1991 [1969], 305.

11 Ibid., 309.

12 John Esposito and John Voll, eds, *Makers of Contemporary Islam*, Oxford: Oxford University Press, 2001, 13.

had not been very far from political influence to begin with. A couple of years after the Free Officers coup in 1952, the Muslim Brotherhood and other Islamist organizations entered their darkest decade: though not destroyed, they had to lead an underground existence. Whereas the endowments lost their social importance and the Islamist organizations stuck to their political independence, al-Azhar struck a middle way. Its educational infrastructure remained intact and legal, which would allow it to adjust to (and have a limited Islamizing influence on) the twists and turns within Egyptian secularism.

The Free Officers regime disbanded all political parties in its first months.[13] Riding on the shoulders of the military, and in parallel fashion to Iran, the initial years of the modernizing regime were thoroughly opposed to political society (unlike Kemal's Turkey, which blended the military and the political party in imposing modernization). Even though Nasser initially became a hero, the defeat of his pan-Arabist strategy by 1967,[14] as well as the slowing down of development toward the end of his term in 1970,[15] discredited both him and his regime. However, ongoing repression ensured that all competing parties (the liberal Wafd, the conservative Ahrar, and others) remained marginal and uninfluential. This repressive structure was one of the reasons that allowed illegal Islamic organizations (including the Muslim Brotherhood) to become major players in the political arena and civil society. Exceptions include the non-Islamic Labour Party, which became Islamic at the end of the 1980s: even those civic actors with some potential felt the need to Islamize.

Between 1952 and 1956, the Egyptian economy resembled the Turkish pattern of the 1920s. State enterprise and intervention were mostly meant to enhance further private accumulation.[16] This strategy changed after the nationalization of the Suez Canal, which created a huge state patrimony, and 1961 witnessed large-scale

---

13 Tamir Moustafa, 'Law versus the State: The Judicialization of Politics in Egypt', *Law & Social Inquiry* 28 (2003): 888.

14 Manar Shorbagy, 'The Egyptian Movement for Change – Kefaya: Redefining Politics in Egypt', *Public Culture* 19 (2007): 179.

15 John Waterbury, *The Egypt of Nasser and Sadat: The Political Economy of Two Regimes*, Princeton, NJ: Princeton University Press, 1983.

16 Alan Richards and John Waterbury, *A Political Economy of the Middle East*, Boulder, CO: Westview Press, 2007, 188.

nationalizations of big industry, banking, insurance, foreign trade, utilities, marine transport, airlines, hotels and department stores.[17] As a precursor to these moves, the regime established an economic planning mechanism in 1957.

But import substitution, the emergent developmental strategy of the Egyptian regime, proved very fragile. The foreign-exchange problem was even more serious than in Turkey, since Egyptian industries did not have economies of scale to allow exports (as did Turkey). Soviet financing (which started in 1957) did not help much after the first five-year plan. The second five-year plan was a disaster, and things got worse after military defeat in 1967.

Initially, 'Arab socialism' aimed to extend social services and even employment to the whole population and distribute these equitably. The Egyptian vision was thus bolder than Turkish corporatism. But with sluggish development, it became clear that social benefits were going to be restricted to formal employees in the public and private sectors. As in Turkey, informal workers were the losers under corporatism.[18]

The regime based these policies on two (overlapping) social strata: the rural middle class and the public employees.[19] Land reform undermined the rural aristocracy, but the government redistributed the land to relatively better off country-dwellers rather than to the mass of the peasantry.[20] This class further benefited from Nasserism by sending their offspring to the universities and thereby becoming eligible for the jobs guaranteed to university graduates under 'socialism'.[21] The Egyptian regime tried to make amends for this restricted class base through subsidies for basic necessities (most of all, bread) that would spread to the whole population. Yet, especially under Sadat (a Free Officer, and Nasser's anti-Nasserite successor) and later Mubarak, even bread subsidies became much less systematic. The inconsistency

17 Ibid., 189.

18 Waterbury, *The Egypt of Nasser and Sadat*, 223.

19 Hazem Kandil, 'Why Did the Egyptian Middle Class March to Tahrir Square?', *Mediterranean Politics* 17:2 (2012): 197–215.

20 S. Yunis, *Al-Zahf al-muqadas: Muzaharat al-tanahi wa tashkil 'ebadet Abd al-Nasser*, Cairo: Dar Merit, 2005, 69.

21 R. A. Brooks, *Shaping Strategy: The Civil–Military Politics of Strategic Assessment*, Princeton, NJ: Princeton University Press, 2008, 72–3.

of policies throughout the initial decades of corporatism prevented the formation of blocs as solidly separated from each other as in Turkey.

Tunisia, even though a smaller and richer country, followed a path similar to Egypt's. The Tunisian leadership also developed a Kemalist-type relation with Islam. While dismantling or subordinating traditional religious institutions (most importantly, the Zaytouna mosque), it also set up new official ones (such as modern theology faculties). Moreover, it generously mobilized religious imagery and vocabulary to legitimize the nationalist project. Just as Kemal officially became Gazi, the founding leader Habib Bourguiba (who ruled Tunisia from 1956 to 1987) took on the name of the Great Warrior (*mujahid al-akbar*).[22] Atatürk was also a direct inspiration for the personal status code (of 1956), which equalized men and women regarding inheritance, abolished polygamy and raised the minimum age for marriage to eighteen. Nevertheless, Bourguiba decided to modernize Islamic law rather than abolish it, and was in fact critical of Atatürk's all-out attack on Islamic law.

Unlike many other Arab states (including republics such as Libya, Iraq and Syria), Tunisia's centralization led to a more or less united and homogenized population with a strong national identity,[23] making it more comparable to Turkey and Egypt.[24] After gaining its independence from France in 1956 Tunisia also subscribed to a version of Arab socialism. Regarding growth policy, the country followed the Turkish model of import-substituting industrialization, like many other countries in the region (Algeria, Egypt, Syria, Iraq and Iran). Unlike Turkey, it followed Egypt and Algeria (especially between 1962 and 1969) in giving its statist economy a radical and 'socialist' twist by subordinating the private sector.

---

22 Mehdi Mabrouk, 'Tunisia: The Radicalization of Religious Policy', in George Joffé, ed., *Islamist Radicalization in North Africa: Politics and Process*, London: Routledge, 2012, 50–2.

23 Kenneth J. Perkins, *A History of Modern Tunisia*, Cambridge: Cambridge University Press, 2004.

24 This certainly had to do with the premodern balance of the administrative centre and the tribes, as much as nineteenth- and twentieth-century political reforms. See Mounira Charrad, *States and Women's Rights: The Making of Postcolonial Tunisia, Algeria, and Morocco*, Berkeley: University of California Press, 2001.

As distinct from Egypt and Turkey, an initially independent labour union was one of the main protagonists of Tunisia's war of independence. This trade union federation (UGTT) retained independence and power as long as the country remained on a social-corporatist path. UGTT usually supported the regime, but had the clout to oppose it whenever the interests of organized labour were threatened. Another important difference to Egypt was the salience of a political party (neo-Destour, founded in 1934), which articulated diverse groups such as small commercial capitalists, intellectuals, professionals and trade unions.

Iran

Since the 1920s, Iran had been held together by a monarchic dictatorship with a secularist ideology.[25] Reza Shah (the founder of the modernizing Pahlavi dynasty) attempted reforms quite similar to the Turkish ones. In fact, his own coterie compared him to both Mussolini and Atatürk.[26] The Shah and his entourage showed an interest in Kemal's reforms well before his famous visit to Turkey in 1934,[27] after which he took more directly Turkish-like, top-down secularist steps. In some issues such as language reform,[28] Iran's intelligentsia studied Turkey closely.

The obsession with clothing, which marks today's Islamist and secularist politics, also shaped much of the two countries' interactions at the time, as the appointment of a new ambassador (Mohammad Ali Foroughi) to Ankara demonstrates:

> Foroughi was quite aware of the sartorial dimension of his new appointment. He happened to be in Paris when he learnt of it, and immediately rushed out to buy himself a dinner jacket, tails and a morning coat. In Turkey, he got along well with Mustafa

25 Fred Halliday, *Iran: Dictatorship and Development*, New York: Penguin, 1978.

26 Matthew Elliot, 'New Iran and the Dissolution of Party Politics under Reza Shah', in Touraj Atabaki and Eric J. Zürcher, eds, *Men of Order: Authoritarian Modernization under Atatürk and Reza Shah*, London: I. B. Tauris, 2004, 87.

27 Ibid., 68.

28 John R. Perry, 'Language Reform in Turkey and Iran', in Atabaki and Zürcher, eds, *Men of Order*, 238–59.

> Kemal and Ismet Pasha, and saw them often. But it was not easy for a man of Forughi's urbanity to have to keep his Pahlavi hat on while all other diplomats were bareheaded, and so on 28 April 1928 he sent a secret letter to Taimurtash, in which he pressed the powerful court minister to work for the adoption of the European hat . . . Forughi returned to Iran in 1930, but his work endured. By 1932 bilateral negotiations had led to a marked improvement in Irano-Turkish relations.[29]

The influence was not unidirectional. During a train journey through Anatolia with the Shah in 1934, Atatürk threw a tantrum when they saw a turbaned cleric. This internationally embarrassing sign of backwardness led Atatürk to ban (male) clerical garb in public spaces. The Shah was impressed and, upon his return, expedited hat reform in Iran.[30]

Yet the Shah ended up a much more arbitrary (and less political party–based) leader than Atatürk, partially due to the much less developed economic, political and administrative centralization that preceded his rule.[31] As Eric Zürcher and Ervand Abrahamian have both pointed out,[32] Kemalism and Pahlavism (despite all of their similarities) differed in one core aspect: Kemalism's organization of consent through a political party, which left a marked difference between the two countries. The Shah in fact did try out consent-formation through several parties, one of them explicitly based on the Kemalist model, but these experiments were short-lived due to the Shah's fear of republicanism.[33] This divergence even spilled into the contrasting formations of their Islamic movements. The obsession with clothing rules has remained a constant in both countries until today, but consent for them was organized by a party in one context (and was more 'voluntary' and therefore more insidious), whereas in

29 Houchang Chehabi, 'Dress Codes for Men in Turkey and Iran', in Atabaki and Zürcher, ed, *Men of Order*, 220–1.

30 Ibid., 221–2.

31 Atabaki and Zürcher, eds, *Men of Order*, 9–11.

32 Eric J. Zürcher, 'Institution Building in the Kemalist Republic: The Role of the People's Party', in Atabaki and Zürcher, eds, *Men of Order*, 98–112; Ervand Abrahamian, *Iran between Two Revolutions*, Princeton, NJ: Princeton University Press, 1982, 148–9.

33 Abrahamian, *Iran between Two Revolutions*, 138–9.

the other different kinds of clothing were imposed by the state (and later on, by paramilitaries) in different periods. The political party remains the most effective tool for merging the voluntary and forced faces of subordination.

In the 1970s, Iran faced multiple problems. The failure to industrialize and secularize the country discredited a range of secular authority figures, most of all Mohammad Reza Pahlavi (Reza Shah's son, who had replaced him in 1941).[34] These failures were paralleled by internationally imposed, indecisive political openings.[35] In the meantime, even some secular intellectuals, students and middle-class sectors were thoroughly dissatisfied with secular-modern lifestyles and turned to religion as an answer – a trend that had been in the making for several decades but that intensified in the 1970s.

Although most clerics were not opposed to this modernizing dictatorship during its first decade,[36] the leading node of Islamic resistance became the clergy and remained so up until the 1979 revolution. The turning point was the 1960s, when the Shah undertook a 'White Revolution', which sought to industrialize the country while undermining the prerogatives of the landlords, merchants and the clergy. Non-mainstream clergy led the mobilization against the Shah's half-hearted revolution from above, resisting the regime's moves to break up landholdings (including those owned by religious foundations), grant women the right to vote and equality in marriage and allow religious minorities to hold government office. Khomeini, a maverick cleric, became nationally renowned during this opposition.

The old regime in Iran took the first decades of the Turkish regime as a model, but was occasionally bolder in its intervention in everyday life (for example, an all-out ban on veiling that extended to public places and lasted for several years, rather than a ban restricted to

---

34 John Foran, *Fragile Resistance: Social Transformation in Iran from 1500 to the Revolution*, Boulder, CO: Westview Press, 1993.

35 See Said A. Arjomand, *The Turban for the Crown: The Islamic Revolution in Iran*, Oxford: Oxford University Press, 1988; Michael M. J. Fischer, *Iran: From Religious Dispute to Revolution*, Cambridge, MA: Harvard University Press, 1980; and Misagh Parsa, *Social Origins of the Iranian Revolution*, New Brunswick, NJ: Rutgers University Press, 1989.

36 Anthony Gill and Arang Keshavarzian, 'State Building and Religious Resources: An Institutional Theory of Church–State Relations in Iran and Mexico', *Politics and Society* 27:3 (1999): 442–5.

educational and official sites, as in Turkey). This seeming boldness set a precedent for its Islamic opposition. Moreover, the monarchy in Iran became more authoritarian while Turkey partially democratized. Bazaar and clerical networks frequently resisted (during the 1930s and 1960s) and intermittently negotiated (in the 1920s and early 1950s) with the state, and thereby constituted the core civil society tradition in the twentieth century. However, there was no autonomous and strong political society, since the major parties had been banned after a coup in 1953 against Mohammad Mossadegh's elected nationalist government. Political opposition remained mostly clandestine and restricted.

As in its other policies, the monarchy's developmental path drew on the republican models of Turkey and Egypt rather than following the path of the Gulf, despite abundant oil wealth that made the Gulf model a possibility for Iran. From the 1920s to the 1940s, social protection programmes expanded from the civil bureaucracy to industrial workers. Later expansion came in jolts followed by setbacks, most importantly during Mossadegh's short tenure.[37] The overall structural results were similar to Turkey and Egypt (and to Latin American welfare systems as well): both development and welfare benefited formal employees more than informal employees (and urban more than rural regions), especially after the White Revolution of the 1960s. The result was an exclusionary corporatism that left large swaths of society outside the formal sectors of production and protection. Hence, bloc-ness was at low levels within the ruling strata, and the power bloc sealed weaker articulations at the societal level when compared to its secularizing counterparts in Turkey, Egypt and Tunisia.

Neoliberal Undoing of Corporatism

In so far as the secular republics are concerned, Turkey's and Egypt's experiences were trendsetters in neoliberalization, though Algeria and Tunisia quickly followed suit, and Turkey was a latecomer in the transition to neoliberalism. Turkey's initial neoliberal moves, though, were

37 Kevan Harris, 'A Martyrs' Welfare State and Its Contradictions: Regime Resilience and Limits through the Lens of Social Policy in Iran', in Steven Heydemann and Reinoud Leenders, eds, *Middle East Authoritarianisms: Governance, Contestation, and Regime Resilience in Syria and Iran*, Stanford, CA: Stanford University Press, 2013, 61–80.

stronger than those of Egypt, and the two countries converged again in the 2000s in deepening their neoliberalization. Iraq and Syria have done much less in regards to liberalizing their economies. In Yemen, there were some signs of neoliberalization, yet these did not go very far in an extremely impoverished and territorially torn country. Algeria's experiment was quickly interrupted by civil war. Hence, Turkey, Egypt and Tunisia became the main neoliberalizing republics in the region.

Turkey

In Turkey, the September 1980 junta put into effect the neoliberal reforms suggested by policymakers on 24 January of that year. As well as a response to the threat posed by organized labour and the left, neoliberalization was also a pragmatic way of dealing with the budgetary problems that import substitution strategies had created. Turkey's growth in previous decades had been possible only through massive foreign subsidies and debt, for the protected industries required expensive, high-technology machinery (which had to be imported). These difficulties fostered an overreliance on flows of foreign currencies. The other import substituting modernizers in the region were also hit by the same problem.[38]

The 1980 coup simultaneously expanded official Islam's sphere of influence in order to fight the left while suppressing autonomous expressions of Islam. The generals in fact declared the new regime in Iran as one of Turkey's biggest enemies. Following the military's dissolution of all existing parties and civil organizations, a new centre-right party (the Motherland Party or ANAP, led by Özal) led the neoliberalization process. Secular businessmen, pious tradesmen and a new secular professional class concentrated in the private sector constituted the core of the party. The subordinate wing of the power bloc seemed to be taking over, but the completion of this transition within the boundaries of the old regime (and therefore preservation of the existing power bloc) would prove impossible.

Very quickly, Turkey became an export-oriented country, with manufactured goods constituting a big part of the exporting strategy. Buğra and Savaşkan note: 'The share of total exports in GDP, which was 3.1 per cent in 1980, reached 10.5 per cent in 2000 and continued

38 Richards and Waterbury, *A Political Economy of the Middle* East.

to increase'.[39] By 2012, 90 per cent of exports were manufactured goods. Contradicting free-market prescriptions, the government took a very active hand in promoting the export-oriented bourgeoisie through subsidies and preferential credits.[40]

Society remained divided along class lines. Grievances against neoliberalization were mostly expressed in support for the Social Democratic Populist Party (SHP), an offshoot of the CHP. However, this party was a weaker version of the CHP of the 1970s; in the absence of a strong socialist and communist left (whose leaders and members had been hanged, imprisoned and exiled en masse), the SHP was free from strong pressure on its left. Hence, rather than opposing neoliberalization, the SHP promised to temper it, after the example of the Third Way parties in the West such as New Labour in Britain. Even so, the SHP's municipal and governmental performance was dismal. Mired in corruption, it could not deliver even as much as Western and Latin American Third Way options, effectively closing the route to a standard (secular) social liberalism in Turkey. This, among many other factors, would gradually push social liberals, mainstream(ed) social democrats, liberalized Marxists and other proponents of Third Way–style policies to invest their hopes in what they perceived to be an Islamic version of Blairism.

Egypt

Sadat and Mubarak, the two presidents who succeeded Nasser, combined neoliberalization with uneven doses of cooperation with Islamists. Even though this paralleled the post-1980 Turkish pattern (of absorbing Islamists to soothe neoliberalism-induced distress), Egypt remained the more authoritarian of the two. Nevertheless, real opportunities, to the extent they were granted at all, were provided to the Islamists. As important as his incorporation of Islamic activists

---

39 Ayşe Buğra and Osman Savaşkan, *New Capitalism in Turkey: The Relationship between Politics, Religion and Business*, Cheltenham, UK: Edward Elgar, 2014.

40 Ziya Öniş, 'Anatomy of Unorthodox Liberalism: The Political Economy of Turkey in the 1980s', in Metin Heper, ed., *Strong State and Economic Interest Groups: The Post-1980 Turkish Experience*, Berlin: De Gruyter, 1991, 27–41; and Öniş, 'Turgut Özal and His Economic Legacy: Turkish Neo-liberalism in Critical Perspective', *Middle Eastern Studies* 40:4 (2007): 113–34.

was Sadat's turn to religion as a basis of legitimacy between 1970 and 1981. Nasser had also deployed Islam to build support, but Sadat did so much more systematically. He generously resorted to Islamic vocabulary to help mobilize Egyptians against Israel during the 1973 war. Right after the war, he came to be known as the 'Believer President' or Al-Ra'is Al-Mu'min.[41] The pro-government press engaged in debates of what constitutes an Islamic economy, unsurprisingly putting emphasis on individual ownership and initiative. Islamic investment companies and banks proliferated under the protection of the regime. Moreover, the 1971 constitution stipulated that Islam has a primary role in legislation,[42] and an historic 1980 amendment underlined *sharia* as the principal source of legislation. This recruitment of Islam did not necessarily result in a solid bloc of forces aligned with the regime in a hegemonic way, though it certainly helped spread religiosity throughout Egypt in a diffuse manner. Ironically, Sadat was assassinated by Islamists in the following year.

Mubarak did not have Sadat's religious appeal as a believing president. But he also sought to incorporate Islamic activists through elections and other mechanisms, even though he somewhat tightened controls on religious activity on campuses. He also tried to expand the regime's religious legitimacy by using al-Azhar, but his moves in this sphere might have partly delegitimized this institution as much as bolster the regime's Islamic credentials.[43]

US involvement in this regime–Islam cooperation has long been a matter of speculation. Documents recently provided through WikiLeaks suggest that Henry Kissinger perceived the Brotherhood as Sadat's 'stick' against leftists. According to these documents, the regime supported the Islamists both financially and organizationally. Most crucially, it filled the university campuses with Brotherhood members and other Islamists to counterbalance Marxists and Nasserists.[44] (An organization with origins on campuses ultimately assassinated Sadat.) The US was most probably on board with (and

41 Hesham al-Awadi, *In Pursuit of Legitimacy: The Muslim Brothers and Mubarak, 1982–2000*, London: I. B. Tauris, 2005, 37.

42 Ibid., 37, 41.

43 See al-Awadi, *In Pursuit of Legitimacy,* chapter 3.

44 'al-Ikhwan: ʿasa al-Sadat li darb al-Nasseriyyin', *almasryalyoum.com*, 7 April 2013.

perhaps actively involved in) these efforts to create an official Islam against the left.

Despite having comparable opportunities, Egyptian and Turkish Islamists diverged in their strategies. This divergence suggests that we need to take into account the structure of political society in analysing how similar political opportunities might sometimes give rise to contrasting results. The section on Islamist opposition below will address this question.

The regime's top-down Islamizing strategies were intertwined with its policies of economic liberalization. Egypt was home to extensive privatization and deregulation from the 1970s to the 1990s. These reforms brought with them sustained growth in the first half of the 1980s, along with declining real wages and increasing unemployment and poverty.[45] IMF-imposed subsidy cuts of bread, sugar and other necessities resulted in riots and seventy-seven deaths in 1977. The IMF quickly gave out huge loans and the subsidies were restored. After that point, the subsidies were gradually and covertly eliminated.[46]

Luckily for the regime, the boost in oil prices meant increased remittances from the Gulf and some oil revenue from the Sinai Peninsula. When oil prices dropped again in the 1980s and Islamists attacked tourist targets, both oil and tourist revenues declined again. Egypt became one of the most heavily indebted countries in the world. The government attempted to finance the debt by overvaluing the currency, a strategy that further discouraged exports and made the trade gap more serious.[47]

After Sadat's liberalizing ('Open Door') policies, cuts in government credits to farmers and rural provision increased poverty in the countryside,[48] transformations which were comparable to those Turkey underwent from the 1980s onward. Political opposition to

45 Eberhard Kienle, 'More Than a Response to Islamism: The Political Deliberalization of Egypt in the 1990s', *Middle East Journal* 52 (1998): 219–35.

46 John W. Salevurakis and S. Mohamed Abdel-Haleim, 'Bread Subsidies in Egypt: Choosing Social Stability or Fiscal Responsibility', *Review of Radical Political Economics* 40:1 (2008): 35–49.

47 Richards and Waterbury, *A Political Economy of the Middle East*, 222–4, 249.

48 Ray Bush,. 'Politics, Power and Poverty: Twenty Years of Agricultural Reform and Market Liberalisation in Egypt', *Third World Quarterly* 28:8 (2007): 1603–5.

these rural reforms was weak.[49] However, Sadat's neoliberalization (and even the first few years of Mubarak's rule) retrospectively seems to have been half-hearted, despite the protests it generated. Deregulation, privatization and the shift of emphasis from industry to services and finance were inconclusive.[50]

The regime tried out an economically orthodox IMF standby agreement in 1993, with the US forgiving military debts in return for fiscal discipline (as well as a reward for political obedience during the Gulf War in 1990–91). The government cut spending, increased its international reserves and rolled back its budget deficits. Plummeting oil prices, the resulting state bankruptcy and the IMF agreement led to a thorough privatization.[51] However, most of Egypt's economic growth resulted from public investments (such as irrigation projects) and not from exports. In fact, integration with the world economy actually declined.[52]

Some reasons for the failure of this renewed neoliberal attempt at growth were the Asian financial crisis, continuing attacks against tourists, low labour productivity, and crony capitalism. At the beginning of the 1990s, the privatization programme was proceeding rapidly, yet its pace soon declined. Most of the newly privatized companies in any case went to the regime insiders.[53] The military resolved the Islamist insurgency (and the attacks on tourists) by the mid-1990s. However, much damage had already been done. The explicitly public nature of the regime's cronyism also further delegitimized neoliberalization, and marketization under these circumstances became more and more difficult to sustain.

In sum, the secularist undoing of Egyptian corporatism remained a top-down affair. Turkish neoliberalization, by contrast, came to be a hegemonic ideology only through bottom-up Islamization. Sadat

49 Ibid., 1606–8.

50 See Relli Shechter, 'The Cultural Economy of Development in Egypt: Economic Nationalism, Hidden Economy and the Emergence of Mass Consumer Society during Sadat's Infitah', *Middle Eastern Studies* 44:4 (2008): 571–83; and Dona J. Stewart, 'Changing Cairo: The Political Economy of Urban Form', *International Journal of Urban and Regional Research* 23:1 (1999): 142.

51 S. Suleiman, *Al-Nizam al-qawi wa al-dawla al-da'ifa: Edaret al-azma al-maliya wa al-taghir al-siyasi fi 'ahd Mubarak*, Cairo: Dar Merit, 2005, 9, 54.

52 Richards and Waterbury, *A Political Economy of the Middle East*, 250.

53 Ibid., 251.

and Mubarak's mixture of Islamization from above and control over Islamists postponed experimentation with a full Islamic neoliberalization for decades.

Tunisia

Like Egypt and Turkey (and unlike oil-rich Iran), industrialization through an import substitution strategy led to unresolvable balance of payments crises in Tunisia and resulted in a shift to export-led (and market-oriented) growth. The shift arguably started at the end of the 1960s, but picked up pace during the 1980s.[54] Change had become palpable by 1969, when founding leader Habib Bourguiba turned on more left-wing elements within the regime in order to win back small capitalists and landholders. The weight of the state in national planning and promoting economic growth significantly declined after this point.[55] The regime also started a policy of top-down Islamization in the 1970s. Most notably, Bourguiba established the Association for the Safeguard of the Koran,[56] which served to counterbalance the left.[57] Rather than simply covering regime policies in Islamic garb, as was perhaps intended by Bourguiba, this organization had a bold vision: it claimed that it wanted to create an Islamic society and state working from the bottom up, transforming individuals one by one.

As in Egypt, the Tunisian state's quick withdrawal from provision of necessities led to social unrest. Prompted by bread riots, the officially recognized union, the UGTT, called for a general strike in 1977, the same year as the Egyptian bread riots. Throughout the 1980s, the UGTT's relations with the regime remained fraught with tension, and became more and more repressive of the union, though the latter

---

54 Alan Richards, John Waterbury, Melanie Cammett, and Ishac Diwan, *A Political Economy of the Middle East*, 3rd edn, Boulder, CO: Westview Press, 2013, 25–9.

55 Ibid., 195–6.

56 Similar to the disagreements regarding regime-Islamist relations in Egypt, the import of such active support or involvement of the Tunisian state in fostering the Islamic movement in the 1960s is a matter of unresolved dispute. Mehdi Mabrouk, 2012. 'Tunisia: The Radicalization of Religious Policy', in George Joffé, ed., *Islamist Radicalization in North Africa: Politics and Process*, London: Routledge, 2012, 54.

57 François Burgat and William Dowell, *The Islamic Movement in North Africa*, 2nd edn, Austin: University of Texas Press, 1997, 184.

was able to retain some autonomy – a room of manoeuvre whose scope depended on the region and the sector.[58]

As in many countries throughout the world, more neoliberalization was seen as the medicine for the shortcomings of initial neoliberal reform. When consumer subsidy cuts resulted in further riots in 1984 (again backed by the UGTT), the increasingly neoliberal regime decided to knock on the IMF's door. The IMF imposed a harsh standby agreement as a condition, putting Tunisia on the path to become the most orthodox neoliberal regime in the Arab world. The result was sustainable growth in the following years, along with increasing exports and untaxed imports. Levels of unemployment remained a problem, despite labour's negotiations with the regime to slow unemployment as much as possible.[59]

The Crisis of Neoliberal Authoritarianisms

Neoliberalization, coupled with varying degrees and kinds of 'secular' authoritarianism in these three core countries, started to run up against more difficulties in the 1990s and 2000s. Divided and inept, IMF-monitored centrist parties mismanaged (though still erratically 'liberalized') the Turkish economy throughout the 1990s, a mismanagement that ultimately led to the financial meltdown of 2001, when the whole country became much poorer overnight.[60] The roots of the crisis lay in financialization: growth during the 1990s had come to depend more and more on spirals of debt, government borrowing and then governmental and private reinvestment in risky bonds and securities.[61]

As Jamie Peck notes, in our times the failures of free market economics are resolved through free market economics.[62] Kemal

58 Chris Toensing, 'Tunisian Labor Leaders Reflect upon Revolt', *Middle East Report* 41:258 (Spring 2011): 30.

59 Richards et al., *A Political Economy of the Middle East*, 3rd edn, 240–2.

60 See Çağlar Keyder, 'The Turkish Bell Jar', *New Left Review* 2:28 (July/August 2004): 65–84.

61 Buğra and Savaşkan, *New Capitalism in Turkey*; Ziya Öniş, 'Beyond the 2001 Financial Crisis: The Political Economy of the New Phase of Neo-Liberal Restructuring in Turkey', *Review of International Political Economy* 16:3 (2009): 409–32.

62 See Neil Brenner, Jamie Peck and Nik Theodore, 'Variegated Neoliberalization: Geographies, Modalities, Pathways', *Global Networks* 10:2 (2010): 209–10.

Derviş, a top-level World Bank figure, was hastily summoned. He created the blueprint for aggressive deregulation and privatization measures that gripped Turkey for the coming decade. The already tight links with (and subordination to) Washington Consensus institutions such as the IMF and the World Bank were further strengthened.[63] The question now became whether these policies would result in mass unrest under (Islamized) secular authoritarianism. A bloc of leaders, intellectuals, entrepreneurs and activists answered with a resounding 'no!'. IMF/World Bank interventions had very different outcomes in Turkey compared to Tunisia and Egypt.

In Egypt, the decisive neoliberal shift came at the beginning of the 2000s. The business class, which had remained in a subordinate position within the power bloc, gained the upper hand.[64] After 2004, even the cabinet came to be dominated by businessmen, the peak of the neoliberalization of the state apparatus. The cabinet revamped the official outlook on inequality, poverty and unemployment and solidly redefined these as managerial rather than social problems.[65] Losing its relative autonomy, moreover, the state was gradually plundered by this class. De-statization of the economy, rather than resolving corruption, as expected by mainstream Western circles, instead led to more corruption.

Despite many differences, Turkey and Egypt also displayed certain parallels in their marketization processes. In both countries industrialization had slowed in recent decades. The motors of growth became tourism, finance and construction (though with some manufacturing on the margins, such as the textile sector, which was significant in both Turkey and Egypt). The predominance of tourism, construction

63 The AKP government, self-confident due to the credibility it gained as a result of its pursuit of free market policies, loosened its ties with the IMF in the 2010s.

64 While Kandil provides one of the best accounts of this process, his insistence on calling the Egyptian bourgeoisie (including the richest families of the country) a 'middle class' sector takes away from the analysis. A critical distinction between the bourgeoisie and the new petty bourgeoisie deals with the analytical problems this institutionalist baggage (which takes the ruling class as the upper class) creates. Furthermore, the dominant class has to be differentiated from the ruling class.

65 See Timothy Mitchell, *Rule of Experts: Egypt, Techno-Politics, Modernity*, Berkeley: University of California Press, 2002.

and finance prevented big leaps in industrialization or technological development despite sustained growth in both cases,[66] and contrasting sharply to the high-tech-oriented neoliberalization of India.

Egypt stopped being an oil exporter in 2007, and its Suez Canal revenues declined after the 2008 global crisis. Though none of this plunged Egypt into a fatal economic crisis, it prepared the ground for economic disarray that would further sharpen after 2011. The following sections and the next chapter will analyse why a hegemonic Islamic bloc similar to the Turkish one could not emerge despite this crisis (and sweep away the corrupt neoliberal secularism).

Tunisia was virtually the only country in the whole Middle East where secular neoliberalization seemed to be proceeding smoothly. The only apparent cost was dictatorial policies and intense cronyism,[67] along with a chronic unemployment problem that was characteristic of all other neoliberalizations in the region. Ben Ali, a general who had replaced the founding (and ailing) leader Bourguiba through a coup in 1987, curtailed the civilian makeup of the regime and invigorated the security apparatus. However, this did not prevent the regime from boasting of a steady growth based, most importantly, on a sustained export strategy (which included a huge chunk of exported industrial goods). Tunisia was unique in this regard, and its success was comparable only to that of Turkey.

Due to its comparatively successful neoliberalization, Tunisia came to be regarded as the IMF's and World Bank's poster child. International agencies noted the problems of authoritarianism and cronyism, but these were considered unimportant footnotes in an overall positive evaluation, and were regarded much less serious than cronyism and 'corruption' elsewhere in the world, including Italy and Greece.[68] Tunisia got a standing ovation for its seeming progress in international competitiveness, poverty reduction, the advancement of

---

66 Thomas Richter and Christian Steiner, 'Politics, Economics and Tourism Development in Egypt: Insights into the Sectoral Transformations of a Neo-patrimonial Rentier State', *Third World Quarterly* 29:5 (2008): 955.

67 Stephen King, *Liberalization against Democracy*, Bloomington: Indiana University Press, 2003.

68 Emma C. Murphy, 'Under the Emperor's Neoliberal Clothes! Why the International Financial Institutions Got It Wrong in Tunisia', in Nouri Gana, ed., *The Making of the Tunisian Revolution: Contexts, Architects, Prospects*, Edinburgh: Edinburgh University Press, 2013, 37–41, 45.

women, fiscal management, human development and economic growth.

It was only after the revolution that analysts started to uncover the social costs of the Ben Ali regime, such as the exclusion of traditional merchants and the rising middle classes in favour of Ben Ali's cronies. Analysts also started to pay more attention to the problems of unemployment, regional disparities and poverty. The problem is that most of these were post-hoc explanations of regime crisis.[69] These weaknesses were discovered quickly after the fact, which makes one doubt how much of the 2010–11 revolt can be attributed to them. We are more likely to have a balanced evaluation of neoliberalization under Ben Ali after the heat of the moment passes.

The Challenge of the Iranian Revolution: Corporatism Revolutionized

Previously on a comparable path, Iran ultimately constructed its own way of exiting secular corporatism. Rather than simply dismantling it through marketization, it revolutionized and Islamized corporatism. The revolution was a non-neoliberal response to stagnant national development and its injustices, secularism and authoritarianism. Due to this very originality, Iran became a force to contend with throughout the region (as much as the decaying old regimes and their elites). In other words, the secular and Islamic varieties of neoliberalization that flowered in the Middle East in the 1980s and onwards were responses not only to the failure of secular corporatism, but to the Iranian revolution as well.

The 1979 Islamic revolution thus introduced novel dynamics not only to Iran but to the region as a whole. It went beyond simply putting Islam at the centre of politics, society and economics. It empowered the poor, the working classes, and the middle classes in paradoxical and militarized ways. Its electrifying message shook the region so much that the Middle East has yet to recover. It can even be argued that the Islamic revolution, as a threat to which regional elites had to respond in some coordinated way, contributed to the making of 'the Middle East' (originally a Cold War category and construct).

69 See Murphy, 'Under the Emperor's Neoliberal Clothes!', for a rare self-criticism of a past favourable assessment.

Political Dynamics of the Revolution

Who brought about the Islamic revolution? Which political actors played the decisive role in the construction of the Islamic regime? During the Islamic revolution, as before, there was no effective Iranian political organization (in parties or other sociopolitical organizations).[70] There were established secular and religious parties (or rather, factions), but with no strong, widespread roots in the population.[71] The official party of the revolution (the Islamic Republican Party) did not pre-exist the revolution, but was established in 1979.[72] Islamic and secular sociopolitical organizations such as the People's Feda'iyan and the People's Mojahedin were active in toppling the Shah,[73] but were not strong enough to protect the revolution's popular gains against the clerics.[74]

The weak link in Iranian political society has thus been the constitution of leadership through parties and sociopolitical organizations. Between 1979 and 1983, the clerics pushed most political organizations out of legality and then out of existence. The violent response of sociopolitical organizations to this repressive atmosphere terrorized the country and provided excuses to the new regime to increase repression, eventually leading to an almost wholesale destruction of the organizations and their sympathizers. After the suppression of Islamic and secular unofficial parties by 1983, the Islamic regime gave rise to quasi-parties (rather than open ones) in the form of radicals, pragmatic moderates, conservatives and (later) Islamic liberals organizing in state

70 I reserve the term *sociopolitical organization* for groupings that have broad (shared and contested) political, social and economic visions, but are not as institutionalized as parties.

71 One of the most prominent of these, the Freedom Movement of Iran, for instance, was not even comparable to the Turkish National Salvation Party/Welfare Party or the Egyptian Muslim Brotherhood in terms of the scope and depth of its organization.

72 Bahman Baktiari, *Parliamentary Politics in Revolutionary Iran: The Institutionalization of Factional Politics*, Gainesville: University Press of Florida, 1996, 55.

73 Nikki R. Keddie, *Modern Iran: Roots and Results of Revolution*, New Haven, CT: Yale University Press, 2006 [2003], 238; Charles Kurzman, *The Unthinkable Revolution in Iran*, Cambridge, MA: Harvard University Press, 2004, 146–7.

74 Ervand Abrahamian, *The Iranian Mojahedin*, New Haven, CT: Yale University Press, 1989.

agencies, parliament and civil society (for example, pious foundations) under different factions (without explicit programmes and organizations). Ali Gheissari and Vali Nasr underline how these factions differed from political actors in the usual sense:

> The . . . factions existed only informally. There was no actual organization, charter, rules, or platforms to define membership; nor were there any grassroots movements and party structures. The factions functioned as informal circles within the revolutionary elite, with ill-defined and often changing boundaries. The factions became proto-party structures, however, especially because they shaped electoral results directly.[75]

These factions did form a political society, but not a strong, autonomous and professionalized one. As a result, they have not penetrated civil society to the degree that Turkish Islamists have. The point is not that there was no political society in Iran, but that political society was not organized in a structure comparable to the Turkish one. These factions *were* organized in terms of colonizing different parts of the state machinery;[76] but *were not* organized in terms of constituting *sustainable* links with and mobilizing society. Even during the revolution, sociopolitical organizations and parties had intervened very late, and during most of 1978 mobilization was controlled by clerics and clerical students.[77] This factor blurred the boundaries between the state, political society and civil society.

These particular ways that political society interacted with state and civil society led to construction of a quite original power bloc. As distinct from the Egyptian case, the Iranian power bloc had more meat to it; it was also, relatively speaking, based more on mobilization of subordinate strata. As distinct from the Turkish case, however, the power bloc was both *volatile* and *frail*, and the lines between its dominant and subordinate sectors were quite blurred. By the end of the 1980s, the conservative clerics and the merchants constituted the

75 Ali Gheissari and Vali Nasr, *Democracy in Iran: History and the Quest for Liberty*, Oxford: Oxford University Press, 2006, 101.

76 Baktiari, *Parliamentary Politics in Revolutionary Iran*.

77 See Kurzman, *Unthinkable Revolution*, chapter 2.

dominant, and the radical clerics and religious (urban) middle strata the subordinate, sectors of the bloc (even though they were more influential at the beginning of the decade). These sectors mobilized the subproletariat for their projects, but the proletariat and the secular middle classes were gradually demobilized (and repressed). The old regime's upper classes (the landlords and the bourgeoisie) were decisively excluded from the power bloc. These balances were to change decisively in the 1990s.

Changes in Religious Life

This dispersed structure of political society (and the resulting volatility of the power bloc) set limits to what the Islamic Republic could accomplish. Everyday life transformations after the revolution depended, to a large degree, on the state and paramilitary organizations, not on political parties. The state imposed gender segregation and dress codes (veiling and dark-coloured clothing for women), and from time to time it banned music. The regime also restricted relationships between girls and boys. It outlawed daytime eating during the fasting month. These regulations were enforced not only by the official police, but also by paramilitary organizations such as the Basij.

In the Shah's Iran, whereas public places were always open to women on paper, this openness was a reality only in secularized, wealthy and westernized northern Teheran.[78] The Islamic Republic promised to end urban domination over the periphery and also to segregate urban space along gender lines (class egalitarianism coupled with gender inegalitarianism).[79] For almost a decade, this crystallized as tight gender control of the urban centre by paramilitary groups staffed by squatter and provincial youth.

There were some countertrends as well. With worsening economic conditions at the end of the Iraq–Iran war, the regime had to allow women access to public spaces. Ironically, by opening up the city to

78 Masserat Amir-Ebrahimi, 'Conquering Enclosed Public Spaces', *Cities* 23 (2006): 455–61.

79 For the incredibly contradictory, sometimes liberating, aspects and outcomes of segregation policies, see Nazanin Shahrokni, 'The Mother's Paradise: Women-Only Parks and the Dynamics of State Power in the Islamic Republic of Iran', *Journal of Middle East Women's Studies* (forthcoming).

all those who donned the veil, the regime incorporated more women from squatter areas into public city life when compared to the Shah's time.[80] These developments were restricted, however, due to the structure of political society and the state, which tolerated them but did not adopt them as core elements of its own project.

In sum, the spirituality of the revolution, which some (most notably Michel Foucault) had hoped would result in a less authoritarian structure, actually led to more authoritarianism. The reason, however, could be sought not only in spirituality and religiosity as such, but in the political forms through which spirituality and religiosity were experienced and imposed. State- and paramilitary-dominated Islamization in Iran kept alive the hope among many intellectuals that a religiosity exercised through organization in democratic parties and civil society would lead to quite different results. This implicit or explicit contrast with Iran formed one of the intellectual components of the Turkish model and its version of Islam.

Improvising the Islamic Economy

In the first decade of the revolution, Iranian Islamic political society was bifurcated along the axis of support for two different class forces: the middle-class sectors of the bazaar versus the subproletariat. The small shopkeepers and artisans (henceforth 'small merchants') were the primary class forces in the overthrow of the Shah.[81] The subproletarian sectors constituted a secondary class, at best.

Workers and their allies occupied many enterprises during the revolution. Whether willingly or not, the emergent Islamic state recognized and confirmed the occupations by declaring that the major industries and national trade and banking would be a part of the public sector. Article 44 of the revolutionary constitution declared, at the same time, that the public sector would be paralleled by a cooperative sector based on Islamic principles. The private sector would only supplement these two core sectors.

In the early 1980s, the radical, pro-subproletariat quasi-party comprised Bani-Sadr (the first president), the Revolutionary Council,

80 Amir-Ebrahimi, 'Conquering Enclosed Public Spaces'.

81 Misagh Parsa, *Social Origins of the Iranian Revolution*, New Brunswick, NJ: Rutgers University Press, 1989, 91–5, 105–25.

the Revolutionary Guard, the Revolutionary Committees, a majority of the members in the first two assemblies and a few prominent clerics. This party propounded full nationalization, land reform, progressive taxation and equality. The conservative, pro–small merchant party (composed of the majority of the clerics and the Council of Guardians) opposed these measures. By the end of the 1980s, the conservatives (who had become the dominant wing of the power bloc) had blocked most of the radical measures.[82]

In the first years of the Islamic revolution, populist measures won the hearts of the poor.[83] Despite ambiguities and differences within political society regarding 'capitalism' in general, big capital was defined as un-Islamic.[84] For example, real estate prices were frozen between 1980 and 1982 in order to help the poor gain access to housing.

The early progressive measures of the revolution led to improvements in income distribution, but this improvement had abated by the mid-1980s.[85] The net effect of the first revolutionary decade was the expansion of petty commodity production along with the establishment of an ethos based on blaming 'capitalists' and 'imperialists' for social problems. In other words, small-scale, predominantly merchant capitalism emerged as the main economic victor of the revolution. However, since control over the state machinery gave the chance for further capital accumulation, the gradual transformation of these small merchants into full-fledged capitalists remained a possibility.

Throughout this process, the conservatives interacted with networks in the bazaar, but the radical wing of political society lacked

---

82 See Mehrdad Valibeigi, 'Islamic Economics and Economic Policy Formation in Post-Revolutionary Iran: A Critique', *Journal of Economic Issues* 27:3 (1993): 793–812. Some commentators have questioned the radical faction's commitment to radicalism. Khomeini's exact role in these factional battles is also open to more than one interpretation (e.g., see Kevan Harris, 'The Rise of The Subcontractor State: Politics of Pseudo-Privatization in the Islamic Republic of Iran', *International Journal of Middle East Studies* 45:1 [2013]: 50).

83 Elizabeth Sanasarian, 'Ayatollah Khomeini and the Institutionalization of Charismatic Rule in Iran, 1979–1989', *Journal of Developing Societies* 11 (1995): 189–205.

84 Farhad Nomani and Sohrab Behdad, *Class and Labor in Iran: Did the Revolution Matter?* Syracuse, NY: Syracuse University Press, 2006, 2–3, 38.

85 Sohrab Behdad, 'Winners and Losers of the Iranian Revolution: A Study in Income Distribution', *International Journal of Middle Eastern Studies* 21:3 (1989): 327–58.

similar backing in civil society, since workers' councils had been reduced to state organs early in the revolution,[86] and the subproletariat lacked self-organization. Finally, sociopolitical organizations (including Islamic ones) that could have backed radical measures were savagely suppressed during the first four years of the revolution,[87] so the 'bloc-ness' of the radical wing was restricted. The initial push of nationalization in the early 1980s depended on social pressures from below and the exigencies of war,[88] as well as on the organization of the radical wing of the power bloc. The removal of these social and political pressures (and the end of the war with Iraq) therefore ultimately led to a relatively more liberal decade in the economy.

Revolutionized Corporatism

These fluctuating political battles ultimately led to a bifurcated welfare and developmental system.[89] On the one hand, the Islamic regime not only preserved but expanded the corporatist policies of the Shah: the working class and the new middle classes were supported through industrialization and sector-specific welfare benefits. On the other hand, the regime built a third sector meant specifically to employ and militarily empower the poor (Abrahamian calls this a 'martyrs welfare state'). A set of foundations (*bonyads*) and paramilitary organizations became the poor's sources of livelihood and avenues for upward mobility.

Some of the welfare institutions of the Islamic Republic had their roots in revolutionary mobilization. Khomeinist activists organized networks of aid in the bazaar using revolutionary language. Their goal was not only to aid the poor financially but also to elevate them symbolically. The word *mostazafan* (the Persian pronunciation of the Qur'anic *mustadafin*) had been updated by Islamic leftists during the previous decades, under the influence of Franz Fanon and other Marxists, to picture the subproletariat as the saviours of the late modern age. This symbolic angle was taken up by activists such as the

86 Nomani and Behdad, *Class and Labor in Iran*, 206.
87 Abrahamian, *Iranian Mojahedin*.
88 Kevan Harris, 'Martyrs' Welfare State', 49–50.
89 Harris, 'The Rise of the Subcontractor State'.

cleric Karroubi during the revolution and popularized in the bazaar. He and others also brought these emergent networks under an umbrella organization a few weeks before the Shah's fall, culminating in the major aid organization of the republic, the Imam Khomeini Relief Committee.[90] Karroubi would later become a key figure, first in the subordinate wing of the power bloc, and then in the liberal Islamic movement.

Bonyads, which control a good chunk of Iran's economy, are among the most controversial institutions of the Islamic Republic. According to their critics, they are the central nodes of corruption in Iranian society and the main impediments in the way of market reforms. Bonyads were set up to help the poor and eradicate poverty. Most of their property was confiscated from the Shah's family and other local and foreign elites. Since they were meant to serve the mostazafan, they have been kept immune from planning and tight central regulation, as well as from market rules. They are accountable to themselves and, at least on paper, to the mostazafan. In practice, regime-friendly merchants and clerics control these autonomous organizations and staff them with pro-regime workers. Bonyads, theoretically non-profit organizations, invest in everything from textile to metal-working enterprises and make profits (their proponents could say that their surpluses are not profits but self-empowerment of the mostazafan). While foreign and local free-market critics have focused on the inefficiency of bonyads and called for their privatization, left-wing critics have emphasized that these institutions transform social justice into patronage and produce fanatically pro-regime workers, merchants and clerics (which could be described, from a more analytical angle, as the formation of the conservative bloc). In any event, these huge nonmarket and nonstate organizations redistribute wealth and alleviate poverty – but more among the regime's supporters than throughout the wider population. The largest bonyad in Iran is interestingly called Bonyad-e Mostazafan va Janbazan (the Bonyad of the Dispossessed and the Disabled).

Unlike the institutions inherited from the old regime, these new institutions cut across classes and sectors, though they mostly

90 Harris, *Martyrs' Welfare State*, 175–7.

incorporated those excluded from the corporatist regime. These two sets of welfare regimes (the one inherited from the Shah and the other created by the revolution) did not fuse. The revolutionary institutions not only depended on the state treasury, but also on citizens' voluntary donations based on traditions of Islamic giving (in many cases, even on those of citizens who might have detested the regime).[91] These institutions were also run by revolutionary cadres (wearing revolutionary clothing and using revolutionary rhetoric) and avoided professionalization. They used contextual rather than standardized and technical evaluations to determine who received aid, and cash and vouchers heavily outweighed ATM and smart card distribution systems. Such institutions of aid also mobilized hundreds of thousands of volunteers and preferred fervour and spirit over bureaucratized functioning.[92] The recipients of aid frequently mimicked the revolutionary culture of these institutions, though there are studies that show some sections of the poor just avoided them. After the Iran–Iraq war in the 1980s, the regime was able to reduce absolute poverty significantly, possibly as a result of these institutions (as well as stable growth).

Central to the consolidation of corporatism was the war with Iraq. Even though devastating, the war effort helped entrench corporatism and sideline its conservative and revolutionary critics. The emergent 'war corporatism' also allowed the regime to break up the ulama's and the bazaar's traditional horizontal networks and definitively merge them with the corporatist state, a modernist 'success' which would have been unimaginable under the Shah.[93] Hence, even though these two strata benefited immensely from the revolution, their gains were never unchecked, and their power was ultimately subordinated to the state.

As important as their policies of aid and reproduction of revolutionary discourse among the elite and the populace was the relief organizations' political and economic empowerment of subproletarian actors. These organizations became the primary venues of upward

91 Ibid., 70–2.

92 Kevan Harris, 'The Martyrs' Welfare State: Politics of Social Policy in the Islamic Republic of Iran', Ph.D. diss. (Johns Hopkins University, 2012), 185.

93 Ibid.; Arang Keshavarzian, *Bazaar and State in Iran: Politics of the Tehran Marketplace*, Cambridge: Cambridge University Press, 2007.

mobility and political assertion for this 'class' which is not a class. Comparable only partially to the peasants of Marx's Eighteenth Brumaire, the subproletariat depends on the expansion of this third sector (rather than simply governmental bureaucracy, as in nineteenth-century France). The Islamic Republic, invested rhetorically so much in the empowerment of the oppressed, indeed gives them power, but only by subordinating them to a huge, decentralized machine. This non-class has not been able to organize itself, yet its top-down organization by the revolutionary regime has become a core source of willing and active consent from the bottom up.

The Rise of Islamist Opposition

In the rest of the region, Islamist opposition came into its own over several decades through frictions, clashes and sometimes engagements with the regimes. The Iranian revolution boosted the Islamist opposition's self-confidence and encouraged its independence from the conservative wings of the secularist regimes.[94] Despite many differences from each other, Islamisms throughout the region distinguished themselves both from secularist republicanism and the emergent liberal alternative to it. They held that an Islamic state and an Islamic economy would cure all the ills created by the republicanisms and the liberalisms. However, what an Islamic economy would look like (and in what sense it would be distinct from corporatism and neoliberalism) was poorly formulated. What an Islamic state entailed was not entirely clear either. The ultimate, and perhaps unintended, contribution of Islamist opposition in the rest of the region (outside Iran) would be the creation of mass organizations that would allow political society to link the existing states to their citizenry.

The spectre of the Iranian revolution, rather than the exact economic and political makeup of the actual Islamic regime, thoroughly shaped opposition. Islamists had to position themselves either for or against it.[95] A journalist from the semi-official newspaper of the

---

94 Yet, as we will later see, Islamism's initial and harsh criticisms of the conservative *regional* bloc were quickly watered down, as a result of which it became less and less distinguishable from Sunni conservatism during the Arab Spring.

95 For instance, see Abdelkader Zghal, 'The New Strategy of the Movement of the Islamic Way', for early attempts by Tunisian Islamists to prove to the world that they were different from the Iranian ones. Zghal, 'The New Strategy of the

AKP regime reflects back on these revolutionary days and recalls how Islamization from above stumbled under this overbearing spectre:

> [The junta of 12 September 1980] took a veritable step to regulate religious life. It [undertook] restoration and conservative interventions based on [modernized] religion. But its restrictive and regulatory interventions were frustrated [*bozguna uğradı*]. The Muslim generations of the 1980s and 1990s took their intellectual nourishment not from [the junta's] curriculum, but from [the event] that incited the most intense excitement in those days (the Iranian Revolution) and from its ideologues.[96]

Mehmet Metiner, one of Turkey's prominent Islamist activists, praised how the Iranian regime was able to reproduce revolutionary fervour ten years after the revolution, which he had witnessed in a visit in 1989. In his book on Iran, Metiner drew attention to how poor crowds mobilized to commemorate the revolution's martyrs:

> I pay attention to the outward appearance of the people who gathered at the martyrs' graveyard; they are all poor-looking people. You can tell their poverty also by their behaviour. They are the [mostazafan] that Imam Khomeini always carefully underlines. That is, they are *the real owners of the revolution*.[97]

But why did these people so fervently mobilize in favour of the regime? The author focused on loyalty to Khomeini's person throughout the book (as well as Islam itself, of course), but on one page he specified an institutional reason. The hotel where the author stayed was owned by Bonyad-e Mostazafan:

> The hotel used to belong to one of the Shah's men. It was transferred to the foundation after its owners escaped the

---

Movement of the Islamic Way: Manipulation or Expression of Political Culture?', in I. Williams Zartman, ed., *Tunisia: The Political Economy of Reform*, Boulder, CO: Lynne Rienner Publishers, 1991.

96 Süleyman Seyfi Öğün, *Yeni Şafak*, 6 October 2014.

97 Mehmet Metiner, *Şafak'ta 10 Gün: İran Notları*, Istanbul: Birim, 1989, 24 (emphasis mine).

> revolution. All of the hotel's revenues go to the foundation and from there it is distributed to the deprived and the poor. The poor and the deprived are without doubt the revolution's own children [*öz evletları*] . . . The Iranian Islamic Revolution . . . adapted the responsibility to protect . . . and honor its own children.[98]

Similar words of praise filled the pages of the most influential Islamic intellectual magazine of the 1980s, *Girişim*, to which Metiner was a regular contributor. In 2013, a member of the Egyptian organization al-Jihad expressed similar views, but also cautioned against the sectarian nature of the Iranian regime: 'In the early 1980s, we were all inspired by the Iranian Revolution and admired Khomeini and we still admire much about the Islamic government of Iran. But we are different and we don't want them to rule over us.'[99] Even (Sunni) Islamists sympathetic to the revolution were worried about Shiite influence. Metiner himself spent years fighting this concern, but also acknowledged that due to the special place of Shiite clergy and jurisprudence in Iran, a direct export of the regime to Turkey was out of the question.[100]

First and most obviously, the Iranian revolution brought hope and power, since it demonstrated that the tables could be turned back on the secularists. But it also encouraged Islamists to think outside the box and consequently increased their ability to form new coalitions. In Tunisia, for example, Islamists increased their emphasis on equality and similar left-wing themes after 1979, which allowed them new venues for mobilization (such as the student and labour movements).[101] The Iranian revolution was among the key factors that diverted the attention of Tunisian Islamists from moral and individual issues and channelled it towards the topics of social justice and anti-imperialism.[102]

98 Ibid., 55.

99 Reported in Shibley Telhami, 'Arab Perspectives on Iran's Role in a Changing Middle East', *Wilson Center*. Available wilsoncenter.org/.

100 Metiner, *Şafak'ta 10 Gün*, 109–10.

101 Christopher Alexander, 'Opportunities, Organizations, and Ideas: Islamists and Workers in Tunisia and Algeria', *International Journal of Middle East Studies* 32 (2000): 465–90; Elbaki Hermassi, 'The Islamicist Movement and November 7', in Zartman, ed., *Tunisia: The Political Economy of Reform*, 194.

102 Murphy, 'Under the Emperor's Neoliberal Clothes!', 64, 71.

Turkey

The rise of Turkish Islamism challenged both Kemalism and conservatism. During the early 1970s, Islamist politics was mainly the resort of small provincial entrepreneurs, on the defensive against the state's industrial policies, rising labour militancy and rapid Westernization. The lack of response from the established business organizations and parties to the needs of small enterprises, facing extinction in an import-substitution economy, led the ex-president of the Union of Chambers of Turkey, Necmettin Erbakan, to found the National Order Party (MNP), in 1970. As well as defending the economic interests of provincial businessmen and traders, the MNP also appealed to their religious feelings and their distaste for Western consumer culture. This stance won support from the more pious of peasant farmers and artisans, who were also attracted by Erbakan's rather sketchy programme of economic development based on communally owned private enterprise, shielded and regulated by the state: Erbakan's promise of a 'third/communal sector' seemed to be a barrier against the growing power of big business. Some of the religious intellectuals and communities shifted their support from the centre-right to this party during the 1970s. There were two dynamics behind this shift: some of the more staunchly pious communities found the centre-right too secular and modern, while at the other end of the spectrum, many intellectuals, publishers and clerics (along with their students) wanted an Islamic line independent from the state. Against the communist East and a state allied with the West, their motto was 'Neither the East nor the West'.

Closed down by the military in 1971, the MNP was refounded in 1972 as the Milli Salvation Party (MSP), with virtually no change in its programme. The MSP's most significant gain during the 1970s was increased freedom of operation for the country's Imam-Hatip schools, whose graduates would provide the main activists and leaders of the Islamist movement in the coming decades. These schools were officially intended to educate prospective preachers (*hatips*) and prayer leaders (imams). But since it was not possible for students to observe the precepts of Islam in regular public schools, they also attracted enrolment from religious families who did not necessarily want their children to become preachers or prayer leaders. In time, this generation of Imam-Hatip graduates came to occupy important public positions, constituting a religious new middle class capable of competing with the secularist intelligentsia in economic, cultural and political realms. In a country where intellectuals had previously been equated with the left, the emergence of this new, avowedly Muslim intelligentsia would be a significant element in the construction of Islamism as a hegemonic alternative.

The 1980 coup crushed the challenge from the left and also initiated a controlled opening to religious groups. It introduced Islamic studies as part of the national school curriculum. Certain hitherto semi-clandestine religious communities were now afforded increased public visibility. In this environment, especially the 'post-Sufi' Gülen and Süleymancı communities (which combined tenets of mystic Sufi Islam with a systematic embrace of the natural sciences, Turkish nationalism and a somewhat rationalistic understanding of scripture) expanded.[103] In the 1982 constitution, the definition of 'Turkishness' included unprecedented references to Islam.[104]

These concessions can be seen as an attempt to contain and defuse the appeal of the Iranian revolution and socially radical Islamism through a 'politics of absorption'. The other side of this process was the demobilization of potential revolutionary forces. This 'revolution–restoration' kept the power bloc (temporarily) intact while partially satisfying the popular sectors. During the 1980–83 military dictatorship, the Turkish regime took some steps towards implementing Islamist demands while defusing their insurgent potential.

Yet while these changes were intended to consolidate (rather than undermine) secularization, they nevertheless opened the way to further conflict, since they increased the weight of religious actors throughout the country. If the post-Sufi religious communities were the intended beneficiaries of these reforms, Islamist circles and parties were the unintended victors. The Islamist vote rose from 8 per cent in 1987 to 16 per cent in 1991 and then passed 20 per cent in 1994 and 1995 (whereas all other parties gradually became stuck below 20 per cent).

103 Ruşen Çakır, *Ayet ve slogan: Türkiye' de İslami oluşumlar*, İstanbul: Metis Yayınları, 1990.

104 Taha Parla, *Türkiye'nin Siyasal Rejimi*, Istanbul: İletişim, 1995.

The Turkish Vision for Islamic Economics and Its Deradicalization

The military closed down the MSP in 1980. When parties were once again allowed to organize in 1983, Erbakan's Welfare Party (RP) incorporated the revolutionary wind that blew from Iran. The Islamist party now had an anti-liberal, social justice–oriented platform. This religious mobilization also developed a communitarian market vision, parallel to that of Karl Polanyi, but mixed inconsistently with free market and national developmentalist elements. The new RP programme combined contradictory themes. The party voiced the interests of an expanding pious business class which was more likely to adapt to neoliberalization than the state-protected bourgeoisie (though it was going to become clear in a few years that this new, allegedly independent class fraction was as interested in state protection as its competitor, the established secular bourgeoisie). 'Heavy' (state-led, massive, non-flexible) industrialization was dropped from the programme to instead emphasize market dynamism. Hence, the party clearly had *some* neoliberal inclinations. Nevertheless, the programme also assigned a central role to moral, collectivist communities as regulators of the market.[105] Due to such moral control, there would be no exploitation even in private enterprises.

Hence the party (its newspapers, ideologues and politicians) claimed to be 'anti-capitalist', some of them citing non-Marxist socialists such as Robert Owen (one of Polanyi's main inspirations). Owenite socialism had arrived in Turkey in Islamic garb. Party manuals promised living wages and unionization for every worker; party rallies were adorned with slogans that announced the 'end of exploitation'. This contradictory discourse, which articulated an acceptance of open markets together with communitarian socialism, resulted in immense support from the urban poor.

In Turkey, as throughout the Middle East, Islamist intellectuals of this era were developing notions of the ideal Muslim city – centred on a mosque, further surrounded by markets, schools and cultural centres.[106]

---

105 Necmettin Erbakan, *Adil Ekonomik Düzen*, Ankara, 1991.

106 The discussions of urban Islamism in this chapter and the next integrate a few paragraphs from Tuğal, 'The Greening of Istanbul', *New Left Review* 2:51 (May/June 2008): 64–80.

This constituted the spatial dimension of the Islamic economy. Architectural modesty and harmony with nature would be the city's defining features; development would respect the historical texture of the city. Buildings would reflect humility before God. High-rise developments were to be banned.[107]

The victory of the RP's Erdoğan in the 1994 metropolitan municipal elections created both panic and euphoria in the city at the prospect that this Islamist urban *imaginaire* would be applied wholesale. In fact, the Islamist intellectuals were divided over their plans for urban development, and not least in their attitudes towards squatters. Some glorified the pious squatters as agents of retribution on the godless urban elite.[108] Others were more ambivalent, at times applauding their creative contribution to the cityscape, at others scolding them for pillaging history and nature. But an influential section of the RP leadership saw the sidelining of the secularist establishment as a way to integrate Istanbul more successfully into the world economy and exploit its rich Ottoman history to attract more tourists. These strategists were also less forgiving towards the squatters, whom they perceived as nomads at odds with the urban spirit of Islam.[109]

The RP was at the intersection of these cross-currents, and its moves responded to all of them. Under Mayor Erdoğan, the Istanbul metropolitan authority redistributed resources, tightened control on alcohol consumption, recentred Islamic symbols in public places and introduced prayer rooms in municipal buildings.[110] However, even though Erdoğan's election speeches promised to remove high-rises from the city, his administration was quite pro-finance and therefore left these houses of cash flow untouched.

---

107 For the best exemplars, see Mustafa Armağan, *Şehir, ey Şehir*, Istanbul: Şule Yayınları, 1997; Turgut Cansever, *Kubbeyi Yere Koymamak*, Istanbul: Timas Yayınları, 1997; and Rasim Özdenören, *Kent İlişkileri*, Istanbul: Iz Yayıncılık, 1998.

108 For this populist line, see İdris Özyol, *Lanetli Sınıf*, Istanbul: Birey Yayıncılık, 1999.

109 These views were voiced in Mustafa Kutlu, *Şehir Mektupları*, Istanbul: Dergah Yayınları, 1995; and İhsan Sezal, *Şehirleşme*, Istanbul: Ağaç Yayınevı, 1992.

110 Menderes Çınar, 'Turkey's Transformation under the AKP Rule', *Muslim World* 96:3 (2006): 469–86.

The party reaped the benefits of its efficient municipal administration, emerging as the country's leading party from the 1995 national elections. The RP-led coalition government implemented high wage increases and moved to limit bank interest. In the municipalities, the RP started to organize events to advertise its sympathy for Islamic causes. Initially Erbakan signalled his attention to work toward a 'global democracy' based on the cooperation of Muslim nations under Turkish leadership.[111] However, he soon caved in to pressure from the Turkish military elite, even signing a historic military cooperation agreement with Israel.

Other religious trends of the 1980s and 1990s included expansion of the place for ritual in everyday life, especially in poorer neighbourhoods; a flourishing of Islamic publishers, radio and television channels, and newspapers and magazines; further growth of pious schools and dormitories; increasing numbers of mosques and Qur'anic schools; and an increasingly public struggle among Islamic groups regarding the correct definition and practice of Islam. Along with an Islamic attack on secularism, Turkey thus witnessed Islamist attacks on many beliefs and practices hitherto believed to be Islamic (tomb visits, the Sufi *dhikr* and even the Friday prayer in a secular republic). While the post-Sufi groups (such as the Gülen community) participated in some of these trends, they did not join the struggle against traditional Sufi practices (though they had themselves dropped most of these practices, most notably the dhikr).

Party leader Erbakan also talked frequently about the need to open more Imam-Hatip schools and hosted a prime ministerial dinner to which prominent Sufi *şeyhs* were invited. Such a gathering was a first in the history of the republic, and the secularist hard-liners interpreted it as a formal recognition of religious orders that had been banned since the early Kemalist reforms. All of these acts and trends did not go unnoticed by the old power bloc. In February 1997, the military stepped in to demand that the government restrict Imam-Hatip schools, increase obligatory secular education from five to eight years and control religious orders. The RP was too divided to

111 Elizabeth Özdalga, 'Necmettin Erbakan: Democracy for the Sake of Power', in Metin Heper and Sabri Sayarı, eds, *Political Leaders and Democracy in Turkey*, New York: Lexington Books, 2002.

mount an effective resistance, and the government resigned. The generals initiated another round of repression and torture, though not on the scale of the 1980s, climaxing in the closing down of the RP. At this stage, too, the military undertook a thorough purging of Islamists from its ranks.

Islamists immediately established another party. The Virtue Party (Fazilet Partisi, henceforth FP) got rid of the anticapitalist rhetoric in the RP's programme. This was a clear sign that the neoliberal wing of the defunct RP was starting to gain the upper hand within the party. This pro-Western wing could now also hope to gain some external backing from the European Union. The EU had started to actively promote human rights in Turkey, and the country was granted candidate status for accession in December 1999. The Islamists toned down their criticism of the establishment, but they also ventured to put up a headscarfed woman as a parliamentary candidate. The ban on covering in government buildings was a linchpin of Turkish secularization, and even the RP had never dared to take such a major step while in office. Now the FP's ideologues started to reframe covering as a matter of human rights, rather than of religious obligation, in the expectation that the EU would intervene on their behalf. In the short term, their tactics backfired: in 1999, Merve Kavakçı, the covered deputy, was precluded from taking her oath.

This early experiment in (neo)liberal Islam was a failure only in appearance and in the short term. It was in fact the first in a series of steps towards a new, flexible strategy of Islamization: pious actors tested the boundaries of Turkish secularism in gradual fashion and by trial and error rather than attempting to overthrow secularism in one stroke. The next decade would witness the gradual marginalization of all other strategies of Islamization by this new strategy – a shift that was possible due to the *political* structure of Turkish Islamism.

Dramatic confrontation with secular authorities became more and more marginalized by the end of the 1990s, a trend which was prepared by the post-coup events. Some Islamists organized demonstrations to challenge the steps the military took against Islamic education and clothing. However, RP and FP leaders effectively controlled most radicals and party youth. Islamist radicals who could escape their control were ultimately marginalized. The radicals could neither sustain street mobilization in the absence of political leverage nor build new organizations or parties that could supply such leverage. Disappointed and disillusioned radicals repented and started to seek Islamic change from within the system. Most of them would join the party in the following decade. Some disillusioned radicals even became top bureaucrats in the 2000s.

The significant difference from Egypt at this juncture was not the interplay between radicalization–repression–deradicalization–reradicalization (of which there was plenty in both cases). Turkish Islamists lacked any alternative, organized religio-political institution to turn to (such as an effective radical party, or alternative and effective sociopolitical organizations). Islamic political society was unified in Turkey (that is, a legal Islamist party gradually monopolized religio-political authority). There were multiple Sufi communities, but they institutionalized their impact through cooperating with centre-left, centre-right, and Islamist parties, instead of building their own, separate party; and (as opposed to Egypt) there was only one major Islamist political party in Turkey.

Egypt

Egyptian Islamism also evolved from a belief in the distinctiveness of Islamic economics to a deradicalized, even gradually market-oriented stance. This change of heart regarding the economy was married more unevenly to Egyptian Islamists' shift from the fight for an Islamic caliphate to an Islamic law–focused movement. However, the road to liberal Islam proved to be much rockier than in Turkey, and political and cultural liberalism remained much less developed. Egyptian Islamism came to be distinguished from the Turkish one by its relatively more rigid pietism as well as its more solid focus on implementing Islamic law. In these senses, it became 'legalistic', defined in this book not as a preference for legal rather than illegal existence, but as a staunch support for Islamic law.

The gradual rise of a law-, piety- and modesty-oriented Islam in Egypt, with no clear break from its corporatist past, contrasts starkly with the relatively more liberal and free market turn of Islam in Turkey. The roots of the difference can be partly traced back to the organization of religion in the two cases. As different from Turkey, courts and al-Azhar scholars (as experts of Islamic law) also propelled Islamization in Egypt, in order to claim radical Islam's ground and limit its effectiveness.[112] Still, the Muslim Brotherhood was the central node in Egyptian Islamic political society, though it shared the religious field with other significant opponents (such as Jamaa Islamiyya, Sufi groups and various preachers and organizations known as the Salafis, which all reject the Brotherhood's spiritual and political leadership).

It was not only the Brotherhood's inability to monopolize the Islamic field, but its organizational dispositions as well that led to a starkly different organization of religion from that in Turkey.[113] The Brotherhood had been founded in 1928 by Hasan al-Banna and, in its first decades, developed as a socio-political movement organizing itself around athletic clubs, evening schools, welfare provision and anticolonial activism.[114] The Brotherhood's founding leaders had an anti-institutionalist bias: they did not want to be established as an association, club, or anything 'official', but rather presented themselves primarily as 'an Idea'.[115] To clarify this further, the Brotherhood was never against *organization* (indeed, from the early years onward, it had a complex organizational structure, called the *tandhim*), but it remained suspicious of legal and formal institutionalization (and hence, also of establishing a formal political party), in sharp opposition to the institutionally disposed Turkish Islamists.

The economic visions of the Islamists in the two contexts were also different, though they tended to converge after the 1970s. Factions within the early Brotherhood propagated Islamic socialism,[116] which

112 See, e.g., Samia Mehrez, 'Take Them Out of the Ball Game: Egypt's Cultural Players in Crisis', *Middle East Report* 31:219 (Summer 2001): 11–12.

113 Most of the following six paragraphs are taken from Cihan Tuğal, 'Religious Politics, Hegemony, and the Market Economy: Parties in the Making of Turkey's Liberal–Conservative Bloc and Egypt's Diffuse Islamization' in Cedric De Leon, Manali Desai, and Cihan Tuğal, eds, *Building Blocs: How Parties Organize Society*, Stanford, CA: Stanford University Press, 2015.

114 Brynjar Lia, *The Society of the Muslim Brothers in Egypt: The Rise of an Islamic Mass Movement 1928–1942*, Reading, UK: Ithaca Press, 1998; Richard P. Mitchell, *The Society of the Muslim Brothers*, London: Oxford University Press, 1969.

115 Olivier Carré, *Les Frères Musulmans Egypte et Syrie, 1928–1982*, Paris: Gallimard/Julliard, 1983, 12.

116 Salwa Ismail, 'Confronting the Other: Identity, Culture, Politics, and Conservative Islamism in Egypt', *International Journal of Middle East Studies* 30 (1998): 207.

was never a clear position among Turkish Islamists. Their understanding of socialism was, in the spirit of the times, mostly state-based. After prosecution by Nasser in the 1960s, Brotherhood members escaped abroad and engaged in economic activity, which they continued in Egypt after President Sadat's *infitah* ('Open Door' or trade deregulation policies after 1973). Since the 1970s, the creation of jobs in the private sector and explosion of foreign trade benefited these Brotherhood members. Many became wealthy.[117] The emigrant money coming from the Gulf escaped state control and was invested in Islamic banks, and the financialization of the economy was legitimized as Islamic in the 1970s and 1980s. Trading with the West or on the black market was also deemed Islamic through religious verdicts.[118] Subsequently, the Brothers started to shift to favouring a mixed economy agenda and quitting their allegiance to 'socialism'.

In the 1960s, the Brotherhood advocated a violent overthrow of the regime by a revolutionary vanguard. Both the increasing authoritarianism of the regime and the group's radicalism isolated the Muslim Brotherhood, preventing it from operating in conjunction with civil society during this decade. Privatization and deregulation from the 1970s to the 1990s, however, moderated the Muslim Brotherhood's position in political matters as well.[119] In addition, Islamists were allowed during the 1970s to organize within the student body (in secular universities as well as in al-Azhar), and the public influence of al-Azhar was bolstered because Sadat wanted to use both Islamists and al-Azhar against the left.[120] This strategy enhanced the influence of al-Azhar and increased the importance of Islamic legal scholarship.

The Muslim Brotherhood tried to help the regime prevent Islamist students from taking part in demonstrations, strikes and sabotage,

---

117 See Davut Ates, 'Economic Liberalization and Changes in Fundamentalism: The Case of Egypt', *Middle East Policy* 12 (2005): 133–44.

118 Ismail, 'Confronting the Other', 213–14.

119 See Barbara Zollner, 'Prison Talk: The Muslim Brotherhood's Internal Struggle during Gamal Abdel Nasser's Persecution, 1954 to 1971', *International Journal of Middle East Studies* 39 (2007): 411–33, for the political roots of this moderation in a split within the Muslim Brotherhood in the 1960s.

120 Malika Zeghal 'Religion and Politics in Egypt: The Ulema of Al-Azhar, Radical Islam, and the State (1952–94)', *International Journal of Middle East Studies* 31 (1999): 371–99.

but it could not control the students completely since it was not organized as a political party.[121] This provides an important contrast to the Turkish Islamic political party, which had considerable control over Islamist students in the 1980s – a crucial difference between the Islamic political societies of the two nations. However, Sadat's monopolization of power at the end of the 1970s interrupted the cooperation with Islamists. After Sadat's assassination in 1981 and the regime's relative liberalization, the Muslim Brotherhood started to participate in municipal, associational and parliamentary elections. This participation taught the Brotherhood how to play by the rules of the game. Could this constitute the groundwork for the application of the Turkish model in Egypt?

In this decade, as before, the Brotherhood defined its own goal and the goal of the state as enhancing individual piety – including intensified worship, good manners and overall abidance by Islam.[122] As in the Turkey of the 1970s through the 1990s, Egyptian Islamic parties of different stripes enforced cleanliness, correct worship and Islamic morality through their newspapers, magazines, books and conferences,[123] as well as monitoring neighbourhoods and streets and providing cheap urban services and low-cost Islamic clothing.[124] Ever since the 1970s, Islamic groups in universities had been instituting gender segregation.[125] Despite this similarity in the everyday implications of earlier Islamization, Egyptian activists came to focus more on implementing Islamic law than did their Turkish counterparts. This seems, on the surface, to reflect contextual differences only (the Egyptian state recognizes a restricted version of Islamic law, whereas the Turkish state does

---

121 Raymond W. Baker, 'Afraid for Islam: Egypt's Muslim Centrists between Pharaohs and Fundamentalists', *Daedalus* 120 (1991): 41–68.

122 Mohammed Zahid and Michael Medley. 'Muslim Brotherhood in Egypt and Sudan', *Review of African Political Economy* 33 (2006): 693–708.

123 Salwa Ismail, 'Confronting the Other: Identity, Culture, Politics, and Conservative Islamism in Egypt', *International Journal of Middle East Studies* 30 (1998): 211–12.

124 Salwa Ismail, *Political Life in Cairo's New Quarters: Encountering the Everyday State*, Minneapolis: University of Minnesota Press, 2006; Gilles Kepel, 'Islamists versus the State in Egypt and Algeria', *Daedalus* 124 (1995): 113.

125 Salwa Ismail, 'Religious "Orthodoxy" as Public Morality: The State, Islamism and Cultural Politics in Egypt', *Critique: Critical Middle Eastern Studies* 8 (1999): 25–47; Maha Abdel Rahman, 'The Politics of "UnCivil" Society in Egypt', *Review of African Political Economy* 29 (2002): 21–36.

not). However, this divergence also reflects a contrast in religious strategy due partly to differences in the organizations of political society.

The Islamist movement in Egypt was always concerned with Islamic law. However, at the beginning of the 1980s Islamic law became a greater priority for the Brotherhood. The tone of the Brotherhood thus became conciliatory, particularly after the government declared Islamic law as the principal source of legislation in May 1980. After this, the Muslim Brotherhood dropped its confrontational stance.[126]

Institutional legacies perpetrated an Islamic political society quite different in structure from the Turkish one. The Brotherhood's anti-party stance persisted well into the 1980s. Omar Tilmesani, the leader of the organization in the 1970s and 1980s, remained a consistent critic of political pluralism and partisanship or 'party-ness' (*hizbiyya*). Islamic organizations like the Brotherhood could defend the interests of the nation and the umma, but, he held, parties changed their platforms based on personal whim and political situations. He also repeated al-Banna's views on the issue: parties were based on disputes and therefore divisive of the Islamic community.[127] Based on this logic, when Sadat offered the Brotherhood the chance to become a legal political platform (he had no intention of allowing a party), the organization refused. Nevertheless, by 1983 Tilmesani had reconsidered some of his thoughts. He decided that the organization would participate in the elections through coalitions with legal parties.[128] He had dismissed this option in the 1970s (when the organization fielded only individual candidates).

In sum, in the early years of the Mubarak regime, Islamic political society offered a hodgepodge of political, religious and economic alternatives to neoliberalizing secularism. Neither a novel political bloc nor a systematic reshuffling of the existing blocs could result from this. The next chapter will trace how the prospects changed as a result of Western and Turkish influences, as well as more autochthonous dynamics of liberalization.

---

126 Denis J. Sullivan and Sana Adeb-Kotob, *Islam in Contemporary Egypt: Civil Society vs. the State*, Boulder, CO: Lynne Rienner Publishers, 1999, 57.

127 Al-Awadi, *In Pursuit of Legitimacy*, 39.

128 See Al-Awadi, *In Pursuit of Legitimacy*, chapter 3.

Tunisia

Al-Nahda, the major Tunisian Islamist party, was formed in the 1970s (but named as such only in the late 1980s), when a group of activists decided to break from a mainstream Islamic organization. The Association for the Safeguard of the Koran had preached religious transformation at the individual level, holding that this would in time result in a more Islamized state. Partly under the impact of politicization elsewhere, Tunisian Islamists had also come to think such cultural gradualism was not the way to go.[129] They entered the political scene, influenced especially by their contact with the Muslim Brotherhood (from which they learned not only an organizational model, but an Islamic way of thinking about current politics and society).[130] As distinct from all three major cases covered, however, Tunisian Islamists did not develop complicated political positions until the 1980s. Even at the end of the 1970s, they remained fixated on preventing a leftist takeover of the country and were much less interested in opposing the ruling regime than were their counterparts.[131]

The Tunisian Islamist movement decided to participate in the system. One reason was encouragement by the regime, which also made the same calculation as its neighbours: support the Islamists to fight the leftists. However, al-Nahda's electoral showing in 1989 (around 15 per cent nationwide, but 30 per cent in urban centres) led to a clampdown by the authorities. The organization responded by calling for an uprising and allegedly planned a coup.[132] If successful, these steps could have put Tunisia on an Algerian path towards bloody civil war. However, the Tunisian military was much more

---

129 Alexander, 'Islamists and Workers in Tunisia and Algeria'.

130 For one of the biographical accounts regarding how this contact took place among the top leaders, see François Burgat and and William Dowell, *The Islamic Movement in North Africa*, 2nd edn, Austin: University of Texas Press, 1997, 185.

131 The almost obsessive anti-socialism of the movement comes forth much more clearly in the French version of Burgat's interview with Enneifer, one of the founders and primary leaders (François Burgat, *L'Islamisme au Maghreb: La voix du sud*, Paris: Karthala, 1988, 208–9). For more on the regime-al-Nahda cooperation against Marxism at the end of the 1970s and the early 1980s, as well as the fluctuating repression and persecution faced by the Islamists, with 1981 as the apex, see Burgat *L'Islamisme au Maghreb*, 214–16, 218–20.

132 Burgat and Dowell, *Islamic Movement in North Africa*.

effective than the Algerian (a good indicator, and maker, of a territorially integrated state). The uprising was put down and the party (apparently) destroyed.

The standard account of the post-crackdown situation holds that the party was out of the picture. Not only were its leaders exiled or imprisoned, but it was not allowed to organize or even operate underground. Whereas it had come to control some key institutions at the end of the 1980s (such as student councils in science programmes), it ultimately lost these institutions to the Salafis.[133]

In the absence of a serious competitor, it is usually held, Salafi organizations blossomed throughout Tunisia in the coming two decades. Previously treading behind their counterparts in the region, Tunisian Salafis became quite well organized. Just as under the Mubarak regime in Egypt, some of these organizations had quite shady relations with the state. While doctrinally distanced to political involvement, some of them seemed to have been infiltrated by the regime so that they would serve as fighters against al-Nahda.[134]

The Tunisian Islamists' economic positions were much less clear than those of the Turkish and Egyptian Islamists. Rashid al-Ghannouchi, al-Nahda's spiritual leader, persistently emphasized social justice, putting him in the camp of left-leaning Islamists in the eyes of some, though he was never as socially radical as Shariati or the early Qutb. Moreover, al-Nahda had placed little emphasis on social justice and labour issues in the 1970s, even during the bread riots that shook the country. It did elaborate a pro-labour rhetoric only in the 1980s, when opportunities to do so presented themselves:[135] ideological commitment to these issues may have played a lesser role than in the cases of Egypt, Turkey and Iran. Al-Nahda did not develop a consistent line on issues of structural adjustment and unionization. It vacillated on these topics, based on its perceptions

133 Mehdi Mabrouk, 'Tunisia: The Radicalization of Religious Policy', in George Joffé, ed., *Islamist Radicalization in North Africa: Politics and Process*, London: Routledge, 2012, 61. This account is questionable because al-Nahda emerged as the most organized force immediately after the ouster of Ben Ali. It must therefore have kept some of its organization intact underground.

134 See Mabrouk, 'Tunisia: The Radicalization of Religious Policy', 63, on the 'scientific' Salafis, though his comments need to be taken with a grain of salt due to his partisanship on behalf of al-Nahda and against other Islamist groups.

135 Alexander, 'Islamists and Workers in Tunisia and Algeria', 470–6.

of how much the labour movement (and in particular, al-Nahda's involvement with the official union) would help stabilize the expansion of its own organization and limit the authoritarianism of the regime.

Ghannouchi and others also lacked an Islamic vocabulary that could be employed to talk about issues of exploitation, poverty and labour before the Iranian revolution, from the rhetoric of which they learned considerably.[136] By contrast, Egyptian Islamism had already developed a language of its own in this regard by the 1950s. This centrality of Iran and its socially radical Islam in deepening the politicization of religion across the larger region further demonstrates why the global elites badly needed to find an 'authentic' model to counter its appeal.

Ghannouchi criticized both capitalism and socialism harshly, just as did other Islamists. Yet even in the writings of this key Tunisian thinker, liberalism, utilitarianism, individualism, materialism and capitalism remained undifferentiated from each other (an ambiguous use of concepts not atypical of other Islamists). Ghannouchi loosely attacked all of them because they conferred on the rich the freedom to exploit the poor – basically, a vulgarized version of the Marxist critique of capitalism.[137] Echoing other Islamist formulations, Ghannouchi emphasized in a speech in 1980 that property belonged to God: its accumulation could be permitted only as long as it served religion and the community of believers. Workers and people who worked the land had the primary right to reap the benefits.[138] Up until the late 1990s, Ghannouchi also remained committed to the idea of social welfare, arguing that as welfare systems declined, Western nations plunged into 'barbarism'.[139]

Tunisian Islamism, in short, offered an even more ambiguous alternative to the existing order. As the following chapters will point out, however, it partly made up for this weakness by developing a tradition of strategic thinking.

---

136 Ibid., 472.

137 Azzam S. Tamimi, *Rachid Ghannouchi: A Democrat within Islamism*, New York: Oxford University Press, 2001, 103, 144.

138 Ibid., 52–3.

139 Ibid., 146.

The Scene Ready for Islamic Liberalism

By the turn of the twenty-first century, global centres of power and influence were looking for a medicine to reinvigorate their debilitated secularist props in the region. The neoliberal pill had not been sufficient and had caused many complications. They needed something stronger – and they also needed to find an antidote to what they now perceived to be the most dangerous poison, the Islamic threat. Neoliberal Islam would provide them with both the medicine and the antidote.

The search for alternatives had local as well as global dynamics. The secularist modernization effort, first in its corporatist and then in its neoliberal varieties, could not deliver any of its central promises (development, independence, liberty). It prepared its own demise by injecting religiosity into its own veins. The only surviving mass opposition to it, Islamism, was devoid of real content, though it developed (in uneven fashion throughout the region) the organizations and blocs that could grease the wheels of the bankrupt social order. The contradictory combination of struggle, clash, competition and engagement between Islamism and secular neoliberalism led to the absorption of the Islamic challenge into the existing regional order (even if this absorption later turned out to be explosive). The next two chapters discuss how the resulting marriage of Islam on the one hand and political and economic liberalism on the other came to constitute 'the Turkish model'. While boosting development of one kind, this model also perpetuated authoritarianism and inequality. Its export to the rest of the Middle East would lead to further consequences intended by neither its proponents among the global elite nor activists at home.

CHAPTER 2

The Liberalization of Islam

Local and global elites could wish for a liberalized Islam as much as they wanted but one could not be simply conjured up into existence. Most important, the Islamist actors themselves would have to desire such a revised religious line, and this desire, moreover, could not turn into a social force without effective organization. Only in some places were there the preconditions for such a fundamental religio-political transformation.

The Liberal Islamic Experience

The (perhaps temporary) exceptional case of Turkey allows us to appreciate the contingency of factors that made a popularized liberal Islam possible. How could Turkish Islamists move in a liberalized direction? How did the intellectual and political landscape enable a liberalized religious life?

The Intellectual and Social Roots of Liberal Islam

After the crisis of 1997, when it became clear that larger concessions were necessary to win the toleration of the ruling elite, a new generation of Islamists began to challenge Erbakan's leadership. In the late 1970s, 1980s and early 1990s, this generational conflict had been expressed as a clash between ardent young radicals and a more conservative mainstream.[1] Charles Kurzman has argued that the expansion of mass education, literacy, journalism and alternative religious institutions bolstered liberal Islam in the first two and last three decades of the twentieth century.[2] While this may be true, until

1 Parts of the following four sections were published as Cihan Tuğal, 'Conservatism, Victorious: Islam and the Retrenchment of the Secular Turkish State', in Asef Bayat, ed., *Post-Islamism at Large*, Oxford: Oxford University Press, 2013.

2 Charles Kurzman, *Liberal Islam: A Sourcebook*, New York: Oxford University Press, 1998.

the 1990s the semi-self-fashioned intellectuals who were partly the products of these changes were quite likely to become radicals.[3]

The youth had become avid readers of the Egyptian thinker Sayyid Qutb and the Iranian Islamist Ali Shariati, shifting Islamist discourse in a more revolutionary direction and reducing the influence of the relatively more party-sanctioned Pakistani Abul A'la Mawdudi. Turkey's most influential Islamist intellectual during that period, Ali Bulaç (who later fell out of favour), gives an insight into what the youth learned from Shariati. In a book on the Iranian revolution, in which Shariati was the only thinker whose position was discussed in concentrated fashion, Bulaç summarized the latter's views regarding why almost all Islamic states and empires were actually non-Islamic:

> The first caliphs led a very simple life. The [real] caliphate system does not excuse a luxurious life. But later, [under the Umayyads], the caliphate was turned into a monarchy . . . Throughout history . . . the oppressed have always struggled and the [nominally Islamic states] have exploited . . . The real Islam can only be realized if the oppressed and the intellectuals work hand-in-hand.[4]

In the late 1990s, liberalizing Islamists steadfastly repudiated such views, which put into question all of post-Umayyad Islam. An influential book by Akdoğan attacked (in his words) such 'radical' ideas: these had presumably resulted from extensive reliance on translated authors, and hence were 'alien' to Turkey.[5] Akdoğan particularly targeted Sayyid Qutb.

Though intellectually not as deep and sustained, similar radical ideas were voiced by Turkish figures such as İsmet Özel. All of these thinkers envisioned an Islamic society and state entirely different from secular, democratic capitalism, though there were also differences

3 The divergence of the analysis from Kurzman's is in part due to our different definitions of liberalism. The same difference also impacts our classification of major modern-era Islamic thinkers.

4 Mehmed Kerim, *İran İslam Devrimi*, İstanbul: Düşünce Yayınları, 1980 [1979], 103.

5 Yalçın Akdoğan, *Siyasal İslam: Refah Partisi'nin anatomisi*, İstanbul: Şehir Yayınları, 2000, 69, 71, 152.

among them. Ali Shariati propounded a more egalitarian order, and Abul A'la Mawdudi remained loyal to free private property. Qutb's views lay between the two, and he shifted away from socio-economic egalitarianism at the end of his life, while also moving towards a more exclusivist vision of the ideal Islamic community. Similar differences existed among radical Islamic youth in Turkey as well, but the rifts weren't systematized in the form of well-differentiated programmes and platforms. The main venues where these influences became visible were intellectual magazines (such as the *Girişim* of the 1980s).

By the end of the 1990s, intellectual attention was shifting away from Qutb, Mawdudi and Shariati to Abdulkarim Soroush and Muhammad al-Jabiri. Their more liberal Islamic theologies, which reject not only the viability but even the idea of an 'Islamic state', started to dominate public debate. At the same time, journalists such as Abdurrahman Dilipak and religious scholars such as Hayrettin Karaman, known for their arguments about the distinctiveness and superiority of Islamic political structures and states, started to argue that democracy was the closest political structure to Islamic ideals under existing conditions. This position kept open the option of imposing Islamic rule in the longer term, but the time frame they had in mind was not spelled out.

Most theological debates centred on the legitimation of democracy. Secondary commonplaces in the decade that followed the 1997 coup were the desirability of coexistence with other religions (rather than struggle or war with them), the religious need to promote the Turkish state's strength (indeed, an old conservative theme) and the necessity of working with Western states (while at the same time opening towards the Islamic world). These theological shifts were mostly articulated in the newspapers *Yeni Şafak* and *Vakit* (later *Akit*) and partly in the official party booklet *Conservative Democracy*.

Yalçın Akdoğan, the author of the booklet, was an academic (and later a top advisor to Erdoğan). This ideologically definitive booklet drew on Western conservative and liberal theory more than on Islamic sources. Soroush was the only Islamic thinker quoted at length. Here is how the booklet paraphrased and endorsed his ideas:

> Human rights have to be defined as independent from religion . . . Pluralism has to be accepted . . . Religion and religious

> interpretation and understanding are different . . . Religion is one, religious understanding is not. The acceptance of this opens the door to pluralism . . . Religion has recognized the freedom to reject religion.[6]

As a culmination of these theological steps, the booklet declared that state-building should be based on the social sciences, since it cannot be based on religion (which has left this area to human conduct and its trial-and-error methods).

The symbolic weight of Soroush was as important as the content of his ideas. Even though active in the initial years of the Iranian regime, Soroush later turned against it as an Islamic liberal (but some see in him a critical insider rather than an anti-regime figure). Honouring him, rather than any other Islamic thinker, was also a way to keep some distance from the Iranian regime. Islamic newspapers and party booklets thus waged a now open, now covert fight against the Iranian regime throughout the 2000s.

Mehmet Metiner, the radical Islamist quoted on Iran in the previous chapter, was at the forefront of the open struggle against Iran. Metiner had flirted with liberalism and Kurdish nationalism before ultimately joining the AKP and becoming a member of parliament. In his 1989 book on Iran he had lauded the revolution for being exceptional since it had not devoured its own children. Two decades and one passive revolution later, the reverse characteristic came to define the regime for him:

> Iran is destroying its own revolution and revolutionary values [by supporting the Syrian regime] . . . The revolution in Iran first devoured its own children. Those who carried out a revolution for liberty . . . built a rigid dictatorship that destroyed other people's liberties.[7]

---

6 Yalçın Akdoğan, *Muhafazakar demokrasi*, Ankara: Ak Parti, n.d., 104.

7 Mehmet Metiner, 'Kendi devrimini bitiren ülke: İran', *Yeni Şafak*, 30 August 2012. Metiner, who supported AKP rule through liberal values during these years, would end up as an organizer of authoritarian-conservative obedience by 2014. See 'Mehmet Metiner: "Biatsa biat, itaatsa itaat"', hurriyet.com.tr, 6 January 2014.

While some hard-liners interpreted these changes as selling out (as charged by the newspaper *Milli Gazete*), most interpreted them in two different (though sometimes overlapping) ways. The public line was that the old goal of a completely different Islamic order was unrealistic and that the righteous therefore had to adjust to the realities of Turkey and the world. Another line, mostly circulated among activists rather than argued to the larger public, was that the old Islamist goal was intact but that the leaders had discovered longer-term and more roundabout ways of realizing it, adjusting their strategies to the realities of Turkey and the modern world. In my extended ethnography of a formerly radical Islamic region within Istanbul,[8] I found that people could shift frequently between these positions, or sometimes even combine them, in a far-from-consistent fashion. The straight and uncompromising rejection of these two standpoints remained restricted to a minority.

Liberal Islam's Rise to Predominance in Turkey

Similar liberalized ideas were in circulation throughout the 1990s. However, they would not have become a *mass line*, the more or less consistent *project of a bloc*, without political organization. The former radicals' engagement in trade raised doubts about their old dream of a wholly distinct 'Islamic economy'. Nevertheless, this half-hearted questioning did not amount to a complete rejection of the Islamic economy until a new political party, the AKP, normalized the market economy among its constituencies. More and more intellectuals and activists gradually abandoned their puritanism as the party rose to prominence and fell under the influence of those who had been pushing for the separation of religion from politics and economics. How did this party emerge? The neoliberal, (relatively) pro-democratic, and pro-US younger generation of the Virtue Party first tried to take over the existing party structure. Its leaders lost on a vote during a major party congress on 15 May 2000, then established a new organization in 2001, the AKP. The AKP leaders promised the secular media and the military that they would not use religion for political purposes. But what did they mean by this?

8 Cihan Tuğal, *Passive Revolution: Absorbing the Islamic Challenge to Capitalism*, Stanford, CA: Stanford University Press, 2009.

The AKP would not challenge the headscarf ban, they reassured the old elite. They emphasized their allegiance to the free market (in line with the interests of their own increasingly bourgeois support base) and parliamentary democracy. The leaders were also vociferously pro-European and committed to the process of EU accession. They made frequent trips to the United States, holding meetings the agendas of which remained private. Abdullah Gül helpfully explained to an American audience that the members of the AKP were 'the WASPs of Turkey'. The new leadership was thus trying to reclaim the territory of the centre-right in Turkish politics – in effect, to reconstitute an updated version of that alliance of export-oriented businessmen, religious intellectuals and the state elite at which the subordinate fraction of the power bloc had traditionally aimed but which had become impossible with the rise of radical Islamism. As a logical consequence, the AKP incorporated politicians from the now failed centre-right parties. The liberal (less rigidly secularist, more pro-American and less authoritarian) wing of the military, as well as centre-rightists in the secular media, gave signals that they would be willing to work with such a reformed Islamic party. This convergence crowned decades-old efforts by liberal academics, Turkish and Western.

Post-Sufis: From Foe to Friend

Central to this transformation were the changing fortunes of a post-Sufi community. The Gülen community (named after its spiritual leader, Fethullah Gülen) was a frequent target of Islamist attack before the coup in 1997. Islamists perceived the community as an ally of the Turkish and American states. In the 2000s, the community became not only a necessary ally against an oppressive secularism, but a respected member of the now expanded Islamic-conservative bloc as well. Through its inclusion of the post-Sufi community, the AKP regime also gained further liberal credit.

The Gülen community was based on some of the central themes of the Said-i Nursi line (that is, it was 'Nurcu').[9] The Nurcu

9 Said was one of the most prominent clerics of twentieth-century Turkish Islam. His followers splintered into several groups after his death. All of them are known as 'Nurcu'.

interpretation of Islam is based on a scientific (some would say positivistic)[10] understanding of Islam, a silent (rather than armed and public) struggle against the left, support for the centre-right (rather than an independent Islamic political party), a synthesis of the Sufi and textualistic elements of Islam, and an overall strategy that focuses on Islamizing the individual rather than the state. However, this community significantly shifted more towards the centre than did other Nurcu groups, especially by supporting cooperation between Turkey and the West and dialogue among religions. The community was Turkish nationalist, and the schools it built all over the world emphasized Turkification more than Islamization. Covering was not one of the priorities of the community, but some have commented that in all other issues pertaining to gender, its internal relations are quite patriarchal.[11] The public discourse of the community (as voiced by quite powerful media channels such as the newspaper *Zaman* and the television channel *Samanyolu*) was not based heavily on Islamic references but rather sought to instil national pride, a mainstream and pragmatic foreign policy vision and a stance against authoritarian secularism. However, the internal structure of the Gülen community was quite complex. The inner circles (which were much less public) were more committed to Islamic piety. Finally, the key word in the Gülen community was *responsibility*. Its understanding of responsibility was more individualist and market-oriented in comparison to that of the Islamists. In all these senses, the community was Islamic conservative and nationalist, rather than Islamist.

Before 1997, relations between Islamists in Turkey and the Gülen community were not only conflict-ridden but also sometimes violent, as Islamists struggled to save the youth from Gülen's pro-Western understanding of Islam. In the 1980s and 1990s, the conservative wing of the power bloc marketed the Gülen community (along with another post-Sufi community, the Süleymancıs) as antidotes to Islamism. Up until the 1999 elections, the Gülen community publicly supported centre-right (and once, even centre/left-nationalist) parties

10 For the argument that Said interpreted Islam in a positivist way, see Şerif Mardin, *Religion and Social Change in Modern Turkey: The Case of Bediüzzaman Said Nursi*, Albany: State University of New York Press, 1989.

11 Berna Turam, *Between Islam and the State: The Politics of Engagement*, Stanford, CA: Stanford University Press, 2007.

and openly criticized Islamists (for example, Gülen verbally attacked the mobilization for the legalization of the veil on university campuses). The community welcomed the military coup in 1980 and (in oblique fashion) the 1997 coup (though it eventually fell victim to the latter intervention).

After 1997, Islamists started to think that Gülen had a more realistic agenda than old-style Islamism. Key to this turn was the purge of Gülen followers from the army in the aftermath of the 1997 coup. Gülen emigrated to the United States after the coup, reinforcing his image as a victim of rigid secularism. He settled in Pennsylvania and aimed to build a bridge between the Islamic world and Washington, based on dozens of quite influential NGOs inspired by his reinterpretation of Islam. In Turkey itself, the community's influence was restored after the AKP came to power in 2002. In this process, the tone of the Islamist press gradually switched from critique to praise and admiration. The Gülen community was perceived, in the 2000s, as an unquestioned member of the Islamic bloc against the Kemalists. The relation between the AKP and the community went beyond a simple alliance and (despite many lingering tensions) resembled a merger, as many Gülen followers became AKP members and leaders.

The Emergent Authoritarianism of Liberal Islam

Even though the AKP's appeal to liberals rested primarily on its pro-democratic stance, the party never actually demonstrated more than a pro forma commitment on this front. Erdoğan was already known for his authoritarian tendencies. Between 1994 and 1998, he had ruled Istanbul with an iron fist.[12] At the AKP founding congress its leadership pledged itself to internal party democracy, but initial moves in this direction were soon overturned. In 2003, the AKP's Board of Founders annulled internal elections to the party's Central Committee and invested the party president, Erdoğan, with sole authority to appoint or dismiss its members. The Turkish liberals and conservatives (as well as their Western allies) were willing to ignore these open signs of authoritarianism, since the AKP was their only hope against the vestiges of corporatist secularism and an Iran-style Islamic threat.

---

12 Mehmet Metiner, 'Dünden bugüne Tayyip Erdoğan', *Radikal İki*, 6 July 2003.

A further test of democratization was the official approach to the Armenian massacres of 1915. The power bloc had always denied any responsibility for these killings. It is still a criminal offense in Turkey to say that they constituted genocide. In 2005, with expectations of democratization rising, an international group of scholars attempted to organize a conference at which the genocide thesis could be openly debated. AKP Interior Minister Cemil Çiçek reacted by saying that the conference organizers were 'stabbing the nation in the back'. The scholars first called the meeting off and then moved it to a different university due to this semi-veiled threat. While holding such a gathering would have been hard, if not impossible, under any previous government, the incident was a stark reminder of the nationalist-authoritarian tendency within the AKP, of which Çiçek was a leading figure. Despite this, liberal academics remained staunch supporters of the party, seeing only Çiçek as the villain. Even today, some liberals date the AKP's authoritarianism back to 2007, before which the party had been allegedly committed to democratic reform. They thus choose to paint over their own mistreatment at the hands of the party during the golden age of Islamic liberalism.

These authoritarian moves had their counterparts in the relation of the party to the people in the mid-2000s. While Erdoğan's government legislated a series of democratic reforms at the instigation of the EU, it also disregarded the most basic norms of representativeness and accountability with regard to its electorate. Rather than taking popular grievances seriously, Erdoğan publicly scolded anybody who talked to him about hunger, unemployment or housing problems. At party rallies he told the poor to pull themselves together and do something for themselves, instead of expecting the government to do it for them.

In May 2010, he told the families of the victims of a mining accident that the suffering of miners was an inseparable part of their job, indeed their 'fate'. Erdoğan had likewise blamed flood and earthquake victims in poverty-stricken areas of being responsible for their plight (since they had picked dangerous locations to live in and used low-quality construction materials in their buildings) and denied official responsibility in the face of social protest (which followed these events). When his proclamations about 'fate' aroused criticism in the press, the prime minister questioned the faith of his critics, telling them to discuss the matter with the Directorate General of Religious Affairs. In this manner, Erdoğan manipulated religious discourse to shut off public debate about the mining industry and other social issues.

Some analysts perceived demilitarization and the government's position on the Kurds as proofs of its allegiance to democracy. Since the AKP was able to marginalize the military – which had come to constitute the root of all evil in this new, liberal, revisionist and quite simplistic interpretation of Turkish history – its 'minor' infringements on rights could be forgiven. But even here the outcome was mixed. During the course of the 'Ergenekon' trials, the pro-government prosecutors and journalists courageously attacked some murderous groups within the state. A network called Ergenekon (after a Central Asian–Turkic legend) had been allegedly assassinating minorities and fomenting violence. However, a number of opposition figures (at best) loosely or ideologically connected to these murderous groups were also imprisoned. Moreover, any opposition to the government after that point was labelled publicly as 'pro-Ergenekon' without any proof (such as a major strike in 2010 by Tekel workers who had lost their rights as a result of privatization). On the one hand, ethnically oppressive laws were rescinded. On the other hand, the courts and security forces ratcheted up the pressure against legal Kurdish parties and associations, alleging that they had ties to the illegal guerrilla organization, the Kurdistan Workers' Party (Partiya Karkerên Kurdistanê, or PKK). Even children were put on trial for participating in demonstrations organized by legal Kurdish parties. While secular and religious liberals celebrated the Ergenekon and Kurdish processes, critics (Kemalists, secular-nationalist Kurds, and socialists, who were all losing support to an endlessly expanding pro-AKP liberal intelligentsia in the 2000s) raised the suspicion that the AKP was democratic only to the extent that doing so benefited the party and its bloc.

Consolidation of the New Power Bloc

During the late 2000s, not only Islamists but also many liberals and Marxists were absorbed into the AKP's conservative agenda. Partly based on the social science of the last three decades (the common argument of which tended to be that pious people represent the 'periphery' and 'civil society' in opposition to the centre and the authoritarian state tradition), partly motivated by the European and American search for a 'moderate Islam', these liberals and leftists joined forces with the ex-Islamists to fight the bureaucracy, Kemalist intelligentsia and the intensifying labour, environmental and youth activism – all of which they now perceived as one bloc against democracy. Another hope was that the AKP would resolve the Kurdish issue through its mix of Islamic conservatism and democracy.

Not surprisingly, therefore, many Turkish and Western liberals and leftists were mobilized to help pass constitutional amendments that would increase the scope of the executive's powers through curbing the powers of the judiciary (which remained, quite mistakenly, perceived as a secularist stronghold) and the military. After a successful referendum in 2010, the 1980 constitution was indeed amended. Instead of curbing military excesses, however, the government ratcheted up military pressure on the Kurdish national movement (and to the dismay of only a few of the leftists in its coalition) police pressure on labour and other Turkish activism. The AKP also received carte blanche from these forces in its pre- and post-referendum cleansing of the media from 'anti-democratic' (read anti-AKP) elements. In sum, what marked AKP success was not deploying authoritarianism (as all neoliberal parties since 1980 have done), but dressing it in 'democratic' and 'Islamic' garb. Liberalism, like any other project, needs to repress some of its enemies; its relative success lies in its more persistent blending of such repression with fluctuating inclusiveness.

The failed manoeuvres of a new CHP leader (Kemal Kılıçdaroğlu) to push the party to the left demonstrated that the new power bloc's articulations had become so 'common sense' that nobody could take a step without falling back on the oppositions between Islam, democracy and the free market on one hand, and secularism, authoritarianism and statism on the other. The pro-AKP media (ranging from conservatives and ex-Islamists to secular liberals and liberalized ex-Marxists) repeatedly accused the new CHP leadership of having a hidden agenda: the new leader was, at best, just a naïve prop fronting a coup plan. Pro-AKP journalists also held that student protests against privatization and massive strikes were parts of the same coup plot.[13] Subsequently, all attempts to bolster a leftward move in the CHP were interpreted as militarist conspiracies. The authoritarian forces in the CHP used this environment to render moves by the new leader ineffective. Kılıçdaroğlu himself shifted to old-style Kemalism as a response to these pressures.[14] What was more important than the AKP's sweeping electoral victories, then, was its success in destabilizing and marginalizing its opponents.

In sum, before the Arab revolts of late 2010 and 2011, Turkey (backed by its Western allies) revelled in a dystopia of near-total consensus. A reshuffling of Islamic political society had led to the formation of the most hegemonic bloc in Turkish history. The top academics, the most revered public intellectuals, many activists and a large proportion of the popular classes had become one with the regime, even if they attributed contrasting meanings to their adherence.

Conservative Liberalization of Religious Life

By the mid-2000s, Turkey witnessed a molecular absorption of pious life patterns to capitalism . The result was what we can call liberal Islamization. In distinction from legalistic and revolutionary Islamization, liberal Islamization is individualist, oriented towards business and consumption, and flexible. It is pragmatic and its application easily adjusts to circumstances. However, these characteristics do not mean that liberal Islamization is completely devoid of legalism and force. They suggest instead that Islamic law and force (if applied at all) will be absorbed within economistic and individualistic dispositions. In short, liberal Islamization can be defined as a flexible implementation of gender segregation and female covering; flexibility and (business and political) utility orientation regarding

13 Many influential former Marxists joined the neoliberal Islamic bloc due to such concerns. For a prominent example, see Murat Belge's interview in *Radikal*, 4 July 2011, where he argued that 'fascists' were behind the apparently leftist strikes, student movements and environmental protests of the last few years.

14 After the AKP's conservative turn in 2013, Kılıçdaroğlu attempted, in vain, to refashion the CHP as the true representative of the original AKP's project (by running a former AKP figure as the presidential candidate).

the daily and Friday prayers; flexibility, 'tolerance' and attention to economic implications in the restriction of 'un-Islamic' practices (such as alcohol consumption, cohabitation and mixed schooling).

As distinct from its usage in everyday language, therefore, 'liberal' in this case does not denote 'completely free and democratic'. A liberal project is one in which the individual, his/her freedom from the state, and her property are put in the centre; and state and society are summoned to develop and expand the market-oriented responsibility and productive and financial capability of this individual (and by implication, his freedoms and property as well). I base this definition of liberalism on John Locke's *Second Treatise of Civil Government*, which not only defines freedom/liberty as the right to life and property, but also posits that private property is at the basis of all freedom (see, for example chapter 16, sec. 192); and sees the uninhibited accumulation of that property as the cornerstone of the good life.

Moreover, the goals and strategies of Turkish Islamism were 'liberalized', but they were not consistently liberal. This liberalization should be taken relatively and contextually. Turkish Islamism could appear conservative in the American context, but it was 'liberal' in comparison to its own past and to other major movements in the region. For example, creationism and anti-gay mobilization (*Yeni Şafak*, 23 March 2010) were becoming core aspects of Islamism, replacing pro-sharia and pro-Islamic state mobilization, bringing Turkish Islamism closer to American conservatism, but more unlike Egyptian and Iranian conservatism.

How did Turkish Islamists shift from propagating a comprehensive and rigid understanding of religion to this new interpretation? Political society was central to liberalizing Turkish Islamism. The AKP hijacked Islamism to further consolidate liberal-conservatism.[15] For example, while prayer lost its centrality to everyday life, Islamic leaders and activists made a point of praying before and after public

---

15 Parts of the following four paragraphs draw on Cihan Tuğal, 'Religious Politics, Hegemony, and the Market Economy: Parties In the Making of Turkey's Liberal-Conservative Bloc and Egypt's Diffuse Islamization' in Cedric De Leon, Manali Desai and Cihan Tuğal, eds, *Building Blocs: How Parties Organize Society*, Stanford, CA: Stanford University Press, 2015.

political meetings.[16] Such public shows had been central to the careers of centre-rightist politicians throughout the history of the Turkish Republic. These politicians led westernized lives but mobilized Islamic symbols for mass appeal. As centre-right parties weakened in Turkey, Islamic parties moved in to fill the gap but internalized some long-standing centre-right strategies while doing so. The changes in the place of prayer in social and political life thus resulted from changes in the structure of political society rather than solely from the secularist impositions of the state.

Interlocking movements in political society and civil society put an end to the separation of sexes in workplaces while reproducing a tamed variety of gender segregation in less visible neighbourhoods. Segregation was unofficially practiced, but in official venues like municipalities or party meetings it lost its prominence. Professional and business-oriented women gained more visibility in this new, more flexible social climate. Instead of attempting to ban alcohol everywhere (the Islamist utopia), AKP imposed restrictions on alcohol sale and use, after the American conservative model. Political economic structures, such as the upward mobility of women and the importance of alcohol in Turkey's economy (not least in tourism), constitute a context for understanding these changes. However, women (including pious women) had been upwardly mobile for the last two decades and it was never a secret that banning alcohol everywhere would hurt the Turkish economy. It was ultimately shifts in political society (from the rigidity of the RP to the flexibility and 'tolerance' of the AKP) and political decisions that changed the Islamic position regarding female visibility and alcohol.

We can take the AKP's flexible attempts to apply Islamic law and force as further demonstrations of liberalized Islam. In 2005, the government attempted to criminalize adultery. Even though it did not mention Islamic law, it was clear that the latter had inspired this initiative, which provoked reactions from Europe and secular liberal intellectuals in Turkey (the AKP's allies). The government decided to abandon the attempt. This was a sign of both an ongoing commitment to legal precepts of Islam *and* an ability to be flexible in this commitment so as not to anger allies (a degree of flexibility that

16 Tuğal, *Passive Revolution*, 193–5.

neither the major Islamist organizations in Egypt nor the Iranian regime has so far exhibited).

In the 2000s, cultural centres and networks of friends, mosques and Islamic schools manufactured a pragmatic and business-oriented spirituality. For example, whereas the Welfare Party and Virtue Party leaders encouraged their members and contacts to pray whenever the call to prayer was sounded, the AKP leaders and members chose to emphasize how hard work itself was a part of religion and did not publicly encourage people to pray.[17] Religious observance became more individualized (for example, former activists no longer put pressure on people around them to perform the daily prayers communally). Finally, some sectors of the elite appropriated this emergent religiosity and became more observant themselves.

How stable were these religious configurations? The liberalization of piety depended on the parameters outlined in the first three chapters of this book: Turkey's integration with Western political, diplomatic and economic structures; stable economic growth; the AKP's professionalism, monopolization of the Islamic field and control over Islamic radicals and ex-radicals; and, if an absence can be counted as a factor, the near-global lack of hope regarding the imminence of Islamic revolutions, which contributed to the de-radicalization of Islamists. These factors, however, would mutate in irregular ways by the end of the 2000s. After that point, the place of piety would prove to be one of the most unpredictable elements in the Turkish passive revolution.

Limits of Islamic Liberalization in Egypt

Much hope has been invested in policy and academic circles in the liberalization of the Muslim Brotherhood. For instance, Sullivan and Abed-Kotob charged that the Mubarak regime failed to represent the interests of Egypt and the (mostly 'civil') Egyptian society. Islamist movements (except the militant ones) were a part of this civil society, and in the long run, these authors held, they would further civilize and democratize the country: the Islamist movements were *inevitable* and *tameable*.[18]

---

17 Ibid., 103–7, 193–7, 217–24.

18 See Denis J. Sullivan and Sana Adeb-Kotob, *Islam in Contemporary Egypt: Civil Society vs. the State*, Boulder, CO: Lynne Rienner Publishers, 1999, chapter 1.

Many other scholars drew attention to an increasing trend within Egyptian Islamic groups to emphasize gradual change, hard work, technological competition and economic growth-oriented education.[19] Why didn't these hopes materialize? Why didn't the taming (of which there was a lot) result in political and economic liberalization?

The Muslim Brotherhood indeed gave up many of its radical ideas. From the 1980s onwards, it moved from calling for a transnational Khilafa state[20] to supporting democracy, women's rights and minority rights – though some scholars and activists remained suspicious of the sincerity of these declarations.[21] The Brotherhood even started to use Islamic modernist arguments (for example, *shura* as an Islamic equivalent of democracy) in favour of democracy and a plural party system (abandoning al-Banna's condemnation of parties). Was liberalized Islam finally arriving in Egypt?

Such moves away from an anti-state understanding of Islamization were indeed paralleled by the commodification of religion (the refashioning of Islamic symbols as artefacts that can be bought and sold) among some urban sectors, just as in Turkey in the 1990s.[22] Veiling became less conservative, more revealing and a component of new urban chic.[23] Among the poor, religiosity maintained its salience by integrating them to the city, but everyday life became less puritan through an acceptance of fashionable dancers, singers and expensive vacations. The poor could care less about whether these practices abided by the Brotherhood's understanding of a comprehensive Islamic life.[24]

Nevertheless, the Islamist leadership refused to accommodate market-oriented practices (such as revealing and flexible Islamic

---

19 Raymond W. Baker, *Islam without Fear: Egypt and the New Islamists*, Cambridge, MA: Harvard University Press, 2003, 12–13, 34–44.

20 Hossam Tamam, *Tahawwulat al-Ikhwan al-Muslimin*, Cairo: Maktab Madbouly, 2010, 8–10.

21 Chris Harnisch and Quinn Mecham, 'Democratic Ideology in Islamist Opposition? The Muslim Brotherhood's "Civil State"', *Middle Eastern Studies* 45 (2009): 199–200.

22 Farha Ghannam, *Remaking the Modern: Space, Relocation, and the Politics of Identity in a Global Cairo*, Berkeley: University of California Press, 2002.

23 Linda Herrera, 'Downveiling: Gender and the Contest over Culture in Cairo', *Middle East Report* 31 (2001): 16–19.

24 See Ghannam, *Remaking the Modern*, chapter 5.

covering that defied the standardization and modesty of the veil or the mobilization of Islamic symbols for consumerist purposes). The fragmented and less-than-professionalized structure of political society ruled out such a liberalizing strategy. The restricted integration of urban middle class and peasant elements into the Egyptian Islamist movement inhibited a monopoly of the Muslim Brotherhood over Islamic political society. In the 1980s and 1990s, a clear class and geographical split marked the Islamic scene: radical armed organizations (Jamaa and Jihad) recruited the urban and rural poor,[25] whereas the Brotherhood mostly appealed to rentier capitalists, the labour aristocracy, petty merchants and professionals.[26] Jamaa was led by university graduates of middle-class and working-class origin and was social justice–oriented). The Brotherhood, by contrast, supported the government's free market policies in the countryside and backed landowners against small farmers.[27]

Such conflict contrasts with Turkey, where conservatives were relatively more integrated through Islamic civil society, patronage and political society. Even though the countryside and the fringes of the cities in Turkey were also marked by poverty, the poor were connected to official institutions (including welfare agencies) through patronage networks of political parties. The relatively peaceful integration of these sectors into political society created a more welcoming environment for liberalized piety as well.

State action also led to further fragmentation of Egyptian Islamic political society. The crackdown in the second half of the 1990s interrupted further strengthening of radical Islamic organizations. The

---

25 Even the more pragmatic and business-oriented Islamic activists in poor quarters remained opposed to the old regime. Salwa Ismail, *Political Life in Cairo's New Quarters: Encountering the Everyday State*, Minneapolis: University of Minnesota Press, 52–7).

26 Salwa Ismail, 'Confronting the Other: Identity, Culture, Politics, and Conservative Islamism in Egypt', *International Journal of Middle East Studies* 30 (1998): 200–1.

27 Mamoun Fandy, 'Egypt's Islamic Group: Regional Revenge?' *Middle East Journal* 48 (1998): 607–25. Egypt's official religious institution al-Azhar also supported Law 96 (abolition of rent control in the countryside) and the expulsion of peasants, while Jamaa opposed it. Anwar Alam, 'The Sociology and Political Economy of "Islamic Terrorism" in Egypt', *Terrorism and Political Violence* 15:4 (2003): 135.

repression was not, however, followed by the Brotherhood's absorption of radical Islamists due to this organization's semi-professionalism: the Brotherhood did not have a spelled out, coherent programme and the structure of a political party,[28] which in combination could provide an alternative route to these radicals. The existence of a programmatic party in a repressive context was what enabled the incorporation and de-radicalization of radical Islamists in Turkey. The reluctance of the Brotherhood leaders well into the 1990s to transform the organization into a political party reflects this legacy of semi-professionalism: political and religious expertise remained poorly differentiated. It was not always clear that the politically most capable people controlled the organization. Official repression does not dictate social outcomes. Political society shapes the ramifications of state terror. The Egyptian crackdown of the 1990s provided similar opportunities and threats to Islamism (the factors that institutionalist accounts would focus on), but the way political society filtered them led to a liberalizing strategy in Turkey and the further entrenchment of legalistic strategies in Egypt.

The structure of authority, another component of political society alongside sociopolitical organizations, also differentiated Egyptian from Turkish Islamism. An important change from the initial radical decades of the Muslim Brotherhood to its middle decades was transition from leadership by teachers to leadership by merchants, paralleling the shift from radicalism to conservatism. Another shift occurred in the beginning of the twenty-first century, which witnessed the rise of professionals within the organization, who now shared power with the old-guard merchants. The increasing influence of 'professionals' (as a socio-economic stratum) might bring about 'professionalization' in political society, but this is not a deterministic relationship. Professionals might also have legalistic or revolutionary tendencies, with their stance depending on their relations to other strata and the structure of political society.

Paralleling the transformation in Turkey, religion was less and less important in the discourse of the new leaders (who had professional backgrounds), in contrast to both the initial leaders and the leaders

28 Hossam Tamam, *Tahawwulat al-Ikhwan al-Muslimin*, Cairo: Maktab Madbouly, 2010.

of the middle decades.[29] This change could indeed lead to a liberalized Islam. Unlike Turkey, however, these new leaders were not in control of the movement.[30] Professionalization of the authority structure was incomplete, and professionalistic tendencies did not generate the same results in Egypt because of more ingrained capacity within political society in Turkey, the volatility of positive international allies in Egypt and the Muslim Brotherhood's lack of a coherent programme.

At the end of the 1990s, the Brotherhood's leadership was marked by stalemate. The liberalizers were imprisoned and 'the legalists used repression as an excuse to have their candidate appointed as the movement's leader. The liberalizing youth regained influence after 2004, with the death of a key conservative leader.[31] However, even following this partial liberalization, the Egyptian regime continued mildly repressing the Brotherhood.

The 2000s: Further Consolidation of Legalistic Strategies

The Muslim Brotherhood continued to fluctuate between a revival of conservative (more precisely, 'legalist') tendencies and small gains by reformists, with conservatives gaining more ground during 2009 and 2010. The period from 2002 to 2010 witnessed many internal battles and the rise of a key conservative behind the scenes. Khairat al-Shater, who was revealed to be the emerging mastermind only after the events of 2011, slowly sidelined the reformists by gaining complete control of the Guidance Bureau and the Shura Council.

Like some of his fellow 'Qutbists' (as they were called in the larger public), al-Shater was a wealthy, pro-neoliberal businessmen. This

---

29 Mohammed Zahid and Michael Medley, 'Muslim Brotherhood in Egypt and Sudan', *Review of African Political Economy* 33 (2006): 693–708.

30 The class base of legalistic Islam is the commercial bourgeoisie and merchants. But to what degree were professionals under their spell in the 1990s and 2000s? Who was more legalistic: the public sector professionals or those employed by the booming real estate sector and private consultancy firms? What per cent of the Brotherhood professionals are still legalistic today? These are some of the persisting gaps in our knowledge.

31 Mona el-Ghobashy, 'The Metamorphosis of the Egyptian Muslim Brothers', *International Journal of Middle East Studies* 37 (2005): 373–95; Jan Stark, 'Beyond "Terrorism" and "State Hegemony": Assessing the Islamist Mainstream in Egypt and Malaysia', *Third World Quarterly* 26 (2005): 307–27.

distinguished the new 'Qutbism' from that of earlier, more new middle-class-based (and also more social justice–oriented) generations.[32] Unlike Turkey, therefore, the turn to intensified economic liberalism was not articulated to political liberalization. The organization's new online magazine, as well as extensive positions created within its bureaucracy, created a large following loyal directly to the Brotherhood's Guidance Bureau rather than the movement as a whole. Al-Shater's influence was confirmed with Mohammed Badie's replacement of Mahdi Akef as the supreme guide in 2010.[33]

Many of the Islamic liberals were ousted during an internal struggle in 2010.The regime used this crisis as a precept to crack down on the Brotherhood, charging that the organization was now controlled by 'fundamentalists'. The intense circulation of Qutb's name during 2009–10 (though as an uncompromising anti-secularist, rather than a prophet of social justice) also enabled the courts to find excuses for the crackdown. The incomplete professionalization of authority structures thus further impeded the normalization of the relations between the state and Islamic political society. Despite all of this repression, the Brotherhood further recoiled to a legalistic position (and thus sought more common ground with the state), instead of either revolutionizing its understanding of Islam or liberalizing it.

By 2010, the most vibrant currents within Egyptian Islamism accepted existing institutions and did their best to encourage the ('secular') state to put Islamic law to practice.[34] Egyptian Islamists thus started to count on the law to discipline the citizenry along Islamic lines; this meant indirect disciplining through the law along with direct disciplining through a party, while the latter had become the predominant channel of Islamization in the Turkish case. Egyptian Islamists also Islamized society through infiltrating certain

---

32 The marriage of a strict interpretation of Islam and aggressive neoliberalism is not restricted to this Brotherhood contingent. Ismail demonstrates how widespread it is among Egyptian Salafi circles as well. Salwa Ismail, 'Piety, Profit and the Market in Cairo: a Political Economy of Islamisation', *Contemporary Islam* 7:1 (2013): 107–28.

33 Khalil al-Anani, 'The Embattled Brothers', *Egypt Independent*, 19 April 2012.

34 Bruce Rutherford, *Egypt after Mubarak: Liberalism, Islam, and Democracy in the Arab World*, Princeton, NJ: Princeton University Press, 2008, chapter 3.

Islamic civil society organizations (such as the Gamaiyya Sharaiyya), which are themselves based on legalistic understandings of Islam and are much less flexible than political Islamic organizations in their interpretations of Islamic law.[35] For instance, Gamaiyya Sharaiyya proclaims in its brochure (titled *el-Dawa, el-Amal el-Salih, el-Ighatha, el-Tanmiyya*) that it abides by a literal understanding of the Qur'an and opposes reinterpretation of received understanding, while even most Islamist parties avoid defining what kind of Islam they subscribe to. Member of parliament offices provided chances of more direct contact after 2005, but these were naturally restricted before 2011 (in comparison to the AKP's). In short, even though the Brotherhood was a very powerful organization, its direct contact with the popular classes was relatively restricted (when compared to Turkey's Islamic parties). In many cases, its contact was mediated by the state's legal experts and legalistic civil society organizations (signs of a highly fragmented civil and political society). The result was the entrenchment of legalistic Islam.

Legalism and semi-professionalism also shaped the Brotherhood's moves in the parliamentary arena. As a response to regime pressure during 2009 and 2010, some members of the Brotherhood decided to boycott the 2010 parliamentary elections. However, the conservative-dominated Guidance Bureau opposed this idea, and the Brotherhood participated in the elections. The Guidance Bureau used overtly moralistic language in its condemnation of the liberalizers who suggested that the organization should boycott the elections. Questioning the decision of the leaders, the Guidance Bureau held, was 'immoral' and against Brotherhood principles.[36] This argument was typical of the organization's moralistic orientation to politics (which was produced and reinforced by the fragmented Islamic political society).

This political structure helped the Guidance Bureau keep the organization intact, but it did not boost its mass appeal. The Brotherhood could win only one seat in the rigged elections, with the

35 Maha Abdelrahman, *Civil Society Exposed: The Politics of NGOs in Egypt*, London: St Martins Press, 2004.

36 'Tasaa'ud al-talaasun daakhil al-Ikhwaan bayna Jabhat al-Mu'aarada wa Maktab al-Irshaad', almasryalyoum.com, 17 October 2010.

governing National Democratic Party securing about 80 per cent of the seats. After this, the Islamic liberalizers were further emboldened. They started a campaign against the Guidance Bureau, which in turn threatened to expel them. Such was the balance of forces within the Brotherhood when the uprising erupted in 2011.

Turkey and Egypt converged in the mid-1990s in their turn away from the inclusive policies of the 1980s (as a reaction to Islamist advances at home and the civil war in Algeria), but the results were different partly due to differences in the structures of their political societies. In contrast with the Turkish case, state repression did not culminate in the emergence of a successful liberal Islamic organization in Egypt. To understand why, we need to focus on how the internal organization of political society differed in the two countries.

Tunisia: Liberalization with No Room to Breathe

Until 2011, comparisons between Tunisia and Egypt on the one hand, and Iran and Turkey on the other, pose a methodological problem: it is only in the latter countries that Islamic actors were in power. Tunisia is an even more problematic case, since the possible Tunisian followers of the Turkish model were severely repressed until 2011, and whatever sign of Islamic liberalization they could display was severely restricted by the circumstances. Despite these conditions, we see strong signs of political liberalization, though fewer signs of liberalization in economics and everyday life.

Despite an overall similarity with other Middle Eastern Islamisms in its position within the political process (see chapter 1), al-Nahda also featured one distinctive quality: its leader's exceptional strategic thinking, his intellectual depth and his democratic credentials. Ghannouchi produced amazing texts that demonstrated his multilayered and flexible reading of politics and society in the modern age. He mapped out, with dexterity, complex tactics and strategies through which to Islamize society. He combined the Islamic philosopher, the spiritual guide and political leader in his person, a combination which had been lacking since the days of Mawdudi, al-Banna, Qutb, Shariati and Khomeini.

Ghannouchi also built a reputation as an Islamic democrat. Unlike the Islamic thinkers mentioned above, he had a genuine engagement with the strengths of the West (not just its weaknesses) and (apparently) a true appreciation for pluralism. Whereas some of his interviews and writings created the impression that Ghannouchi was in favour of a completely pluralistic political system, other writings insisted on the exclusion of non-Islamic parties.[37] This was a contradiction that liberal scholars and journalists grappled to make sense of as Ghannouchi rose to fame.[38]

Ghannouchi's qualities made al-Nahda of interest to the 'international community': it was a party that could decisively reconcile Islam and democracy. From the standpoint of this book, what is remarkable is the depth of Ghannouchi's strategic thinking (and not just his sincere engagement with democracy). If truly absorbed by his party's cadres, a pragmatic, professional and flexible approach to politics and economics could put Tunisia on a passive revolutionary path. Such an internalization would bring Tunisian Islamic political society closer to the Turkish one. An Islamic neoliberal regime in Tunisia would even enjoy the further advantage of having a *spiritual* guide as the political leader, which could further boost consent. But did the Islamists of Tunisia really internalize Ghannouchi's thinking and transform it into a working *mass* strategy? And could such a strategy be implemented without political experience accumulated through decades of municipal rule, even if the Tunisian system suddenly and unexpectedly opened up to Islamists?

On the question of how much the party internalized its leader's theoretical-theological marriage of Islam and democracy, there is some indication that it might not have moved very far.[39] But for the more interesting question of how much al-Nahda has operationalized

37 It should be noted that leading Turkish Islamists did not frequently voice such radically exclusionary opinions, partly due to the Turkish secularist system and its laws, but partly also due to their internalization of that context: even the most democratic Islamist movement in the Arab context appears to be far less democratic than the Turkish one.

38 Opinions diverged, as some found Ghannouchi more sincere, while others held that behind the thin veneer of liberalism was a staunch fundamentalist committed to pluralism only among Muslims who obeyed Islamic law. Khadija Katja Wöhler-Khalfallah, 'Democracy Concepts of the Fundamentalist Parties of Algeria and Tunisia – Claim and Reality', *International Journal of Conflict and Violence* 1:1 (2007): 76–88.

39 Fadia Faqir, 'Engendering Democracy and Islam in the Arab World', *Third World Quarterly* 18:1 (1997): 170.

his strategic thinking, events and actions (more than the party's declarations and official texts) can be a guide. Some of the following chapters will explore whether Tunisian Islamism indeed liberalized along the axis of political strategizing.

Besieged Liberalization in Iran

If, following Bourdieu and Migdal, we posit that the state is a field rather than a unitary actor, this has been more persistently the case in Iran, where a significant amount of the political competition over the last three decades has occurred within the state, and political society has been subservient. Rather than developing within an easily distinguishable, autonomous, differentiated political society, factions have flexed their muscles at the intersection of political society and the state, within that grey area where the two overlap. The various factions have been in an unending battle to control the various parts of the state; likewise, parts of the state have been at war with each other. How did liberalized Islamists emerge in the context of these internecine battles, and how did their prospects fare in comparison to their Turkish and Egyptian counterparts?

Islamic Liberal Actors in an Islamic State

The radical faction lost its base after the Iraq defeat. Its agenda of anti-imperialism, export of the revolution and militancy was discredited .[40] The conservatives and pragmatic moderates were emboldened and started a general campaign against all tenets of radicalism. After the end of the 1980s, conflicts shaped up mostly between conservative, pragmatic moderate and Islamic liberal factions. The liberals, many of them disillusioned radicals,[41] sought to put the prestige from their radical past and their (westernized) Islamic intellectual rigour in the service of liberal democracy,[42] just as had the former radicals in Turkey.

---

40 Ahmad Ashraf, 'Theocracy and Charisma: New Men of Power in Iran', *International Journal of Politics, Culture and Society* 4 (1990): 113–52.

41 Ahmad Ashraf and Ali Banuazizi, 'Iran's Tortuous Path toward "Islamic Liberalism"', *International Journal of Politics, Culture and Society* 15 (2001): 250–1.

42 Mahmoud Alinejad, 'Coming to Terms with Modernity: Iranian Intellectuals and the Emerging Public Sphere', *Islam & Christian-Muslim Relations* 13 (2002): 34; Nikki R. Keddie, *Modern Iran: Roots and Results of Revolution*, New Haven, CT: Yale University Press, 2006 [2003], 260, 270.

However, the religious liberal faction, leader of a possible liberal Islamization in Iran, never demonstrated the political will and unity that could circumscribe conservatism and build a liberal Islamic society.[43] Trends in civil society reinforced the weaknesses of liberal Islamic political actors. For example, the student movement, Islamic liberalism's main civic ally, openly constructed itself as an 'anti-thesis' of political parties, institutions and political actors: as an agent of a 'critique of power', not of the reconstruction of power.[44]

Mohammad Khatami, the liberal Islamic political leader of the 1990s, was also unwilling to form a party.[45] Liberal Islamic forces remained organized as loose coalitions rather than becoming solid political actors with explicit, consistent programmatic visions. Political society under Khatami was diverse, but fragmented and divisive,[46] very different from the conservative-liberal bloc that was forged around the AKP in Turkey. The Islamic liberals were possibly united *against* the conservatives, but they were not united *for* an articulate and detailed programme. The dispersed nature of civil society and political society organized by the liberals led to many coalitions, but never to a sustained bloc.

The voters gave the Islamic liberals the chance to change this situation in 1997 when Khatami became the president. The liberals, with only weak organization in political society and some organization in civil society and the state, faced a conservative blockage organized tightly at all levels of the state and society, a veritable bloc (which, however, itself proved temporary). The Guardian Council, the Expediency Council, the Parliament and paramilitary forces mobilized to make reform difficult, if not impossible. They intimidated and repressed intellectuals and professors, and they also restricted Khatami's and his supporters' space of manoeuvre, especially by further increasing the funding and capacities of state institutions which were under conservative control.[47]

---

43 Keddie, *Modern Iran: Roots and Results of Revolution*, 323.

44 Asef Bayat, *Street Politics: Poor People's Movements in Iran*, New York: Columbia University Press, 1997, 108.

45 Asef Bayat, *Making Islam Democratic: Social Movements and the Post-Islamist Turn*, Stanford, CA: Stanford University Press, 2007, 108–9.

46 Ibid., 111–13.

47 Ali Gheissari and Vali Nasr, *Democracy in Iran: History and the Quest for Liberty*, Oxford: Oxford University Press, 2006, 136–8.

In May 1999 the conservatives closed down numerous newspapers, and student protests followed. Under pressure from the Revolutionary Guards, Khatami denounced the protests. Faced by a large counter-demonstration, the students gave up: weak political society crippled civil society. In 2000, students commemorated the 1999 riots and were attacked by vigilantes. The remaining reformist newspapers were closed down. The reformists could not do much; they passed a number of bills, but the Council of Guardians blocked most of them. Throughout his term, Khatami tried to support women and students through reform bills and other means, promising to expand 'civil society' (in his own terms), but he did not get very far.[48] In fact, Khatami sought to minimize conflict with the conservatives and encouraged all seekers of reform to avoid clashes with them,[49] further weakening the potential for a political society independent from the state. These developments indicate that, on top of the state's continuous attempts to disorganize the opposition, the approach and manoeuvres of politicians also contributed to the *dispersed structure* of Iranian political society.

The resulting lack of consistent connections between civil society and political society cannot be attributed only to the lack of opportunities (the main explanatory framework in most of political sociology). There were ample opportunities during these years for the construction of solid links with civil society. An Islamic organization as structured as either the AKP or even the Muslim Brotherhood (had it existed in Iran) could have constituted such links.

There was wide participation in the 1999 municipal and local council elections. But because the reformists did not take significant initiative in the following years, participation dropped in 2003.[50] Because of indecisive political leadership, institutional openings eventually narrowed: when the Council of Guardians blocked reformist candidacies in 2003, the street did not protect them,[51] attesting to the lack of solid ties between political society and civil society. The reformists remained middle class, elitist and occupied with dialogue;

48 Bayat, *Street Politics*, 120–3; Keddie, *Modern Iran, Roots and Results of Revolution*, 276–80.

49 Gheissari and Nasr, *Democracy in Iran*, 139–40.

50 Keddie, *Modern Iran: Roots and Results of Revolution*, 276.

51 Bayat, *Street Politics*, 130.

they did nothing to mobilize strikes, protests or civil disobedience in their favour.[52]

The dispersed nature of political organization (and the looseness of links between political society and civil society) was reproduced during the 2009 elections, after which large crowds protested the reportedly rigged results for weeks. The intensity of the protests might have given the impression of a solid opposition, but there were many ambiguities. First, the candidate favoured by the protesters, Mir-Hossein Moussavi, was a regime insider, not an independent political leader like Erbakan or Erdoğan. He had been prime minister during Khomeini's reign, overseeing the state mechanism during its bloody years, but he was also credited with building a fair rationing system for food and petrol.[53] Actors formed within the state *can* become actors within political society, but this transformation requires considerable effort, which was not performed in the case of Moussavi. Moussavi's rise hence reproduced political society's subordination to the state and its lack of autonomy.

Second, there was no unified party or proto-party that could outlast the elections (and the protests) and attest to the existence of a persistent and consistent programme,[54] one that could constitute an alternative to existing policies. The regime further intensified this problem by closing down two of the major reformist parties. This loose organization (and the lack of programme) in Iranian political society can be contrasted to Turkish (Islamic) political society, which has been united and programmatic throughout the last four decades.

Finally, it is unlikely whether the protesters shared a vision, but even more so whether they shared a vision with Moussavi (beyond an insufficiently defined liberalization). During their campaigns, the two top reformist candidates focused more on Ahmedinejad's shortcomings and problems than their policies and promises.[55] Moussavi did not 'lead' in the sense of mobilizing and convincing people to support a certain social-political project. In terms of the conceptual framework used here, he remained an actor with the realm of the state and

52 Ibid., 134–5.

53 James Buchan, 'A Bazaari Bonaparte?', *New Left Review* 2:59 (September/October 2009): 78–9.

54 Ibid., 81.

55 Ibid., 79–80.

did not become a professional politician (in the positive sense of a mobilizing figure with a social-political project).

The main reason why Moussavi received votes was because he was against Ahmedinejad's conservatism: what brought the protesters and Moussavi together was what they were against, not what they were for. Was the reform movement a liberal Islamic movement, a conservative democratic one, a liberal democratic one or none of the above? Did it want to overthrow the Islamic Republic or reform it from within? Speculations abounded. The resulting array of forces was not very different from the wide and loose coalition that carried through the Islamic revolution, which had not produced a strongly hegemonic order. Iranian politics never experienced the formation of blocs as solidly as those in Turkey. The reformists could not strike new balances in this absence of hegemonic order, opening the doors again to impositions from above.

There were indications of bloc formation throughout the 1980s and 1990s but none of these tendencies congealed into durable blocs for more than a decade. The conservative bloc that forged its ranks in opposition to the liberals between the mid-1990s and the mid-2000s is a case in point. It disintegrated into two camps: the conservative clerics and the populist conservative professionals (as represented by Ahmedinejad).

Towards the end of the 2000s, conservative factions within both the professional class and the managerial class started to fight not only the liberal factions within these classes, but also the clerics and the merchants within the conservative bloc. Although these quarrels remained within the boundaries of the conservative camp for a while (and were restricted to disagreements about specific policies and appointments), by the beginnings of the 2010s there was a huge political fallout.[56] Supreme Leader Khamanei (the leader of the conservative bloc's dominant wing) and Ahmedinejad publicly parted ways, a split that opened the way for another (watered-down) liberal electoral victory, that of Hassan Rouhani in 2013.

56 For the gradual intensification of the battle, see Boroujerdi's analysis throughout the years. Most interestingly, these frictions among the conservatives have not simply pitted one institution against another (as was frequently the case throughout the 1980s in the struggles between the conservatives and the radicals), but split some core institutions right down the middle, such as the Revolutionary Guards. See iranprimer.usip.org/.

Similar events throughout the Turkey and Iran of the 2000s shed further doubt on the independence of 'opportunities' as an isolated variable, demonstrating instead that opportunities are influenced by movement within political society. The eventual narrowing of openings in the Iranian case presents a contrast with the Turkish military's failed blockage of Abdullah Gül's presidency in 2007 (which expanded opportunities for Islamic liberals). Some military factions, secularist civil society and the Kemalist party (CHP) lined up to block Gül's presidency, but the AKP's decisive leadership ultimately averted this threat: after Gül's presidency was thwarted by semi-legitimate methods in the spring, the AKP turned this suspect process into the central issue of its election campaign, won the national elections by a much wider margin than expected, and had the parliament elect Gül as the president. Institutional openings, then, had very different repercussion in Iran and Turkey due to political interventions. While one could argue that the 2009 elections in Iran did not constitute a real institutional opening, we could also ask what such a dispersed movement could accomplish even if it had better opportunities, especially given the record of the liberal Islamic government between 1997 and 2005.

In sum, Iranian Islamic political society, dispersed in its political organization, produced frail blocs and inadequately integrated civil society with the state. Professionalistic tendencies existed in Iran, but had less impact on the Islamic movement than in Egypt and Turkey. Professionally oriented politicians also lacked committed international allies (as was the case in Egypt as well). The lack of a strong Islamic business class in Iran meant that the liberal politicians' class base was restricted mostly to other professionals, whereas (one could argue) especially in Turkey the interests of professionals within political society were parallel to the interests of both professionals and the business class in society at large. These political structures are likely to reproduce the weakness of the liberal option in Iran for the foreseeable future even though increasing Western support for liberal Islam in Iran (after its irreversible failure in Turkey) will change the balance of forces.

Incomplete Liberalization of Religious and Everyday life

Due to the dispersion and subordination of political society, official and paramilitary impositions of piety were not bolstered by as strong a (civic or political) mobilization. Unlike Turkey and Egypt, there were no thoroughly organized political parties or professional associations which encouraged Islamic lifestyles. Consequently, people acted out Islamic lifestyles on the street but engaged in non-Islamic practices (such as the consumption of Islamically incorrect videos, tapes, books, magazines and CDs) at home and in other closed spaces.[57] These ethnographic observations are supported by some quantitative evidence as well. Based on value surveys, Mansoor Moaddel shows that Egyptians practice Islam more than Iranians, even though the latter live under an Islamic republic.[58] Moreover, the rate of Iranians who participated in communal prayers at least once a week declined from 56 per cent in 1975 to 40 per cent in 2000,[59] a clear embarrassment for an Islamic revolution.

Whereas chic covering became a symbol of Islamic mobilization in Egypt and Turkey, it became a symbol of resistance against the regime in Iran. There was no well-organized Islamic political society in Iran to appropriate fashion in the name of Islam. There were signs that the women's and youth movements of the 1990s adopted a liberal theology.[60] However, they couldn't push the country in a liberalized Islamic direction without assistance from political society, once again demonstrating that civil society *by itself* cannot lead sweeping social transformation.

Many studies suggest that both poor and middle-class university students, and lower-middle and middle-class women, were far from the grip of Islamization.[61] But the 2005 elections, which witnessed a conservative victory, suggested another pattern, especially for the

---

57 See Masserat Amir-Ebrahimi, 'Conquering Enclosed Public Spaces', *Cities* 23 (2006): 455–61.

58 Mansoor Moaddel, *Values and Perceptions of the Islamic and Middle Eastern Publics*, New York: Palgrave Macmillan 2007, 241.

59 Charles Kurzman, 'The Iranian Revolution at 30: Still Unpredictable', 29 January 2009, mei.edu/.

60 See Bayat, *Street Politics*, chapter 3.

61 For example, Farhad Khosrokhavar, 'Toward an Anthropology of Democratization in Iran', *Critique: Critical Middle Eastern Studies* 16 (2000): 3–29; Seyed H. Serajzadeh, 'Croyants non pratiquants: La religiosite de la jeunesse Iranienne et ses implications pour la theorie de la secularisation', *Social Compass* 49 (2002): 111–32; Seyed Masoud Mousavi Shafaee, 'Globalization and Contradiction between the Nation and the State in Iran: The Internet Case', *Critique: Critical Middle Eastern Studies* 12 (2003): 189–95.

fringe neighbourhoods. Also, some other studies drew attention to how modernization, commercialization and the consolidation of individualism went hand in hand with Islamization in the 1990s, rather than undermining it.[62] All of this can be interpreted as an ongoing, but rather incomplete Islamization: due to the lack of political penetration by sociopolitical organizations or parties, Islamization depended on force more than consent, organized by state institutions as well as paramilitary organizations, which were mobilized through sociopolitical factions.

Let's wrap up this discussion by a simple question: which more fosters piety, the Turkish or the Iranian model? In 2000, a report announced to the international press by Mohammad Ali Zam, the head of Tehran's Cultural and Artistic Affairs, noted that 75 per cent of Iranians did not say their daily prayers.[63] By contrast, a research agency found out that 79 per cent of Turkish citizens performed their daily prayers.[64] While these numbers may be exaggerated because they are based on self-reports, it is clear that there was a mismatch between the aspirations of the Iranian regime and the religiosity of the population, especially when contrasted to the population living under Turkey's secular regime. This partly had to do with the fact that the Iranian theocracy had overblown expectations of piety, which might have alienated the citizenry from performing the simpler religious tasks. Even so, this report suggests that an analysis of political society is necessary to understand how Turkish Islamists were able to sustain piety in a secularized context.

What can an analysis of Islamization in Iran, in comparative perspective, teach us about the spread of certain religious practices? The revolutionary Islamization in Iran provides an informative contrast to the liberalized, partial and mild Islamization in Turkey (and the legalistic Islamization in Egypt), which was built through years of work through political society and civil society, in interaction with partial

62 Fariba Adelkhah, *Being Modern in Iran*, New York: Columbia University Press, 2000, 124–9.

63 'Drugs and Prostitution "Soar" in Iran', BBC, 6 July 2000.

64 Some 44 per cent of the sample reported that they sometimes perform the prayers, while 35 per cent said they always perform them ('Transatlantic Trends 2008', German Marshall Fund of the United States, 20, fn. 5).

Islamization by the state. We can grant the possibility that had the Egyptian and Turkish Islamists carried out a successful revolution, they also would have few scruples in enforcing similar measures (for example, the forced segregation and covering of women). However, it was not only the Turkish and Egyptian secular states' relatively entrenched infrastructural and despotic power (in Michael Mann's terms) that prevented such an outcome (though an institutionalist account would no doubt be justified in underlining this contrast). The more developed civil society and political society in Turkey (and more developed civil society in Egypt, in contrast to pre-revolutionary Iran) also made such outcomes less possible.

We can call the pietization in Iran 'forced revolutionary Islamization', describing a revolutionary process where coercion outweighs consent. I loosely base this description on Gramsci's comparison of the French and Russian revolutions. Any revolution will involve force, but in Russia, coercion gradually replaced the willing participation of broad sectors; participation came to be restricted to a small number of intellectuals and urban workers (who willingly mobilized to subordinate upper classes, peasants and other workers up until 1929). This can be contrasted to the French revolutionary processes of the eighteenth and nineteenth centuries, where a wide range of citizens were repeatedly mobilized in favour of republican ideas and institutions. The Russian decline in willing participation (gradual between 1917 and 1929, quite steep afterwards) can be compared to the Iranian revolution, where (after 1981) willing non-official participation in the revolutionary process came to be restricted to a relatively small body of the subproletariat, clerical students and paramilitary groups,[65] which are still mobilized to safeguard Islamic practices in public spaces.

Politics and Society in the Re-making of Religiosity

Many Islamists across the Middle East shared a comprehensive understanding of Islam during the 1960s and 1970s. Yet their objectives as well as their strategies diverged in the following decades. The

65 However, the ongoing mobilization of these very groups, even if restricted in comparison to nineteenth-century France, is impressive in contrast to post-1929 Russia.

variations in political organizational structure (unified versus fragmented versus dispersed) and mode of identification with authority (professionalized versus moralistic and semi-professionalized) partly account for the ensuing contrasts in Islamization of everyday practices. A unified and professionalized Islamic political society, in interaction with relatively more democratic state traditions, fostered liberalized Islamization in Turkey. A fragmented and semi-professionalized political society, in interaction with a state that partially integrated Islamic law, culminated in a legalistic Islamization in Egypt. A dispersed (and even less professional) political society, in interaction with a revolutionary state, led to forced revolutionary Islamization in Iran. Tunisia could have been home to a more liberalized Islam, thanks to the greater professionalism of some of its Islamic leaders, but an increasingly authoritarian state did not allow such a development.

The composition of political society proves central to understanding these differences. In Turkey, a legal political party was at the centre of political society; it faced only minor challenges from radical political organizations and ultimately absorbed them. In Egypt, an illegal organization that shied away from becoming a party was in the centre. It faced more serious challenges from radical organizations and was not able to absorb them. In Iran, factions were in the centre, and parties were relatively weak and radical organizations were destroyed. The legal political party could have dominated Tunisian political society, but it was prevented from doing so by a repressive state.

This centrality of political society requires major revisions in the ways we think about piety, society and state. Under the influence of the institutionalist turn,[66] many scholars have focused on state-related variables in explaining varieties of Islamization. More concretely,

---

66 Peter Evans, *Dependent Development: The Alliance of Multinational, State, and Local Capital in Brazil*, Princeton, NJ: Princeton University Press, 1979; Peter Evans, Dietrich Rueschemeyer and Theda Skocpol, eds, *Bringing the State Back In*, Cambridge: Cambridge University Press, 1985; Jeff Goodwin, *No Other Way Out: States and Revolutionary Movements, 1945–1991*, Cambridge: Cambridge University Press, 2001; Theda Skocpol, *States and Social Revolutions: A Comparative Analysis of France, Russia and China*, Cambridge: Cambridge University Press, 1979.

they have concentrated on repression and the institutional openings and divisions within the secular state, which Islamists make use of.[67] Others looked at how the secular or nonsecular state becomes an active agent of Islamization.[68] While this denaturalization of religiosity is a good antidote to the romanticization of bottom-up piety, it ignores the active participation of society in the making not only of religion, but also of the state (and the opportunities that the state structure might provide).

The concept of 'political society' addresses this gap in our understanding. Unlike the 'civil society'–focused accounts,[69] a political society approach does not assume that Islamic mobilization develops *against* or independent of the state, while still taking bottom-up creativity seriously.[70] This concept allows us to analytically distinguish the

67 Said A. Arjomand, *The Turban for the Crown: The Islamic Revolution in Iran*, Oxford: Oxford University Press, 1988, 114–28; Anne Marie Baylouny, 'Democratic Inclusion: A Solution to Militancy in Islamist Movements?' *Strategic Insights* 3:4 (April 2004); Mohammed M. Hafez, *Why Muslims Rebel: Repression and Resistance in the Islamic World*, Boulder, CO: Lynne Rienner Publishers, 2003; Mohammed M. Hafez and Quintan Wiktorowicz, 'Violence as Contention in the Egyptian Islamic Movement', in Q. Wiktorowicz, ed., *Islamic Activism: A Social Movement Theory Approach*, Bloomington: Indiana University Press, 2004; Sultan Tepe, 'A Pro-Islamic Party? Promises and Limits of Turkey's Justice and Development Party', in H. Yavuz, ed., *The Emergence of a New Turkey: Democracy and the AK Parti*, Salt Lake City: University of Utah Press, 2006; Sami Zubaida, *Islam, the People and the State: Political Ideas and Movements in the Middle East*, London: Routledge, 1989.

68 Ümit Cizre-Sakallıoğlu, 'Parameters and Strategies of Islam-State Interaction in Republican Turkey', *International Journal of Middle Eastern Studies* 28 (1996): 231–51; Gregory Starrett, *Putting Islam to Work: Education, Politics, and Religious Transformation in Egypt*, Berkeley: University of California Press, 1998; Zubaida, *Islam, the People and the State.*

69 Nilüfer Göle, *The Forbidden Modern: Civilization and Veiling*, Ann Arbor: University of Michigan Press, 1996; Robert Hefner, 'Public Islam and the Problem of Democratization', *Sociology of Religion* 62 (2001): 491–514; Masoud Kamali, 'Civil Society and Islam: A Sociological Perspective', *Archives Europeennes de Sociologie* 42 (2001): 457–82; John Kelsay, 'Civil Society and Government in Islam', in S. H. Hashmi, ed., *Islamic Political Ethics: Civil Society, Pluralism, and Conflict*, Princeton, NJ: Princeton University Press, 2002; A. Norton, ed.,. *Civil Society in the Middle East*, 2 vols, Leiden: Brill, 1995/96.

70 There are strong parallels between a political society approach and state-society accounts in political science and sociology: Adelkhah, *Being Modern in Iran*; Ismail, *Political Life in Cairo's New Quarters*; Turam, *Between Islam and the State*. The differences, which can be traced back to contrasts between the Gramscian analysis of politics and the revised and updated institutionalist

realm of political leadership and strategy (political society) and the associational realm (civil society), even though these realms may overlap empirically (since some actors constituted within the state or civil society may also assume leadership roles). Political actors are also distinct from state actors: though state actors may have broad and comprehensive visions for society, they do not necessarily strive to *lead* society, but may be content with administering and coercing social actors.[71]

In sum, without an active political society, the normalization of a social-political project is at best problematic, even if not impossible. Various political projects vie to shape society. They are organized around political parties, sociopolitical organizations and authority figures. In the process of competing with each other, they interact (in varying degrees of intensity) with civil society and the state. The project with the more developed organization in political society, and with more sustained interactions with civil society and the state, is more likely to determine a nation's fate. The collective making of the religious path a society takes thus depends on the way political society interacts with the state and civil society.

---

theorization of politics (see Peter Evans, *Embedded Autonomy: States and Industrial Transformation*, Princeton, NJ: Princeton University Press, 1995; Kenneth Finegold and Theda Skocpol, *State and Party in America's New Deal*, Madison: University of Wisconsin Press, 1995; Joel Migdal, *State in Society: Studying How States and Societies Transform and Constitute One Another*, Cambridge: Cambridge University Press, 2001; Ann Orloff and Theda Skocpol, 'Why Not Equal Protection? Explaining the Politics of Public Social Spending in Britain, 1900–1911 and the United States, 1880s–1920', *American Sociological Review* 49 [1984]: 726–50; Theda Skocpol, *Protecting Soldiers and Mothers: The Political Origins of Social Policy in the United States*, Cambridge, MA: The Belknap Press of Harvard University Press, 1992; Margaret Weir, 'Political Parties and Social Policymaking', in Margaret Weir, ed., *The Social Divide: Political Parties and the Future of Activist Government*, Washington, DC: Brookings Institution Press, 1998), will be discussed in more detail elsewhere.

71 My use of the concept of 'political society' draws on Juan Linz and Alfred Stepan, *Problems of Democratic Transition and Consolidation: Southern Europe, South America, and Post-Communist Europe*, Baltimore: Johns Hopkins University Press, 1996; Jean L. Cohen and Andrew Arato, *Civil Society and Political Theory*, Cambridge, MA: MIT Press, 1992; and Partha Chatterjee, *The Politics of the Governed: Reflections on Popular Politics in Most of the World*, New York: Columbia University Press, 2004. However, I assign a much more transformative and *constitutive* role to politics when compared to the more *mediating* role of politics in these authors' analyses.

From the Analysis of Blocs to Political Economy

The two preceding chapters traced how a unified and professionalized political society, in its interaction with religious tendencies and practices, constituted solid blocs in Turkey. A dispersed political society in Iran, by contrast, resulted in volatile and frail blocs. Tunisian and Egyptian states remained much more top-down when compared to Turkey and Iran. In Tunisia, there was little sign of any political society and bloc formation. In Egypt, fragmented Islamic political society flourished under a 'secular' dictatorship, but this could not lead to the constitution of firm blocs, not only due to the fragmentation of political society, but also to its partially underground nature in a dictatorship.

The next chapter will analyse how these (actual or potential) political societies and blocs (which themselves rested on certain socio-economic balances) reshaped classes and political economies. Religion and politics, in other words, had a huge impact on the formation, maintenance and revision of socio-economic structures.

CHAPTER 3

Paths of Economic Liberalization

What are the economic preconditions and results of the Turkish model? Liberal Islam has a strongly economic, as well as political and cultural, dimension – though much of the public and scholarly discussion has bifurcated these connected vectors. Moreover, the AKP's economic policies have not drawn as much attention as its 'democratization' of Turkey, but they were arguably at least as transformative.

We can draw a full picture of the Turkish model, of Islamic liberalism, only if we embed the economic remaking of Turkey in the analysis of political and cultural structures. Economic liberalization through Islam was possible only thanks to the forging of Turkey's new hegemonic bloc. Hence, it is groundless to think that economic liberalization can lead to similar results in the absence of a similar bloc. But a new hegemonic bloc is unthinkable without freshly subordinated sectors (as well as the reproduction of some of the old subordinations). Formulated in this way, a comprehensive analysis of liberal Islam cannot be severed from a discussion of who loses and who wins through the ascendancy of liberalized religion.

This chapter first analyses how the new Turkish power bloc creatively apportioned the spoils of marketization. It then discusses whether Islamic and liberal actors in Egypt, Tunisia and Iran have the capacity for such a creative programme. The second part of the chapter draws a balance sheet of 'Turkish success' in comparative perspective, which has important implications for the possible costs of its replication in other contexts.

Marketization and Partial Re-embedding under Liberal Islam

Most pre-2013 coverage of the Turkish economy packaged it as a success, while a small number of critics painted a depressing economic picture of citizens suffering and disaster looming just around the corner. Reality was much more complex, however, and most of the winners and losers were ambiguous and were in fact being reshuffled frequently, though there were simultaneously clear winners (global business) and losers (classical labour) overall.

The AKP (initially) worked with the IMF to privatize both public enterprises and natural resources. The regime intensified privatization and also attracted a record rate of foreign direct investment.[1] Global capital had never felt so at home in Turkey. The AKP also undertook an extensive privatization of public forests and other green areas – justified by the claim that it would sell off only tracts that had 'lost their qualities' as forests. Real-estate speculators knew how to interpret that message. There were 829 fires in the first seven months of 2003 which scorched 1,755 hectares of forest, qualifying them as fit for privatization. Similar legislation was passed throughout the course of the 2000s, increasing forest fires considerably during the course of the decade.[2] The earth became good for business.

Like other IMF-led governments, the AKP also depressed wages, curtailed unions and limited strikes. In this context of an all-out war against labour, the price of growth was sustained (and occasionally) intensified unemployment. Nevertheless, Islamic unions flourished during this period: even though they do not usually win higher wages, they have been able to secure many welfare-like benefits (such as vacation packages, car credits and help with educational expenses).

The neoliberal programmes of the 1980s and 1990s were ultimately able to bring (initially very high) inflation under (relative) control, but the budget deficit had remained high. The new phase of neoliberalism in Turkey was able to resolve this long-standing problem as well, while further reducing inflation to single digits and stabilizing it.[3] Despite its booming export businesses, however, Turkey was not able to close the trade gap as imports increased even more rapidly. The export

1 Ziya Öniş, 'Beyond the 2001 Financial Crisis: The Political Economy of the New Phase of Neo-Liberal Restructuring in Turkey', *Review of International Political Economy* 16:3 (2009): 423.

2 This was accompanied not only by political debates but by a tug of war between pro-AKP and anti-AKP academics, a struggle throughout which numbers were deployed abundantly and, most probably, manipulatively. It is therefore quite difficult to come up with exact numbers regarding deforestation and fires – see, e.g., 'AKP'nin Seçim Beyannamesinde Oman (Y)Alanlari', odatv.com, 30 April 2011 and 'CHP: ormanlar AKP'nin Elinden Kurtarimali', milliyet.com.tr, 23 June 2009.

3 Öniş, 'Beyond the 2001 Financial Crisis', 421–2.

businesses themselves remained dependent on the import of capital and technology, signalling that neoliberalization had not resolved what orthodox political economists perceived as the negative pressures of import substitution. The economy therefore remained dependent on international business confidence and the resulting constant flow of hot capital from abroad.[4] This dependency made the economy exceptionally vulnerable to a possible slowing or reversal in capital flows. Before 2013, the major problem noted in international (and economically orthodox local) circles was therefore the current account deficit.[5]

How was the new regime able to sustain, and even increase, the consent of subordinate strata even as it engineered an unprecedented pro-business turn? This was achieved through a restructuring of the welfare state and what could loosely be called 'real estate Keynesianism'. Thanks to its innovations on these two fronts, the ruling party constituted and reconstituted dynamic class balances and blurred the boundaries between the winners and losers of neoliberalization.

The Turkish welfare state did not collapse, but only recoiled and readjusted. Unlike the Egyptian state's substantial cuts in social provision, the Turkish state restructured welfare to respond to the needs of the most vulnerable, such as the disabled (rather than organized labour and civil servants). There were some spheres of clear welfare-gutting. Education expenditures in Turkey have remained quite low despite student protests in the mid-1990s. However, the AKP government restructured the health system in Turkey, dismantling corporatist privileges and liberalizing the system, hence attacking the advantages of formal employees but serving the informal workers and peddlers.[6] This happened in an overall context of higher health spending when compared to Egypt.

---

4 Ibid., 425.

5 Just as in the case of Tunisia, the tone of international coverage of these 'small' frictions in economic success changed as Turkey started to face political problems. In September 2013, the *Economist*, one of the fans of the Turkish model, announced that Turkey faced a serious current account deficit problem and that its debt payment was more than 150 per cent of its reserve assets. 'The Capital Freeze Index', *Economist*, 7 September 2013. See also 'Turkey's Current Account Deficit Is Economy's Achilles Heel', *Financial Times*, 27 November 2013.

6 See Ayşe Bugra and Çaglar Keyder, 'The Turkish Welfare Regime in Transformation', *Journal of European Social Policy* 16:3 (2006): 211–28.

What remained untouched from the old corporatist package, though, was the assumption that family networks are the primary caretakers. Indeed, the gendered dimension of this assumption (the organization of women's access to the welfare system through the working male) was further strengthened by the AKP's understanding of Islamic codes.[7] Another re-enactment of old-style welfarism was election-time spending (that is, direct provision, especially to the poor, close to election time) and other forms of direct cash transfers.[8] Perhaps due to these 'impurities' of market rule (and the AKP's divergence from the official neoliberal mantra of 'no government involvement in the economy'), as well as to economic growth, absolute poverty did not increase significantly during the AKP period.[9]

The Urban Expressions of Free Market Islam

Another component of consent was the urban vision of free market Islam. Just as the Islamist challenge in its heyday had a spatial dimension, so did the absorption of Islamism into capitalism. Even before 1997, Mayor Erdoğan had used Istanbul's religious heritage as a means of attracting global capital and tourism, rather than as the basis for an Islamic republic. The process accelerated after 2002.

Urban-Islamic neoliberalism appealed not only to the tourists, but even to the popular classes. During the 1990s, fast-breaking tents for

7 Ayşe Buğra and Burcu Yakut-Cakar, 'Structural Change, the Social Policy Environment and Female Employment in Turkey', *Development and Change* 41:3 (May 2010): 530–8.

8 Ayşe Buğra and Aysen Candas, 'Change and Continuity under an Eclectic Social Security Regime: The Case of Turkey', *Middle Eastern Studies* 47:3 (2010): 521, 523.

9 These aspects of Turkish neoliberalization can be compared to Latin American 'neoliberal populism', which is characterized by targeted poverty programmes and election-time spending, as well as by attacks on privileged sectors and the successful management of inflation. Kenneth M. Roberts, 'Populism, Political Conflict, and Grass-Roots Organization in Latin America', *Comparative Politics* 38 (2006): 127–48; Kurt Weyland, 'Neopopulism and Neoliberalism in Latin America: Unexpected Affinities', *Studies in Comparative International Development* 31 (1996): 11–12, 17–21. However, unlike these regimes, the AKP was able to integrate the poor into the party and neoliberalize their orientations to work and the economy. Steve Ellner, 'The Contrasting Variants of the Populism of Hugo Chavez and Alberto Fujimori', *Journal of Latin American Studies* 35 (2003): 151; Roberts, 'Populism, Political Conflict, and Grass-Roots Organization', 140; Tuğal, *Passive Revolution*.

the poor during the month of Ramadan were a symbol of Islamism's rising political challenge. Increasingly, however, fast-breaking tents became sites of collective consumption. The AKP-controlled municipalities began to organize nightly Ramadan festivities that went on till daybreak, where people of all classes would enjoy Sufi music (along with pop and rock), narghile, stand-up shows and a wide variety of food. Muslim tourists came from all over the region, especially to the historic mosques in Sultanahmet and Eyüp, boosting Istanbul's 'world city' image. There was a certain irony here: in the 1990s, Islamist newspapers had contrasted their puritanical Ramadan to the consumer-oriented fast-breaking of wealthy secularized Muslims, with their expensive feasts. The sectors merged into a new bloc, thanks to the passive revolution, which assimilated the month of fasting into the sphere of public entertainment.

Neo-Ottomanism, which spread around so much panic in foreign policy, became another consumerist theme in the urban scene. In commemoration of the Ottoman 'Tulip Era' of the 1720s, the AKP took to decorating the city with the flowers. That period had involved a precocious experiment with petty industrialization, the printing press, and the aestheticization of art and architecture. It was brought to an incendiary end in 1730 by a popular rebellion against aristocratic ostentation, led by the ex-janissary second-hand clothes dealer Patrona Halil: the palaces were pillaged and leading modernizers were killed.[10] The AKP's current tulip mania not only celebrated the Ottoman reformers – and their luxurious excesses – but also signified, through the overflow of tulips from the upper-class neighbourhoods to the squatter districts, that conspicuous consumption was now for the enjoyment of all. Such a strategy was intended to ensure that there would be no Patrona Halils in the republic's Tulip Era. This was indeed sound reasoning, and it did prevent the revolt of the subproletariat. But it also fostered, quite unexpectedly, the revolt of the new petty bourgeoisie (see chapter 6).

10 Halil controlled the city for a while, after which the sultan massacred 7,000 janissaries along with him. John Freely, *Istanbul: The Imperial City*, London: Penguin, 1998 [1996], 252–3. On the impact of the West during the Tulip era, see Fatma Müge Göçek, *East Encounters West: France and the Ottoman Empire in the Eighteenth Century*, New York: Oxford University Press, 1987.

The consent for this destructive creation also had a cash dimension in the 'urban transformation projects' of the AKP years (with their background in the 1980s). Municipal and national authorities bulldozed green areas, parks, historical sites and squatter residences alike to create luxurious residences, government housing projects and shopping malls. The massiveness of these projects brought the cities to the brink of urban ecological disaster.

Throughout this creative destruction, the homeowners among the squatters (especially the better connected among them) were compensated, while tenants were pushed out. In other words, the rentierism of the neoliberal era frequently (but unequally) benefited some urban poor groups. Expectations of 'modernization' also helped squatters invest their own hopes in these projects. They enjoyed transitioning from rural stoves to natural gas and started to frequent shopping malls as sites of socialization. The social costs would become clear later. Utility bills and living costs skyrocketed, and the new social and natural environment marginalized or excluded many of them.[11] However, no coordinated resistance emerged in response, since this marginalization happened in gradual fashion rather than overnight.

Moreover, the natural destruction caused by these projects was spread out quite unevenly. The parks in central (non-squatter) districts were razed more mercilessly, while some of the squatters who ended up in massive governmental housing projects also had less access to green space. However, the AKP municipalities at the same time built smaller parks throughout urban poor neighbourhoods (benefiting not only the Sunni urban poor, the AKP's voting base, but even, occasionally, the Alevis).

To the extent that none of these concessions worked, the regime applied a divide-and-rule strategy, planting seeds of ethnic and sectarian division among the squatters. It repressed the few protests that resulted from urban transformation without much fanfare (thanks to the neglect of the mainstream media). In Istanbul, only two neighbourhoods (Gülsuyu and Başıbüyük) sustained mobilization against the AKP's urban projects.

---

11 Ayfer Bartu-Candan and Biray Kolluoğlu, 'Emerging Spaces of Neoliberalism: A Gated Town and a Public Housing Project in İstanbul', *New Perspectives on Turkey* 39 (2008): 5–46.

In sum, a huge part of the 'successful Turkish model' rested on urban-based consent. The spoils of neoliberalism were materially and symbolically shared, based on urban spatial strategies to create the image and partial reality of a free market Islam that enriched not only the well-to-do but even the poor.

Who Are the Islamic Neoliberalizers in Egypt?

Poverty, unemployment and polarization persisted in Egypt as well. Microfinance, accompanied by inflated expectations, has been the internationally supported solution to this malaise.[12] Like Turkey, Egypt also relied on expanding charity as a solution to the problems stemming from changes in welfare policies. The welfare debate in both Egypt and Turkey also featured a discourse on 'teaching people how to catch fish' rather than giving them fish – that is, making the poor self-reliant rather than 'dependent'.[13] Hence, a new 'welfare governance' based on (mostly nontransparent) government–charity partnerships that mobilize poor people's entrepreneurial capacities tended to replace the formal welfare system in both cases.[14] This opened up a socio-economic space in which a liberalized Muslim Brotherhood could fit easily.

Yet, was the Brotherhood ready to play such a role? Echoing its partial religio-political liberalization, the organization's economic liberalization was half-hearted. Its new agenda consisted of a community-based welfare system contradictorily combined with neoliberalization. In the 1980s and 1990s, the Brotherhood's programme supported the state's and community's taking care of the poor, narrowing of class divisions, and social security for all citizens. The programme of its 1987 election alliance with other Islamic parties included both liberal and illiberal elements: on the one hand, it called for the shrinking of the government bureaucracy, upheld the private sector as the backbone of the economy, and promoted alms-giving; yet, on the other hand, it propounded an interest-free banking system, and

12 Ananya Roy, *Poverty Capital: Microfinance and the Making of Development*, New York: Routledge, 2010.

13 Mona Atia, 'Building a House in Heaven: Islamic Charity in Neoliberal Egypt', Ph.D. diss., University of Washington, Seattle, 2008; Bugra and Keyder, 'The Turkish Welfare Regime in Transformation'.

14 Buğra and Candas, 'Change and Continuity', 522.

comprehensive government regulation and strategic planning of the economy.[15] An article published in the Brotherhood's newspaper in 1987 defended social security for all, narrowing of the class gap, increased welfare spending, encouragement of economic solidarity, support for private property and enforcing all able-bodied citizens to be economically productive.[16] The contradictions here are reminiscent of the Turkish Islamists' 'Just Order' programme in the 1980s and early 1990s (that is, before their turn towards the free market). Was this partial economic liberalization, then, just a transition stage that would result in deeper neoliberalization, as in the case of the Turkish Islamists?

Despite a push for economic liberalization from many directions, the Brotherhood platform and practice did not become thoroughly neoliberal in the 1980s. During this decade, the organization's political economic position was articulated in its main publication, *al-Liwa*. In 1989 and 1990, *al-Liwa* articles defined the responsibilities of the state as follows (I have italicized the most clearly non-neoliberal elements): adjusting prices in order to fight against monopolies and their price-fixing arrangements; assuring the just distribution of land through enforcing the Islamic law that *unused land is forfeited*; *establishing basic industries*; controlling foreign trade; *full employment*; the provision of not only necessities but also making sure that education, a minimum of leisure, decent clothing, and so on are available.[17] Articles also called for investment projects that would prioritize income for the largest number of people, and others that would discourage speculation and luxury.[18] Speeches by Brotherhood members in the People's Assembly also voiced these demands.

Still, there were many tensions in the assembly among the Brotherhood members (as well as between the Brotherhood and its political allies). Both Labour (an Islamic party that harboured many

15 Sana Abed-Kotob,. 'The Accommodationists Speak: Goals and Strategies of the Muslim Brotherhood of Egypt', *International Journal of Middle East Studies* 27 (1995): 326–7; Mona el-Ghobashy, 'The Metamorphosis of the Egyptian Muslim Brothers', *International Journal of Middle East Studies* 37 (2005): 373–95.

16 Denis J. Sullivan and Sana Adeb-Kotob, *Islam in Contemporary Egypt: Civil Society vs. the State*, Boulder, CO: Lynne Rienner Publishers, 1999, 50.

17 Bjørn Olav Utvik, *Islamist Economics in Egypt: The Pious Road to Development*, Boulder, CO: Lynne Rienner Publishers, 2006, 153–4.

18 Ibid., 157–8.

ex-leftists) and the Brotherhood agreed that the public and private sectors should co-exist, but Adil Hussayn (Labour) held the state responsible for social justice while Shahhata and Kamal (Brotherhood) argued that private property is the centre of an Islamic economy. (Hussayn became more and more pro-privatization toward the end of the 1980s.)[19] Shahhata and Kamal were not solitary figures; they clearly voiced the opinions of the Brotherhood's increasingly influential neoliberal business wing.

Despite their overall commitment to private property, there were many disagreements among Brotherhood leaders about how much to privatize and when. Iryan (who maintained good relations with the Egyptian left) was a little more cautious, and al-Banna and Shahhata were impatient.[20] Shahhata even declared that some public employees should be fired in the course of privatization, striking a very interesting contrast to the pro–full employment tone of *al-Liwa*.

The overall commitment to private property was somewhat overshadowed by actual political balances. In the assembly, both Labour and the Brotherhood (contradictorily) pushed for higher wages and better working conditions (as well as greater freedom for unions), while at the same time arguing that wages should be controlled and tied to productivity. Whereas Labour supported some strikes, it was silent about the *right* to strike in a future Islamic state.[21] In the meantime, the Brotherhood executed a left turn towards the end of the 1980s, as can be gleaned from subtle shifts in its discourse (an emergent emphasis on 'dependency', a critique of the impact of IMF and US policies on the Egyptian economy, and so on). This turn was a result of Labour Party influence and occurred in response to political pressures: becoming the main agent of opposition against Mubarak in these years required the Brotherhood to take a position on the question of poverty. Nevertheless, the organization consistently stuck to its definition of social justice as a balance between classes (rather than the abolition of classes) and the eradication of extreme poverty.[22]

19 Ibid., 158–61.

20 Ibid., 162–3.

21 Ibid., 166.

22 Ibid., 173–5. To date, Utvik has produced the most comprehensive survey of the Brotherhood's ideology, platforms and actual interventions and steps on economic issues. Unfortunately, his book lacks any theoretical coherence and

In the 2000s, the Brotherhood's position on neoliberalism was still uneven. Some orthodox economists were associated with the Brotherhood, and the organization also supported liberalization in the countryside. More importantly, a pro-business (though politically anti-liberal) new elite was gradually monopolizing the whole organization (this trend came to be associated with the conservative leader Khairat al-Shater).[23] Nevertheless, the media and election platforms of the Brotherhood still combined support for social protectionism with an emphasis on free market dynamism. In the 2005–10 parliament, Brotherhood MPs fought for higher wages, supported strikes and resisted privatization. The Brotherhood's neoliberalization was still gradual and inconsistent.

Despite all of these inconsistencies and anti-market tendencies, my conversations and interviews with Egyptians in 2009 and 2010 indicated that the left-wing intelligentsia did not have any doubt that the Brotherhood was completely 'neoliberal'. Actually, my conversations with merchants in the organization, and with some of the other leaders, showed that they were indeed neoliberals. However, teachers, workers and engineers in the middle and bottom ranks of the organization were either lukewarm about liberalization, or pragmatic about all economic issues, or completely opposed to free market economics.

Moreover, there was no unification in Islamic political society (in contrast to Turkey). No organization monopolized the representation of practicing Muslims (against the secularists). Hence, by 2011 the Islamist opposition was divided between the Brotherhood and

direction. In the light of the bulk of the book (which provides massive amounts of information on corporatist, collectivist or at least solidaristic tendencies and practices of the Brotherhood), Utvik oddly states in the very beginning of the book that the Brotherhood has a liberal economic position. He then argues, in the conclusion, that Islamist economics is an eclectic search for a non-neoliberal model and a revival of the project of the nationalist bourgeoisie with more emphasis on private initiative.

23 Carrie R. Wickham portrays al-Shater as a pragmatic figure (a liaison between the conservatives and liberals, rather than the leader of the internal, conservative restoration), but this is dubious given his actions in the wake of the 2011 uprisings. His role clearly deserves much more research. Wickham, *The Muslim Brotherhood: Evolution of an Islamist Movement*, Princeton, NJ: Princeton University Press, 2013, 103, 119, 131.

more radical groups, none of which held an *unequivocally* neoliberal position, and all of which were in a deadlock with the regime over establishing control over society.

In sum, the diffusion of Islamization at the religious and everyday life levels had its counterpart in Islamic visions of the economy. There was no consensus on a single economic model that would allow Islamic actors to move as a bloc. This would have devastating consequences for the attempted passive revolution in Egypt, as chapter 5 will show.

Tunisian Islamists' Uncertain Neoliberalization

Regarding the marriage of Islam and economic liberalism, Tunisian Islamism seems to stand on much thinner ice. As pointed out in chapter 1, Ghannouchi and al-Nahda did not have a developed outlook on Islamic economics and a clear stance on development and labour issues. In the 2000s, Tunisian Islamists moved away from a strict adherence to the distinctiveness of Islamic economics, possibly putting them on a Turkish path. However, their commitment to the market never became as clear as the AKP's.

To understand this partial marketization, we need to take into account that Tunisian Islamism was operating in a context of a relatively successful, if still unstable, economic model (as in the case of Turkey), and that it also faced a history of labour and leftist mobilization (more militant than Turkey in some regards). Tunisian Islamism had even incorporated some aspects of this mobilization into its own thinking and strategizing. The first of these factors encouraged Islamic neoliberalization, whereas the second restricted it.

There was some proof of a less than complete neoliberalization. In one interview, Ghannouchi pointed out that his *economic* model was Swedish social democracy: a redistributive welfare state (which, to complicate things a little, was itself neoliberalizing at the time of this interview). The *Basic Law*, al-Nahda's programme, remained dedicated to the principles of Islamic economics. For example, labour is recognized in this programme as the source of legitimate income and growth, and its main principles are redistributive. Despite these, al-Nahda's actual policy proposals after 2011 demonstrated a strong market orientation: the promotion of especially small and medium-sized businesses; the remaking of Tunisia as a regional financial hub; the reduction of taxes on businesses, especially those that are small and medium-sized; and creation of a friendly environment for investment. Still, the policy proposals of the 2011 election platform also emphasized job creation (in both the private and public sectors) and the reduction of poverty through Keynesian policies of housing and infrastructural development.

At the same time, the Tunisian Islamists also referred to 'free market' (in their words) Turkish Islamism as their primary economic model, reflecting profound confusion, if not dishonesty: how could both Sweden and Turkey be economic models? Was one of these messages intended for centrist and right-wing and the other for centre-left audiences? There is also anecdotal information regarding a rising 'middle class' in Tunisia, which is pious, free market–oriented, and politically liberal. However, it is not clear how big this group is when compared to its counterparts within the Turkish and Egyptian business and professional classes.[24]

Just as the Tunisian Islamists of the 1980s were even murkier than their Iranian, Turkish and Egyptian counterparts in formulating their alternative to capitalism and socialism, they remained vague on how they reconciled Islam with their intended continuance of the old regime's neoliberal policies. Some analysts have emphasized al-Nahda's aggressively free market stance, based on its proclamations and positions in 2012.[25] We must also note, however, the confusion in this regard among its top leaders. We also lack any deep understanding of how al-Nahda or Ghannouchi evolved from their anti–free market position in the early 1980s to their new position.

In sum, as is the case in Egypt, it is far from clear that Tunisian Islamists have reached consensus around neoliberal Islam. Even if they are able to forge the kind of coalitions that the Turkish Islamists

24 The weak and problematic discussion of this 'middle class' typically fails to differentiate between business and new middle-class sectors; most of it reads like wishful thinking and projection rather than critical analysis. For an example, see Rikke Hostrup Haugbølle and Francesco Cavatorta, 'Beyond Ghannouchi: Islamism and Social Change in Tunisia', *Middle East Report* 262 (Spring 2012): 20–5.

25 Gilbert Achcar, *The People Want: A Radical Exploration of the Arab Uprising*, Berkeley: University of California Press, 2013, 221–4.

accomplished, it is dubious whether their policies would be as straightforwardly neoliberal (in sustainable fashion). Moreover, as the next two chapters will demonstrate, Tunisian Islamists are less than likely to seal similar (and lasting) deals anyway. Both the socio-economic and political preconditions for liberal Islam are shaky in Tunisia.

Iran: Neoliberalization under Revolutionized Corporatism

Iran did not go very far in liberalizing its economy, despite moves in that direction. With the advent of the pragmatic moderate Akbar Hashemi Rafsanjani in 1989, the main goal of the regime became privatization, but remnants of radical Islamism made this difficult.[26] Even though the regime successfully expelled the radical faction from institutions such as the parliament (in 1992), Rafsanjani's five-year plan ultimately failed due to a collapse in oil prices, high unemployment and protests throughout the country.[27]

The response of the Islamic radicals to the political repression they faced was very similar to their behaviour in Turkey: political and economic liberalization to outflank the international and market credibility of the regime. After their exclusion in 1992, radical figures like Mousavi and Karroubi transformed themselves into Islamic liberals, and that only in the span of a few years.[28] The Khatami plan, drawing on this background of liberalization, had most of the necessary ingredients of neoliberalism.[29] Khatami also attempted to rationalize and standardize Iran's welfare system by combining the two differentiated sets (both revolutionary and corporatist institutions) under one roof. This attempt failed.[30] Due to its poor links

---

26 Farhad Nomani and Sohrab Behdad, *Class and Labor in Iran: Did the Revolution Matter?* Syracuse, NY: Syracuse University Press, 2006, 48, 53–61.

27 Kevan Harris, 'The Rise of the Subcontractor State: Politics of Pseudo-Privatization in the Islamic Republic of Iran', *International Journal of Middle East Studies* 45:1 (2013): 51.

28 It should be noted that their political liberalism was much more developed than their economic liberalism.

29 Bijan Khajehpour, 'Domestic Political Reforms and Private Sector Activity in Iran', *Social Research* 67:2 (2000): 577–98.

30 Kevan Harris, 'A Martyrs' Welfare State and Its Contradictions: Regime Resilience and Limits through the Lens of Social Policy in Iran', in Steven Heydemann and Reinoud Leenders, eds, *Middle East Authoritarianisms: Governance, Contestation, and Regime Resilience in Syria and Iran*, Stanford, CA: Stanford University Press, 2013, 75.

with civil society (which translated as an inability to overcome opposition within the state), Khatami's liberal Islamic government could not fully implement neoliberalism, but it did succeed in drawing foreign capital to the oil sector.[31]

Throughout this process of privatization, construction and finance became the motors of private sector growth, as they had in Turkey. Private companies that had their roots in the Pahlavi era (and which had survived the revolution partly based on black market mechanisms) expanded thanks to cooperation with the liberalizing state.[32] However, unlike Turkey's experience, these developments did not undermine the public sector (let alone the cooperative, 'Islamic' sector). Conservatives used the Islamic leftist arguments of the 1980s and 1990s to fight Khatami's moves to decisively liberalize the economy, though the Khatamists were able to revise Article 44 of the constitution and legalize the privatization of key sectors: heavy industry, downstream oil and gas refineries, mining, power generation, banking, aviation, shipping, insurance, infrastructure and telecommunications.[33]

Ahmadinejad derailed liberalization after 2005 and sought to aid the poor (by raising the minimum wage, distributing shares of state-owned companies, and increasing social spending), in the process scaring off foreign capital. The Ahmadinejad years also reproduced the 'ethos' of blaming the elite (now the new managerial class created by the neoliberal turn of the 1990s, rather than the capitalists) and imperialists for the social problems Iran faced.[34] Along the same lines, the new president revived the solidaristic vocabulary of Third Worldism (especially through the image of a revolutionary regime serving the mostazafan, the downtrodden).[35] As a result, the market was never sacralized in Iran to the degree it was in Turkey, despite ongoing attempts at privatization under Ahmadinejad.

---

31 Akbar Karbassian, 'Islamic Revolution and the Management of the Iranian Economy', *Social Research* 67:2 (2000): 621–40.

32 Kevan Harris, 'The Rise of the Subcontractor State', 53–4.

33 Ibid., 54.

34 Said A. Arjomand, *After Khomeini: Iran under His Successors*, Oxford: Oxford University Press, 2009, 160.

35 Ali Gheissari and Vali Nasr, *Democracy in Iran: History and the Quest for Liberty*, Oxford: Oxford University Press, 2006, 156–7.

To have a better understanding of these privatization efforts (and their contradictions), we must continue tracing the factional struggles within political society. Most notably, by the end of the 2000s, political and clerical leaders have come to accept that privatization is a necessity (with the supreme clerical leader Khamanei declaring in 2006 that 80 per cent of state wealth should be privatized). Nevertheless, pressure from below, as well as starkly different takes on privatization among the leaders, has prevented liberalization. The political battle that produced this 'privatization without liberalization' unfolded within the conservative camp, between the clerics and old conservatives on the one hand, and the professionals with rural origins (who owed their upward mobility to the revolutionary bureaucracy) on the other. (On this division within the conservative bloc, see chapter 2). The professionals with rural origins hijacked the economic agenda of the Islamic liberals and put it to revolutionary corporatist use.

This led to what Kevan Harris has called the 'subcontractor state': an economy which is neither centralized under a governmental authority nor privatized and liberalized. The subcontractor state has decentralized its social and economic roles without liberalizing the economy or even straightforwardly privatizing the state-owned enterprises. As a result, the peculiar third sector of the Iranian economy has expanded in rather complicated and unpredictable ways. Rather than leading to liberalization, privatization under revolutionary corporatism intensified and twisted the significance of organizations such as the bonyads (which, as chapter 1 argued, lie at the core of Iran's distinctive 'Islamic economy'). Privatization under the populist-conservative Ahmedinejad exploited the ambiguities of the tripartite division of the economy in Article 44 of the constitution. 'Privatization' entailed the sale of public assets not to private companies but to nongovernmental public enterprises (such as pension funds, the bonyads and military contractors).[36]

Even though populism frequently goes hand-in-hand with neoliberalization in many cases (such as in Latin America), Ahmedinejad put a further revolutionary spin on such privatizing populism by excluding the business class from huge chunks of the privatization

36 Kevan Harris, 'The Rise of the Subcontractor State', 55.

project. Ahmedinejad's two terms resulted in more privatization schemes than the Rafsanjani and Khatami terms combined. However, only around 10 to 15 per cent of privatization actually went to the private sector.[37] Instead, the so-called nongovernmental public sector or the cooperative sector benefited from the privatization.

These struggles over privatization helped rebalance political society through redefining the relations of political factions with societal actors. A new type of conservative faction emerged strengthened from these battles and forged its links with disadvantaged strata via the entrenchment of the welfare state, as well as populist programmes such as 'justice shares' (the discounted sale of privatized firms' shares to Iran's poor). In the future, this faction could become Iran's new oligarchic business elite by following the Russian model: it could pillage privatization's spoils (for example, by amassing the 'justice shares', gradually turning the cooperative sector into a corporate sector). But ongoing revolutionary mobilization and persistent social justice discourse make this difficult (unlike in the case of Russia). And even if successful, this kind of capitalism would be far from what appeared in Turkey in the 2000s.

During these two decades of instability and fluctuations of economic policy, welfare spending increased (independent of who was in office). Despite the common perception of the foundations (bonyads) as the clientelistic backyard of the conservatives, all the factions used them to their advantage and extended them.[38] A dispersed political society subservient to the state could privatize, but not liberalize.

After the populist leader Mahmoud Ahmedinejad was replaced by a so-called moderate, Hassan Rouhani, the doors were opened again to meeting with Western businessmen and striking a pro-business tone. But even then, pro-business rhetoric always came with qualifications. During a meeting with New York business leaders, Rouhani's chief of staff, Mohammad Nahavandian, reportedly declared that 'Iran is now pro-business and welcomes private investment, if and when

37 Ibid., 54–60.

38 Kevan Harris, 'The Martyrs' Welfare State: Politics of Social Policy in the Islamic Republic of Iran', Ph.D. diss., Johns Hopkins University, 2012.

sanctions are lifted'.[39] When I finalized this book in early 2015, Western powers had announced that they would lift the sanctions (if Iran abides by a provisional agreement reached in April 2015). This would indeed create more opportunities for liberalization in Iran, but the exact effects remain to be seen.

Throughout these two decades of zigzagging 'liberalization', the corporatist part of the health provision system was beefed up (whereas its dismantlement was at the core of Turkey's liberalization). The corporatist Social Security Organization (SSO) covered 41 per cent of the labour force in 2007. Ahmedinejad, in one of his neoliberal rather than corporatist moves, reduced gasoline and food subsidies in 2011, but he left the health system of the SSO untouched.[40] The beneficiaries of the system were mostly those working in the formal sector. In other words, rather than mobilizing the poor to fight benefits going to organized labour and the new middle class (as the Turkish regime did), the Iranian regime protected these strata through its entrenched corporatism. Harris notes: 'If we include a large public sector in the list of policies that forge social insurance against economic risk … then it seems that [Iran] still expends a significant amount of resources attempting to protect and decommodify the formal proletarian and professional middle classes from market risk through this welfare regime'. Decommodification persisted in Iran, not as a side effect, but as a core principle of the regime. It is no surprise that the Iranian middle-class revolt of 2009–11 did not target commodification, which was initially at the centre of Turkish revolt in 2013.

The result of zigzagging liberalization can be conceptualized as an 'economic lack of order': the inability of the country to move (with the support of broad sectors, and of solid power blocs) in a consistent, growth-generating direction – whether in a market-based, mixed economy, state-dominated direction, or even a scenario in which the third sector is innovatively turned into a dynamo of growth. It is not that blocs are lacking in Iran, but they are made and unmade very quickly. While we can understand much about the overall structure of

---

39 Somini Sengupta, 'Blunt and Charming, Making the Case for Iran', *New York Times*, September 27, 2013.

40 Harris, 'A Martyrs' Welfare State and Its Contradictions', 76.

the Iranian economy based on state-centric or plainly economic variables, focusing on political society and blocs allows us to grasp why the economic models tried out over the decades have become neither popular nor sustainable.

If the radical Islamists had united in a professionalized and mass-based organization in the 1980s – rather than being dispersed throughout official institutions without any mobilizing ties to the populace – they could have institutionalized some of the republic's earlier redistributive policies and incited workers and the subproletariat into action when the conservatives and liberals attempted to erode them. Or, by contrast, a (unified and professionalized) liberal Islamic political society, had it existed in Iran, could have mobilized civil society in favour of the technocratic and economically liberal reforms of the 1990s. It could also resist the creeping of an anti-imperialist and anti-elite ethos back into society.

In sum, Iranian Islamic political society, weak in political organization, has inadequately integrated civil society with the state. The urban poor and radical militants, whose hopes have been heightened by decades of revolutionary rhetoric and policies, are still open to (destabilizing) mobilization by parts of the bureaucracy and paramilitary organizations. This might partly explain the rise of Ahmadinejad after years of experimentation with moderate pragmatism and liberalism. However, there is no independent pro-subproletariat civil society and political society to exert pressure on the state, and therefore the influence of the poor is restricted to outbursts – which favour authoritarian and conservative rather than radical solutions, and *volatile*, temporary and *frail* rather than sustainable blocs. Ultimately, no 'new balance of forces' has been established in the economic domain.

Turkish neoliberalization, then, was distinguished not only by the consistency of its policies, but by the Islamic and popular forces behind it. Neither Tunisian nor Egyptian neoliberalization enjoyed such Islamic and popular support (even though the former was more consistent and resembled the Turkish one as far as quantifiable indicators go). Iranian neoliberalism, in contrast to all three, never 'arrived'. The constant reshuffling of political/social blocs in Iran culminated in a dynamic but inefficient amalgam of corporatism, neoliberalism and revolutionary economics.

A Balance Sheet of Neoliberalization in Corporatist Contexts

How did these various paths of neoliberalization impact the overall welfare of citizens in each country? Can we unequivocally say that one of the paths benefited people more than the others? Is dismantling all remnants of corporatism the best way forward, at least from a mainstream perspective?

The rest of this chapter evaluates Islamic neoliberalism quantitatively, through some basic contrasts with 'secular' neoliberalism and irregularly liberalized revolutionary corporatism. It is too early to compare *Islamic* neoliberalizations, since they have not happened yet (except in Turkey, and partially in Iran). The quantitative comparisons that follow focus on neoliberalizations in general, but (in the Tunisian and Egyptian cases) they shed light on what kind of a neoliberalized entity Islamic movements would take over if they were to come to power in sustained fashion. While statistical indicators cannot give us all the answers to this question (and some of the answers should be sought within the historical-qualitative analyses provided throughout the book), numbers can be informative as conventional measures of wealth, inequality, poverty and budget priorities.

However, the numbers in these comparisons should be taken with a grain of salt for several reasons. First, they should not be taken as 'the real story', since the way poverty and wealth are actually *experienced* cannot be reflected in (at least these kinds of) numbers. In other words, the reader should resist the urge to think that these tables tell the whole story. Second, these numbers are manipulated by governments (especially to downplay unemployment and inequality). Since it is almost impossible to provide a measure of how successfully each government manipulates the numbers, publicly available data are not strictly comparable. Third, the numbers might be measuring different kinds of realities in different countries. For instance, earning \$5 a day in Iran and \$5 a day in Turkey have profoundly different implications, due (among many other things) to the different price levels of goods and services. Moreover, even when we control for this factor (through, say, integrating measures of purchasing power), the satisfaction derived from accessing the same good might vary from one country to the other.

Despite all of these disclaimers, the quantitative comparison of Middle Eastern countries is necessary. Orthodox celebrators of the Turkish model can still say: 'The proof is in the pudding. You can criticize many aspects of Turkey's path from 2002 to 2011, but whatever you say, you cannot deny that it *worked*. It delivered wealth to the citizens.' The question, of course, is whether we are looking at a bowl of pudding or a bowl of mud. The numbers suggest that what we instead have is quite a mixed pudding. Experts who still eulogize Turkey's pre-2011 route fail to appreciate the complexity that even mainstream measures reveal. The following chapters also demonstrate that they completely misinterpret the reasons of the post-2011 decline and try to explain it away based on the prime minister's personal style and his Islamist roots instead of looking at the multiple layers of the model that the global mainstream had trumpeted for a decade.

Even though this book makes frequent references to the AKP, what this balance sheet puts on trial is not the current Turkish governing party as such, but Turkish Islamic neoliberalization ever since the 1980s (of which the AKP is the inheritor, the intensifier and reviser). Still, it will be instructive to evaluate how much the AKP's Turkey achieved of what the party promised in its brand-name: Justice and Development.

Rethinking the 'Development' in 'Justice and Development'

Turkey's GDP growth was staggering. As shown in Table 3.1, Turkey surpassed all the countries in question over the last three decades. Most remarkably, it has started out as poorer than Iran and then left the latter well behind. Moreover, as Table 3.2 demonstrates, Turkey's GDP growth rate was unmatchable in its rate and consistency (at least up until 2013), though Turkey has been hit harder by the fallout from the 2008 global financial crisis, probably due to its more advanced integration into world markets.

Table 3.1. Gross domestic product per capita (current prices, US dollars)

	1980	1985	1990	1995	2000	2005	2010
Egypt	552	998	1,779	1,057	1,566	1,283	2,776
Iran	2,445	1,670	1,559	1,417	1,510	2,925	5,638
Tunisia	1,502	1,282	1,658	2,210	2,248	3,218	4,199
Turkey	2,235	1,838	3,863	3,962	4,149	7,044	10,015

Source: IMF, World Economic Outlook Database, October 2013.

Table 3.2. Percentage change in GDP (constant prices)

	2000	2001	2002	2004	2006	2007	2008	2009	2010	2011
Egypt	5.4	3.5	3.2	4.1	6.8	7.1	7.2	4.7	5.1	1.8
Turkey	6.8	-5.7	6.2	9.4	6.9	4.7	0.7	-4.8	9.2	8.8
Tunisia	4.3	4.9	1.7	6.0	5.7	6.3	4.5	3.1	2.9	-1.9
Iran	5.1	3.7	8.2	6.1	6.2	6.4	0.6	4.0	5.9	3.0

Source: IMF, World Economic Outlook Database, October 2013.

But in none of the other core indicators of development (unemployment, education expenditure, expected years of schooling, with the partial exception of health) has Turkey experienced the same relative leap when compared to the other countries. In other words, the economic model it has adopted has led to a phenomenal increase in wealth, but not to a better life for the citizenry at large.

Turkey was a poor performer in what the United Nations Development Programme defines as 'human development'. The Human Development Index (HDI) combines gross national income (GNI) with life expectancy (as an imperfect indicator of health care quality) and actual (mean) and expected years of schooling (as an indicator of educational quality). When we remove GNI from this equation (on which, as Tables 3.1 and 3.2 show, Turkey was doing well), we see that Iran did better than Turkey in some regards and Tunisia surpassed Turkey in others.[41] Turkey was *by far* wealthier than both Iran and Tunisia, but that increased wealth didn't bring with it a better life quality for its citizens. In 1980, Iran was behind Turkey (regarding the mean years of schooling for adults, but not

41 I had first attempted to compare the HDI values of these countries over the years, but this proved to be a less than meaningful task. The measure is not quite stabilized. When I first accessed HDI figures in October 2013, Iran seemed to be doing much better than Turkey. The numbers in the same UN databases were very different in November 2014: Turkish HDI figures appeared significantly higher for the same years under scrutiny, and most of Iran's were lower. (The same applies to the poverty numbers provided in Table 3.16. The reader might encounter different numbers in this area in 2015 and later.) On a related note, the United Nations has reported starkly divergent HDI rankings for these countries in its 2013 and 2014 reports. According to the first report, Iran ranked the 76th worldwide in 2012 and Turkey the 90th. The second report ranked Iran the 73rd and Turkey the 69th for 2012!

expected years of schooling, see United Nations development databases). This reversal in educational fortunes is a significant story of transformation.

Table 3.3. Human Development Index indicators

	Life expectancy at birth (2013)	Mean years of schooling (2012)	Expected years of schooling (2012)
Egypt	71.2	6.4	13.0
Iran	74	7.8	15.2
Tunisia	75.9	6.5	14.6
Turkey	75.3	7.6	14.4

Source: United Nations Human Development Report, 2014.

The four nations' comparative investment in education and health suggests the dynamics that lie behind these differences. Regarding public spending on education, Turkey's condition was especially despicable, as Table 3.4 attests. The only indicator where Turkey had a clear lead was health expenditure.

Table 3.4. Public expenditure on education (per cent of GDP)

	1990	2000	2005	2006	2007
Egypt	..	..	4.8	4	3.7
Iran	4	4.4	4.7	5.1	5.5
Tunisia	5.8	6.2	6.5	6.4	6.5
Turkey	2.1	2.6	..	2.9	..

Source: Based on World Bank Development Indicators, accessed October 2013 and updated November 2014.

One could argue that the concept 'human development', as defined by the United Nations, overemphasizes years of education (rather than the quality of education), and that the HDI tells us nothing about the content of education. The only reason why Iran fared better than Turkey might be its heavy investment in education in order to ideologically discipline its citizenry (as an ideological state). This would be an insufficient criticism. As the rest of the book will show, ideological indoctrination through education (if it was a priority indeed, which has to be demonstrated rather than assumed) has not resulted in an obedient Iranian population. However, it is true that we need more comparative (including qualitative) studies of education in both contexts to get a better sense of what was really involved in Iran's more generous investment. This will become even more relevant as the post-2011 AKP thoroughly Islamizes education: Will Turkey invest more in education as it becomes a less liberal country? How will the quality of education change in both Iran and Turkey as their structural-ideological positions in world capitalism change?

Table 3.5. Expenditure on public health (per cent of GDP)

	2000	2005	2006	2008	2010
Egypt	2.2	2.0	2.3	2.0	1.9
Iran	1.9	2.4	2.4	2.5	2.8
Tunisia	3.0	2.9	3.0	3.0	3.8
Turkey	3.1	3.7	4.0	4.4	5.1

Source: Based on World Bank Development Indicators, accessed October 2013 and updated November 2014.

Turkey's problematic performance on human development indicators thus raises some issues. First, Turkey's phenomenal growth in GDP/GNI did not mean that *even the citizens who benefited from this growth* (that is, even when we neglect persistent inequality) were leading *good lives*. Second, a good life is much more than having a fat wallet; it includes the issues the HDI is trying to measure (education and health), even if the United Nations indicators are far from complete. Third, there is no straightforward correlation between having cash and leading a good life: individuals, groups and nations can be developed more along some axes, but not so much along others. The final word on development: while (Islamic) liberalization can be embraced as increasing incomes, it can hardly be taken as a bearer of a satisfying life overall.

Evaluating the 'Justice' in 'Justice and Development'

Developmental indices do not measure justice. One problem with even the HDI is that it does not integrate inequality, that is, it shares the same assumptions with GDP and GNI.[42] A quick glance at the measures of inequality in Table 3.6 indicates that Iran and Turkey overlapped in one significant detail: they were highly unequal. The Iranian revolution, despite its promises to the oppressed, did not reduce inequality. Gini coefficients remained quite high in both countries, even though Turkey was a little more unequal according to this measure. Turkey experienced some advances in Gini in the last few years, but it is still more inegalitarian than Iran (Table 3.7). Other measures of inequality, such as the quintile income ratio and the share of the poorest and richest in national income/expenditure also highlight that Turkey and Iran were inegalitarian countries. In this sense, they can hardly become models to follow when it comes to the issue of social justice. Quintile ratio (the ratio of the average income of the richest 20 per cent of the population to the average income of the poorest 20 per cent) is very instructive in this regard. According to this measure, Turkey appears to be the most inegalitarian country among the four.

Table 3.6. Inequality in the 2000s

	Share of the poorest 10 per cent in income or expenditure	Share of richest 10 per cent in income or expenditure	Richest 10 per cent to poorest 10 per cent	Gini index
Egypt	3.9	27.6	7.2	32.1
Iran	2.6	29.6	11.6	38.3
Tunisia	2.4	31.6	13.3	40.8
Turkey	1.9	33.2	17.4	43.2

Source: United Nations Human Development Report 2009.

Very little high-quality comparative data are available regarding *wealth* (instead of income) inequalities. Available figures are quite alarming not only for Turkey, but for Egypt as well (see Table 3.8; no figures are available for Iran or Tunisia). As a result of the AKP's rule for ten years, the top 1 per cent of Turkish society has come to control more than a half the nation's wealth. Likewise, it appears that the

42 The UNDP's IHDI index is an important step to integrate measures of inequality and human development.

Arab uprisings' calls for social justice have not prevented the steady increase in wealth disparities. These numbers suggest that the richest of the rich in the Middle East have found ways of both monopolizing property *and* hiding this monopolization from the more established and influential international agencies (such as the IMF, the World Bank and the United Nations), as the latters' numbers do not draw attention to such conspicuous inequality.

Table 3.7. Inequality, 2003–2012.

	Quintile ratio	Gini index
Egypt	4.4	30.8
Iran	7.0	38.3
Tunisia	6.4	36.1
Turkey	8.3	40.0

Source: United Nations Human Development Report 2014.

Note: Even though the Gini index shows that there has been some decline in Tunisian inequality over the decades, regional and urban–rural inequalities have significantly sharpened, a factor that cannot be captured by this measure.

Table 3.8. Wealth share of the richest 1 per cent (per cent of total wealth)

	2000	2010	2011	2012	2013	2014
Egypt	32.3	42.0	43.7	45.6	46.5	48.5
Turkey	38.1	47.3	49.1	51.3	52.3	54.3

Source: Global Wealth Databook 2014, Credit Suisse Research Institute.

We get a more detailed picture when we look at another measure of inequality over the years, the income share held by quintiles of the population.[43] Some of the relevant indicators are summarized in Tables 3.9 to

43 Other measures of inequality could also have been integrated into this account. However, none of the accepted measures resolve some basic problems. As political economists have pointed out, these measures underreport *the wealth* of the rich, especially the top 1 per cent. Moreover, the information collected by even the international agencies is based on government sources, which tend to manipulate

3.12.[44] Note, however, that these tables do not give a perfect measure of shifting inequality, since reliable comparative data exist only for income; no data are available for wealth. Table 3.8 and the following tables show clearly how income data underemphasize skyrocketing inequality.

Table 3.9. Income share by quintiles in the 1980s

	Income share held by highest 20 per cent	Income share held by fourth 20 per cent	Income share held by third 20 per cent	Income share held by second 20 per cent	Income share held by lowest 20 per cent
Egypt	n/a	n/a	n/a	n/a	n/a
Iran, 1986	52.73	20.7	13.39	8.6	4.58
Tunisia, 1985	49.57	21.02	14.24	9.63	5.54
Turkey, 1987	50.03	20.27	13.98	9.81	5.91

Source: World Bank Database, compiled in October 2013 and updated in November 2014.

Table 3.10. Income share by quintiles in the mid-1990s.

	Income share held by highest 20 per cent	Income share held by fourth 20 per cent	Income share held by third 20 per cent	Income share held by second 20 per cent	Income share held by lowest 20 per cent
Egypt, 1996	39.91	21.17	16.4	13.01	9.51
Iran, 1994	49.1	21.35	14.39	9.66	5.5
Tunisia, 1995	47.86	21.84	14.74	9.9	5.66
Turkey, 1994	47.68	21.56	14.81	10.15	5.8

Source: World Bank Database, compiled in October 2013 and updated in November 2014.

numbers in order to downplay levels of inequality. For a discussion of how the Turkish state and its statistical institutions manipulate the numbers, see Mustafa Sönmez, 'TÜİK, bu yalanı, araştırma diye satma artık…' *Yurt*, 24 September 2013.

44 No tables are included for the years after 2005, since data are not available for Iran. In Turkey, the share of national income of the bottom 20 per cent, the second 20 per cent, and the top 20 per cent increased from 2005 to 2010. In Egypt and Tunisia, the bottom 60 per cent experienced an increase throughout these years.

Throughout the decades for which data are available, Egypt appears to be the most egalitarian of these countries; the other three are highly inegalitarian. But even Egypt has become more inegalitarian as its neoliberalism has deepened: the share of national income of the bottom 40 per cent has decreased. From the mid-1980s to 2010, Iran experienced a steady but slow increase in the share of the bottom 20 per cent and a larger decrease among the top 20 per cent. Only Iran and Tunisia have experienced increases in the shares of the bottom 20 per cent over these three decades. In Turkey, both the top and the lowest 20 per cent have lost income share in relation to the strata between them.

Table 3.11. Income share by quintiles circa 2000

	Income share held by highest 20 per cent	Income share held by fourth 20 per cent	Income share held by third 20 per cent	Income share held by second 20 per cent	Income share held by lowest 20 per cent
Egypt, 2000	42.1	20.65	15.83	12.47	8.95
Iran, 1998	49.89	21.46	14.17	9.32	5.16
Tunisia, 2000	47.31	21.64	14.89	10.2	5.96
Turkey, 2002	47.73	21.62	14.79	10.1	5.76

Source: World Bank Database, compiled in October 2013 and updated in November 2014.

Since the share of the second quintile has not shifted as much in Turkey (in contrast to Iran, where we see a slight increase over the decades in the shares of this quintile), the clearest winners have been the third and fourth quintiles, which we can loosely call the middle and upper middle classes (admittedly imprecise categories). Based on these indicators, the Iranian model seems more committed (but only slightly so) to the lot of the bottom 40 per cent when compared to the Turkish model.

Another question of justice involves the issue of integration. How much does the population at large participate in the productive economic life of the nation? Even though there are several ways of measuring this participation,[45] employment is one of the solid indicators. Table 3.13 shows that both Iran and Turkey have been quite poor at generating employment. Tunisia's performance has been the worst, while Egypt's performance has been the strongest, perhaps due to continued corporatism.

Table 3.12. Income share by quintiles in 2005

	Income share held by highest 20 per cent	Income share held by fourth 20 per cent	Income share held by third 20 per cent	Income share held by second 20 per cent	Income share held by lowest 20 per cent
Egypt	41.46	20.89	16.05	12.64	8.96
Iran	45.16	21.96	15.54	10.91	6.43
Tunisia	44.62	22.1	15.73	11.08	6.47
Turkey	47.53	22.01	15.07	10.13	5.26

Source: World Bank Database, compiled in October 2013 and updated in November 2014.

Table 3.13. Unemployment, total (per cent of total labour force)

	1989	1991	1997	2001	2002	2005	2008	2010
Egypt	6.9	9.6	8.4	9.4	10.2	11.2	8.7	9
Iran		11.1			12.8	12.1	10.5	
Tunisia	16.1		15.9	15.1	15.3	14.2	12.4	13
Turkey	8.6	8.2	6.8	8.4	10.4	10.6	11	11.9

Source: World Bank, World Development Indicators (updated November 2014).

Liberalism is most associated with inclusiveness. A standard (social justice–based) criticism of liberalization focuses on how it rigs the game even while including people. But the unemployment numbers suggest that liberalization might actually *exclude* more

45 The United Nations Development Programme measures social integration based on employment, vulnerability, equity, perceptions of individual well-being, perceptions of society and safety. UNDP, *Human Development Report 2013*, 174–7.

people wherever it becomes more entrenched. Data on fatal work injuries reinforce this interpretation, since death is of course the ultimate exclusion. Only a few countries can compete with Turkey when it comes to work-related deaths. The ILO does not have comparable numbers for Tunisia, Egypt and Iran, but the few years for which data are available suggest that fatal injuries are relatively small (though Tunisia, the other neoliberal success story in the region, comes close in terms of the ratio of deaths to the total population). A mining accident in 2014 drew attention to this tragedy, but worker deaths have been systematic in Turkey (Table 3.14).

Table 3.14. Cases of fatal occupational injury, Turkey

2002	2009	2010	2011	2012	2013
878	1171	1454	1710	745	1235

Source: ILO STAT database, accessed 21 November 2014; for 2013 only, İstanbul İşçi Sağlığı ve İş Güvenliği Meclisi, *2013 Yılı İş Cinayetleri Raporu*, 13 January 2014.

Approximately four workers died each day in 2013. This is the staggering human cost of the Turkish economic miracle. The reason why investors (and their media) define Turkey as a safe haven for investment is not simply geopolitical, a factor that is often emphasized. An unstated, but core reason is the ease with which business can get away with brutal labour practices without facing any sustained protest or legal sanction.

Can 'Development' Aid the Poor While Circumventing Justice?

Proponents of the 'good' Turkish model (which lasted until 2013) could argue, in spite of these statistics, that it is still a model to follow because it helps the poorest of the poor. It might not help the industrial working class, but that class is on its way to global extinction anyway. We should therefore focus on turning everybody into professionals and businessmen, rather than increasing the share of organized workers and civil servants in national income, and this is actually a more just way to go. To the extent that the Turkish model pulls people out of poverty, it at least creates the conditions for realizing this dream of everybody becoming business wo/men. But how well do these arguments stand the test of numbers?

Table 3.15. Population below the poverty line

	Population below income poverty line of $1.25 a day, 2000–2009 (per cent)	Population below national poverty line, 2000–2009 (millions)
Egypt	2.0	22.0
Iran	1.5	Not available
Tunisia	2.6	3.8
Turkey	2.7	18.1

Source: United Nations Human Development Report 2011.

The results are mixed, to say the least. As Table 3.15 shows, Turkey was doing poorly in terms of both relative and extreme poverty until 2009 (taking an income of $1.25 a day as the line that defines the latter). However, if we take $2 a day as our cut-off point, Turkey fares a little better. In all four countries the ratio of the population living on incomes of less than $2 a day decreased from the mid-1980s onwards (see Table 3.16). Turkey started with the smallest ratio in the 1980s, but by 2010, its ratio was close to that of Tunisia. Moreover, its rate of reduction of poverty (over two decades) is not phenomenal when compared to Iran, and embarrassing when compared to Tunisia. Still it is remarkable that by 2010, extreme poverty had decreased significantly in Turkey.

Table 3.16. Poverty headcount ratio at $2 a day (per cent of population)

	1985	1986	1987	1990	1991	1994	1996	2000	2002	2005	2010
Egypt					27.6		26.3	19.4		20.08	
Iran		13.8		13.1		8.24				8.03	
Turkey			6.8			8.91			7.38	7.54	3.05
Tunisia	25.1			19				12.8		7.64	4.46

Note: The poverty line figure of $2 a day is based on purchasing power parity.
Source: Based on World Bank World Development Indicators, accessed in October 2013 and updated in November 2014.

Neoliberalizations and Islamic Economies: Accomplishments and Shortcomings

Turkey's neoliberal Islam boosted growth and made Turkey a stronger competitor in regional and global markets. It also extended the welfare state's benefits to some hitherto excluded groups. However, it perpetuated (and in some instances deepened) inequalities and increased unemployment. While it thus alleviated some cases of extreme poverty, it added to inequality. The clearest victims of neoliberalism were workers, if the number of workplace deaths is any indication. The AKP also reproduced Turkish neoliberalism's underinvestment in education. Overall, Islamic neoliberalism did not lead to a high quality of life for citizens. Moreover, it is questionable whether its achievements – economic growth, wider provision of health care, increased competitiveness and mitigation of extreme poverty – are sustainable, given the many weak spots in the economy (especially its dependence on global hot money flows and high levels of capital imports, and thus on a vibrant global economy). This, perhaps, is the Turkish model in a nutshell: the ability of businesses to monopolize most of a country's wealth *combined with* its ability to market this monopolization to the region's downtrodden (and to the rest of the world) as 'justice'.

Turkey's Islamic arch-rival, Iran, did not fare much better in its more strongly 'Islamic' economic programme. Its revolutionized corporatism, now seasoned with some neoliberalization, could not sustain growth. Worse, the revolution failed to deliver one of its central promises, social justice. Still, Iran has boasted levels of human development as high as (and in some regards, higher than) Turkey. It should also be noted that Iran's poor overall performance was not simply due to the inherent inferiority of its economic model, but to a devastating global trade embargo as well as the frailty of bloc formation (when compared to Turkey).

Indeed, solid bloc formation was the distinguishing feature of Islamic neoliberalism, rather than simply the economic robustness of its policies. Tunisia's secular neoliberalization had fared quite well on all the indices that Turkey excelled (growth, export orientation and poverty reduction). That model, though, was fragile due to the top-down nature of its neoliberalization, rather than solely the content of its policies. Hence, the Turkish model should be taken as a whole in order to appreciate what it brings to the table: not only Islamic neoliberalism, but Islamic liberalism as well, if liberalism is understood as an overall political and cultural project that enables the mobilization of broad strata for a business-oriented society.

In sum, consent for neoliberalism was what the Turkish model promised to the region. Cases of neoliberal success, such as Tunisia, could further solidify a business-oriented programme through Islamic consent. Cases of neoliberal stagnation, such as Egypt, could hope to weed out remnants of corporatism and move towards more consistent (and popular) economic policies by drawing on the Turkish model.

These hopes, however, have assumed and neglected too much. They assume the presence of powerful Islamic actors willing to move in such a direction. They neglect the necessary factors (such as the specific structure of political society) needed to render such actors capable of forming solid sociopolitical blocs and thereby ruling with consent.

Towards the 2011 Revolt

The Turkish model has indeed delivered benefits to some strata. At the same time, however, it involves a carefully planned, protracted war against others. Indeed, given the number of occupational fatalities, war might not be only a metaphor. Is the Turkish model, though, really that distinct from straightforward neoliberalism? Quantitative indicators from Tunisia might be interpreted as proof that *Islamization* itself does not add much to *neoliberalization*. A successful version of the latter is possible without the former, if we focus only on numbers (which are quite similar for Tunisia and Turkey in some regards). However, even if the upper classes have been pushing successfully for a more inegalitarian system almost everywhere else in the world (for example, in the United States), few if any have been as successful as their Turkish counterparts in selling their economic policies as just and in the interests of the poor. (The Republicans' 'compassionate conservatism' and their 'Average Joe' packagings did not result in three electoral victories in a row in the US.) Moreover, Islamization seemed to prevent revolution (which was perhaps the main intent of those who promoted the Turkish model). Adoption of liberal Islamization may therefore not usher in an incomparably more developed country, but it might be the right path to ensure that marketization will gain the consent of the broadest strata possible.

The next two chapters will demonstrate, however, that even the likely winners of liberalization elsewhere cannot benefit in the same way from the Turkish model. The social and political structures of other countries in the region had already made replication of the Turkish model difficult, but the recent revolt wave has rendered this path next to impossible. Chapter 6 will further point out that after 2013 the Turkish model plunged into a deep crisis in its home country.

CHAPTER 4

The Revolt Against Authoritarian Liberalism

The events in Tunisia and Egypt in late 2010 and early 2011 were almost completely unexpected. Many self-styled clairvoyants retrospectively argued that they had foreseen the uprisings – claims that are open to ridicule.[1] These explosive events created new realities and are not traceable to what was already known about these countries. Citizens' orientations and national power blocs were deeply shaken over the span of a few weeks. However, whether these events would eventually lead to a durable transformation of sociopolitical structures depended on the existing balance of forces.[2]

Chapters 4, 5, and 6 will demonstrate that these revolts had twisted consequences due to the shape of political societies and power blocs (and their transnational interactions). Rather than resulting in revolutionary transformation, the uprisings rather dynamited the potentials for peaceful liberalization along the lines of the Turkish model (and ultimately the sustainability of the Turkish model in Turkey itself). They may also have planted the seeds of deeper structural transformations in the future, but that remains to be seen.

The Unforeseen Road to 2011

A series of street mobilizations spanning a decade paved the way for the 2011 revolt in Egypt. Since Islamists were building their muscles 'under the radar',[3] most street politics had a non-Islamist face.

1 Charles Kurzman, 'The Arab Spring Uncoiled', *Mobilization* 17:4 (2013): 377–81.

2 The analysis in the coming two chapters shares a beginning point with Sewell's eventful sociology and Badiou's philosophy of the event: explosive events have the potential to transform structures. Yet the analysis diverges from the frameworks of these two figures in its focus on blocs' and political societies' impact on this potential.

3 Nancy J. Davis and Robert V. Robertson, *Claiming Society for God: Religious Movements and Social Welfare in Egypt, Israel, Italy, and the United States*, Bloomington: Indiana University Press, 2012.

Between 1998 and 2008, around 2 million Egyptian workers participated in more than 2,600 factory occupations. Joel Beinin points out that this mobilization 'constitutes the largest and most sustained social movement in Egypt since the campaign to oust the British occupiers following the end of World War II'.[4] The tension escalated after 2006, with more than 600 collective labour actions per year.[5] Textile workers led the actions, but many workers from the private and public sectors, as well as white-collar workers and professionals (teachers, clerks, pharmacists, doctors and university professors) also participated. The actions protested low wages and the failure to pay bonuses following privatization, the establishment of free trade zones and the deregulation of employer–employee relations.[6]

The strikes were initiated by local workers' networks: the union officials adamantly resisted them (and in some cases, they were themselves detained by workers).[7] The strikes not only led to higher bonuses, but the first official recognition of non-regime unions. The workers' movement had no national leadership either: liberal and leftist Cairo activists (such as the coalition group Kefaya) tried to build bonds with the striking workers, but these were short-lived. Workers' economic actions became national in scope partly thanks to the brokerage of human rights and labour NGOs, as well as the efforts of leftist politicians. This broadening led, among other things, to a nationwide minimum wage campaign. But the NGOs and the politicians kept political demands out of their labour activities. Workers resisted outreach by some youth activists who directly pushed for the politicization of the labour movement.[8]

The media-savvy youth movement, a liberal democratic opposition, caught more of the international attention. The first leap forward of the liberal forces on the street was in protest against fraud

---

4 Joel Beinin, 'Workers' Protest in Egypt: Neo-liberalism and Class Struggle in the 21st Century', *Social Movement Studies* 8:4 (2009): 450.

5 Ibid.

6 Ibid., 450–1.

7 Ibid., 452.

8 Killian Clarke, 'Unexpected Brokers of Mobilization: Contingency and Networks in the 2011 Egyptian Uprising', *Journal of Comparative Politics* 46:4 (July 2014): 379–97.

during the 2005 elections.[9] The protestors gathered around an umbrella organization, Kefaya ('Enough', founded in 2004), containing elements of the left as well as the Islamists, but led by the liberals. Kefaya slowly died out after failing to achieve any political reforms. A relatively more left-wing version of Kefaya emerged in 2008, when a group of journalists and bloggers called on Egyptian citizens to engage in a general strike to support striking al-Mahalla al-Kubra workers. The general strike never materialized, but the campaign left behind a more activist and lasting network when compared to Kefaya: the 6 April Youth Movement.

The final major strike of the non-Islamist opposition during the Mubarak years was a movement against torture. The brutal murder of Khalid Sa'eed (a blogger) by the police led to the formation of another blogger–journalist network in 2010, 'We are all Khalid Sa'eed'. These two blogger groups called on Egyptians to follow the example of their Tunisian brothers and sisters on National Police Day, 25 January 2011. This time the call did not fall on deaf ears.

As in Egypt, in Tunisia there was a (shorter) prehistory to the uprising. Yet the pre-2011 protests were even more internationally invisible in the case of this small North African country. The major protests had started out in Gafsa, a provincial mining town just to the south of Sidi Bouzid (the provincial town at the origin of the 2011 protest wave). Street protests shook Gafsa following January 2008, when workers mobilized against a major gas company's unfair hiring practices. As the months evolved, protests started to address unemployment and social justice in more general terms, which led them to target political repression as well. The protests first spread to neighbouring towns and then to university campuses, mostly organized by the student wing of the (illegal) Tunisian Communist Workers Party. Heavy repression and torture ensued, but protests persisted until the summer.[10]

9 Antiwar mobilizations against the Israeli occupation of the West Bank and the Gaza Strip (in 2000) and the Iraq War (2003) also allowed activists to hone in their skills (Clarke, 'Unexpected Brokers of Mobilization'). Many of those who participated in these mobilizations became the leaders during the following decade.

10 Laryssa Chomiak and John P. Entelis, 'The Making of North Africa's Intifadas', *Middle East Report* 259 (2011): 8–15.

Striking a different, more middle-class tone, activists organized an event in May 2010 through Facebook and Twitter in order to criticize government surveillance and control over the Internet. The 'Tunisia in White' campaign invited people to dress in white and have coffee along the cafes on Bourguiba Street (the main street in Tunis, where large protests were to be staged in January 2011). The event lasted for six days and security forces clamped down on the protesters pretty quickly.[11]

Tunisian protest once again shifted to the countryside at the end of the summer of 2010. In Ben Guerdane, a region on the Libyan border, rural Tunisians protested against their life conditions after the tightening of security at the border, which killed smuggling, their major source of livelihood. Though anger was first directed at the decision of the Libyan authorities to close the border, the Ben Ali regime chose to respond by repression and imprisonment, eventually channelling anger towards the Tunisian state. However, militant protest eventually pushed the regime to negotiate with Libyan authorities for a reopening of the border.[12]

Most notable about this prehistory of Tunisian revolt, especially in contrast to Egypt, is the relatively more developed politicization of labour. The links between left-wing political society and left-wing civil society were also more developed in these protests, even though both civil society and political society were very weak because of the dictatorship. The UGTT's semi-autonomy from the regime (see chapter 1) facilitated much of this politicization and linkage. Even though the official union's top ranks were experts in negotiation rather than revolt, some middle-level cadres had revolutionary tendencies, belonged to political groups and were quite active on the streets.[13] Later, in 2011, the continuity between the class composition and demands of the protests in the countryside and the capital city Tunis owed much to them. The class composition and the demands of

---

11 Ibid.

12 Amin Allal, 'Trajectoires "révolutionnaires" en Tunisie: Processus de radicalisations politiques 2007–2011', *Revue française de science politique* 62:5/6 (2012): 821–41.

13 Choukri Hmed, 'Réseaux dormants, contingence et structures: Genèses de la révolution tunisienne', *Revue française de science politique* 62:5/6 (2012): 805–6.

Tahrir and al-Mahalla al-Kubra, by contrast, displayed much less continuity. The different make-up of civil society and political society in the two countries would lead to quite different outcomes in the following years.

The 2011 Revolt and Its Limits

Even if these mobilizations led to the establishment of actual and virtual networks that were crucial to the 2011 revolt (as well as some slogans and framing of issues that became central at that point), their scope and ambitions did not foreshadow what was to come just months later. The networks, resources, tactics and mobilizing frames accumulated by these movements paled in the shadow of the pharaohs. Despite the dictators' and the incumbent elites' incomparably richer resources and networks, however, the regimes and their neoliberal development programmes were shaken and their restoration has been uncertain so far.

Tunisia, the birth place of the 2011 Arab revolt, is a challenging case to decipher: why would socio-economic grievances lead to revolt in a neoliberal heaven? Tunisia was the IMF's and the World Bank's poster child: it had maintained robust growth while at the same time curbing poverty and implementing social programmes. Also crucial from the standpoint of social theorizing about the revolt, it boasted the most professionalized middle class with the best life chances in (the non-oil-rich part of) the Arab world. Education, good job prospects and women's status had all improved over the decades.

But Tunisia also suffered from regional inequality, police brutality, corruption and crony wealth. Could these three factors explain why the revolt erupted in Tunisia rather than elsewhere in the Arab world (much of which also suffered from all three problems)? This is not the place to provide a causal account of what brought about the uprising in Tunisia, since the 2011 wave throws causal explanations of revolt into doubt (as the next chapter will demonstrate). The main goal, rather, is to point out how the process of revolt further deepened the difficulty of applying the Turkish model to Tunisia. A parallel goal of this account is to study the process to understand which issues and which sociopolitical forces took centre stage and were then decentred in the process.

Mohamed Bouazizi, a street vendor in the provincial town of Sidi Bouzid kicked off the protests. He was the son of a construction worker. Manhandled by a female municipal officer who mocked his pleas for employment, he decided to burn himself. The international media insisted that he had a university degree to make his case fit their scenario of a middle-class (and therefore acceptable) revolution. Actually, Bouazizi was a high school dropout.

The political scientist Choukri Hmed points out that Bouazizi's action did not come out of the blue.[14] In fact, peddlers in this provincial town had been confronting the police for a decade. Their altercations had led not only to an accumulation of discontent, but also to 'dormant networks' among the unprivileged and the development of subtle folk knowledge regarding the regime. When Bouazizi set himself on fire, therefore, his act not only resonated with a broad set of people but also quickly mobilized them. Arriving after years of attempted suicides by common folk, the act was perceived to be political (an interpretation local union leaders and politicians also helped spread).

Labour, lawyers and street vendors carried out the first massive protests in front of the Sidi Bouzid municipal building. These were followed by protests by the unemployed and students in neighbouring towns. The increasingly militant protests remained concentrated in rural regions for three weeks. Informal networks (especially in marketplaces) were quite important in these first weeks, but teachers and union leaders also incited action in official venues such as schools.[15] Like the peddler youth, these teachers and union leaders had also developed networks and accumulated tactical knowledge over the previous decade.[16] Trotskyist and Arab socialist primary and secondary teachers were the key to the politicization of the events.[17]

When these provincial protests were faced with police brutality, revolt spread to the whole country and evolved from solely socio-economic to political goals, namely the removal of Ben Ali.[18] This was definitively a multiclass revolt. Middle-class youth as well as

14 Hmed, 'Réseaux dormants, contingence et structures', 801, 807–8.

15 Ibid., 811.

16 Ibid., 812–14.

17 Ibid., 805.

18 James Gelvin, *The Arab Uprisings: What Everyone Needs to Know*, New York: Oxford University Press, 2012, 42–3.

organized labour occupied the town squares until the downfall of the dictator. Some 95 per cent of lawyers went on strike against police brutality in early January 2011. But working-class neighbourhoods also echoed with chants and slogans. The officially recognized union, UGTT, not only organized strikes throughout the country but also mobilized the unemployed and the youth on the streets. There are also indications that labour was active in relaying the provincial protests to the capital city in the first place: the 'urbanization' of the initially provincial protests started right in front of the UGTT's national headquarters.[19] Professional syndicates also supported these moves.[20] Ben Ali was forced to flee to Saudi Arabia in a matter of weeks.

By contrast, the Tahrir Square occupation was heavily middle class. The impact of labour was greater outside Tahrir, especially in the industrial towns of Mahalla and Tanta. Working-class and poor neighbourhoods also joined the protests in Cairo and Alexandria, and some of them even occasionally marched to Tahrir,[21] without, however, becoming a mainstay of the occupation there. By 30 January, tens of thousands of workers all over Egypt had started strikes with both economic and political demands. On 10 February the disparate strikes turned into a general one, and Mubarak had to quit office the next day.

Tahrir's revolutionary youth and Mahalla and Tanta's independent workers were in dialogue,[22] but their actions and platforms were not well coordinated. As a result, social justice issues were among the top items on the agenda of the uprising, but demands addressing the (de)commodification of labour, health care, education and housing could not be formulated. According to some analysts,[23] the

---

19 Hmed, 'Réseaux dormants, contingence et structures', 817.

20 Gelvin, *The Arab Uprisings*, 56.

21 Clarke, 'Unexpected Brokers of Mobilization'; Gelvin, *The Arab Uprisings*, 45–6; Salwa Ismail, 'The Egyptian Revolution against the Police', *Social Research* 79:2 (2012): 435–62.

22 Clarke's essay 'Unexpected Brokers of Mobilization' provides one of the detailed studies of the links between the middle-class Cairo activists and labour and how their coordination contributed to the popularization of revolt, especially between 25 and 28 January.

23 For an overview, see Éric Verdeil, 'Arab Cities in Revolution: Some Observations', Metropolitiques.eu, 25 February 2011, metropolitiques.eu. However, none of these reports have so far constituted solid causal links between

commodification of urban space, and especially of informal poor settlements, was one of the causes of revolt. Even so, this issue was not properly politicized or linked to the commodification of labour and social goods – a linkage that could have changed the course of the revolt. This uneven centrality of labour's commodification to Arab protests is in part related to the continued importance of industrial towns in countries such as Egypt, in contrast to their near-extinction in world capitalism's core countries.

Why were labour's demands and related issues of commodification gradually pushed to the margins of the Egyptian revolutionary agenda? The centrality of the much more fatal and immediate questions of old regime and Muslim Brotherhood authoritarianisms and the low level of alternative political organization due to decades of dictatorship played a role. But so did the huge political and cultural gap between the working class and the middle class. The contrasts with the Tunisian case (where teachers, lawyers, mid-level union cadres and communist parties constituted links over the decades) are instructive. Lacking political organizations that tied them together, the Egyptian working and middle classes went their own ways once their fleeting coalition fulfilled its immediate goal (toppling the dictator) and thereby avoided the arduous task of cross-cultural communication, which becomes even more burdensome in the absence of multiclass political organizations. Both classes would pay a dear price for their lack of interest in each other's concerns in the coming years.

Salwa Ismail has mounted a fierce objection to the characterization of the Egyptian revolt as middle class.[24] She has pointed out that informal workers – who have suffered humiliation and violence at the hands of the police, detentions, displacement and confiscation of vending scales during the neoliberal era – played a key role in the 2011 uprising. They have fought the violent battles in Tahrir's back streets and burned down dozens of police stations in working-class neighbourhoods. These, among other factors, have led to the defeat of the

---

the commodification of urban space and the urban-spatial dimension of the 2011 revolt. This remains a potential avenue for future research.

24 Salwa Ismail, 'Urban Subalterns in the Arab Revolutions: Cairo and Damascus in Comparative Perspective', *Comparative Studies in Society and History* 55:4 (2013): 865–94.

police and the security apparatus.[25] Perhaps the way this role fits into the 2011 revolt's general picture can be compared to the role of informal workers in the Turkish revolt of 2013 (see chapter 6). In both cases, informal workers have taken the most serious risks and paid the highest price without taking much credit for it (due to their low levels of formal organization and visibility, and to class prejudices which reinforce these factors). Ultimately, therefore, the public agenda and the spirit of these revolts have remained middle class, even if some of their crucial participants were far from being so.

Did more conscious class conflict within the camp of revolt also have a hand in marginalizing social issues? In light of Marx's famous analysis of 1848, one could expect the upper-class liberals and the middle classes to be afraid of increasing working-class radicalism and therefore become open to accommodation. In other words, it is possible that the middle classes did not turn their back on the working class due to the lack of communication, the neglect of their demands, or the weakness of political and civic organizations that could sustain coalitions between the two, but due to the *realization* that persistent working-class radicalism could undermine some of their privileges. However, Egypt did not even get to that point. Neither the middle strata nor the militant working class was able to offer alternatives to the old regime, lacking direction and organization. No social blueprint emerged along class lines, so there was no open conflict between class forces. In Tunisia, by contrast, the revolutionary camp was divided by class very early on. The elite elements organized a counter-Kasbah demonstration, for example, where they invited the Kasbah occupiers to return to work.

The Official Revolution

The political representatives of the revolution also turned out to be weak in pronouncing any explicit ways out of the old regime. Aside from the Brotherhood, who represented the Egyptian revolution in the political world? Were they really on the same page with the revolutionaries and the people? It is very difficult to know what the revolutionaries and the people exactly wanted. But based on the core

---

25 Salwa Ismail, 'The Egyptian Revolution against the Police', *Social Research* 79:2 (2012): 435–62.

slogans and some articulated demands, we can at least have a sketch of how the political representatives of the revolutionary camp fared in this regard.

The four central slogans shared by the Egyptian and Tunisian militants were bread, social justice, freedom and dignity. According to the Arab Barometer website, the Tunisian protesters listed economic problems as their main motivation for joining the revolts. Which political forces could indeed speak to these concerns?

In Egypt, the major (non-Brotherhood) political figures who emerged after Mubarak's ouster focused mostly on issues of political liberty, sidelining issues of bread and social justice. The most prominent figure, Mohamed el-Baradei, the would-be inheritor of the liberal tradition in Egypt, promised to continue the neoliberal programmes implemented by the old regime (seasoned with promises of job creation and poverty reduction), to the limited extent that he discussed economic issues at all. All the same, the 6 April youth group, which was formed in solidarity with striking workers, regarded him as their hero. In short, even though Egyptian liberalism was evolving towards a more left-wing liberalism on the ground, its political representatives remained committed to the free market.[26]

Hamdeen Sabahi, a Nasserist in whom so much hope was invested by more subaltern elements of society, spoke more extensively on economic issues. He espoused state involvement in the economy, placing more emphasis on industry, a more just distribution of wealth and resources (across regions and classes), a full welfare state and socially just minimum and maximum wages. But even Sabahi promised he would not touch private property.[27] His statism was less socialist than even Nasser's.

Perhaps most interesting among the nationally recognized leaders was a previous Brotherhood member, Abdel Moneim, who had split from the organization shortly after the anti-Mubarak revolt. After losing the presidential election in 2012, Abul Futouh established his

---

26 'El-Baradei: La aqbal ri'asa Hukumat al-Infadh . . . wa laday mashruʿ li tanmiyya al-iqtisad yanshur khilal al-usbuʿayn', almasryalyoum.com, 12 March 2013.

27 'Q&A with Hamdeen Sabahi', egypttoday.com, 7 May 2012; 'Sabahi baʿad wathiqa al-Azhar: Lam uwaqqiʿ ʿala waqf al-mad al-thawri . . . wa lan nadkhul fi safqat', almasryalyoum.com, 31 January 2013.

own Islamic party on a politically more liberal and economically more social justice–oriented platform than that of the Brotherhood (and slightly to the left of older Islamist splinters such as al-Wasat). Nevertheless, he suffered from the same problems with the other recognizable revolutionary political leaders: sidelining of social justice issues and vague promises rather than a solid outline of a revolutionary economic policy.[28] He became the hope and symbol of a possible revolutionary revised Brotherhood line. However, in time it turned out that he wouldn't be able to mobilize significant numbers of Islamists, who remained loyal either to the Brotherhood or to one of the Salafi groups.[29]

The Unofficial Revolution

Prominent independent political figures occasionally pointed out how both el-Baradei and Sabahi were reluctant to question US hegemony, the political and economic structures of the old regime and the rule of capital.[30] But lacking solid organizations behind them, they were unable to intervene decisively in the unfolding protests and the resulting political balances. Some of these leaders, such as Kamal Khalil, carried some weight among the revolutionary groups, the soccer fans and the workers (in the case of Khalil, this was due to decades of pro-labour activism and imprisonment under Sadat). All of these participants in the revolt lost faith in el-Baradei and Sabahi in the months following February 2011. Nevertheless, the disparate groups were not able to unite around a programme, and none of these leaders had the will to promote such unification.

28 His main argument was basically that wealth had to be redistributed through educational and health programmes, rather than attacking (even illegitimate, 'stolen') property. 'Abdul Futouh li ahali Nazla al-Saman: Barnamiji yastahdif jadhb 80 sayih sanawiyyan', 21 February 2012.

29 While the term 'salafi' is usually reserved for religious actors stricter than the Brotherhood, local and historical usage has been much more complex. In the late nineteenth and early twentieth centuries, the term frequently referred to religious modernizers. The Brotherhood still occasionally uses the term to refer to itself, in the sense that it still follows the first generation of Muslims (and seeks to apply the dictates of Islam as they did). See, e.g., 'Mahdi 'akef fi muwajaha sharsa ma'a Raf'at al-Sa'id', *al-Ahram*, 25 November 2011. Salafi, as a self-designation, is occasionally put on and then taken off the Brotherhood website.

30 See, e.g., 'Kamal Khalil li al-Baradei wa Sabahi: Entum tahraqun enfeskum bi aydikum', almasryalyoum.com, 17 April 2013.

A similar disjuncture emerged in Tunisia. Official voices attempted to marginalize the calls for the radicalization of the revolution in early 2011. Demonstrations and sit-ins in Kasbah Square demanded a swifter transition, whereas more respectable meetings and demonstrations urged patience.[31] Unlike Egypt, however, the less respectable voices had more political and institutional representation. This influence impacted the aftermath of the revolt in deep ways, since the Tunisian process remained more integrative of antisystemic demands.

The occupations in Kasbah Square, which was the home of several ministries of the old regime, became one of the Tunisian uprising's central symbols. The actors of the first occupation were delegates from provincial towns, including Sidi Bouzid. After they were violently dispersed, the occupations became socially more diverse. They demanded a parliamentary regime and a constituent assembly, as well as the removal of all remnants of the old regime. Demands were formulated bottom-up, through discussion groups in which all occupiers participated,[32] in the same spirit with recent revolts elsewhere around the globe. The condition of labour and unemployment were also among the debated topics, but no shared demands followed on this front.

Observers have argued that even the most experienced and institutionalized leftist parties, such as the Tunisian Communist Workers Party, were outpaced by these developments.[33] They could not lead them, and therefore they could not rise as the true representatives of the revolution against the secularist party al-Nidaa (a coalition of old regime remnants, centre-leftists and official labour) and al-Nahda. Still, by 2014 they had a bigger presence in parliament than did their Egyptian counterparts.

None of the Arab revolts resulted in immediate political revolutions, let alone social revolutions. The revolts removed the dictators

31 For the tumultuous months after Ben Ali, see Leyla Dahkli, 'Une révolution trahie? Sur le soulèvement tunisien et la transition démocratique', laviedesidee.fr, 19 February 2013.

32 Hmed, 'Réseaux dormants, contingence et structures'.

33 See 'Interview de Choukri Hmed sur la page Facebook el Kasbah', facebook.com/notes/el-kasbah/10-questions-%C3%A0-choukri-hmed/485249554847950.

(in Egypt, Tunisia, Yemen and Libya), but the actors who replaced them were not able to erect institutions that would replace the old regimes, with the partial exception of Tunisia. Police state techniques mutated and survived – or perhaps, even thrived – in Egypt, Yemen and Libya.

If the political question was far from being resolved, the social question faced a more dismal destiny, being all but dropped from the agenda of the revolt, with the exceptions of Tunisia and Egypt, where it kept reappearing sporadically. The sidelining of social issues developed much more quickly in the other cases. Even though protests started with socio-economic issues in Yemen and rural Syria, for example, they were dropped from the agenda as soon as they met sectarian and political brutality.

Still, the revolts not only overthrew four dictators but made any future filial inheritance of power virtually impossible. There were also more subtle changes. In Tunisia alone, the ouster of Ben Ali was followed by a flowering of political and civil society. There were ninety-five registered parties already in 2011, together with 20,000 civil society organizations.[34] The subtle accomplishments of the revolt wave seemed to be as important as its limits.

The Muslim Brotherhood and the January revolt

After the 2011 protests, a deep split emerged within the Brotherhood. In hindsight, the Brotherhood's major post-revolt success lay in containing this split and solidifying the organization (until the harsh crackdown against it in July 2013). That success did not seem guaranteed in early 2011. Since the main tendency today is to focus on how the Brotherhood 'lost' the revolution, it is important to draw attention to this conservative success to get a sense of the organization's chances of survival and empowerment in the coming years and decades.

The Brotherhood's Guidance Bureau was silent regarding the protests of 25 January, which set off the revolutionary uprising in

34 Laryssa Chomiak, 'The Making of a Revolution in Tunisia', *Middle East Law and Governance* 3 (2011): 68–83.

Egypt.[35] Despite this lack of encouragement, many Brotherhood members went to Tahrir Square. Some of those who joined were part of a 'cross-partisan youth network', in Carrie Wickham's description.[36] Since 2003, they had been participating in pro-Palestine, pro-labour and pro-democracy action together with leftists and liberals. While initially quite worried about the role of Brotherhood youth in these protests, the Guidance Bureau eventually followed in their footsteps. After it became obvious that the protests were turning into a popular uprising, the Guidance Bureau switched its position and declared that it was favourable to them.[37]

A few days after the ouster of Mubarak, two top leaders of the Brotherhood resigned. Their reasons for doing so were shocking: they accused the Guidance Bureau of negotiating with Suleiman (one of Mubarak's top butchers) behind the scenes during the revolt.[38] One of them alleged that the Brotherhood–Suleiman deal failed when the Brotherhood youth occupying Tahrir refused to abide by orders from their leaders.[39] Even though they were initially repudiated by the Bureau, the negotiations held with Suleiman were confirmed in September 2013 when a top Brotherhood leader apologized to the Egyptian people because of their political mistakes (more specifically, their reinforcement of military rule, which would ultimately lead to their downfall).

Regardless of this counter-revolutionary politicking at the top, confusion rather than principled conservatism seemed to guide some of the middle-level cadres. An anecdote, related in a piece co-authored by one of the top experts of Egyptian Islamism (the late Husam Tammam), is quite telling:

35 According to one scholar, the Guidance Bureau consciously and explicitly refused to endorse the 25 January protests when pressured by its own members as well as other opposition forces. Killian Clarke, 'Unexpected Brokers of Mobilization'.

36 Carrie R. Wickham, *The Muslim Brotherhood: Evolution of an Islamist Movement*, Princeton, NJ: Princeton University Press, 2013, 155–7, 160–2.

37 'Bayaan min al-Ikhwaan al-Muslimiin hawla ahdaath yawm 25 Yunaayir 2011 wa tada'aiyaatha', ikhwanonline.com, 26 January 2011.

38 'Hal ʿaqada al-Ikhwan ittifaqan maʿ ʿAmr Sulayman li ijhad al-thawra', masrawy.com, 31 March 2013.

39 'Muhammad Habib: Tarshih al-Shater khataa' istrataji sa yukallif al-watan wa al-jamaʿa aʿda' kathirin', almasryalyoum, 1 April 2012.

> In Alexandria, in one of the mass demonstrations, with the streets overflowing and observers claiming a presence of a million and a half, one of the Brothers' preachers launched into a confrontational sermon that called for revolution, in tune with the mood of the day, and ended begging for its success. Then, abruptly forgetting this revolutionary gesture that had won him such an audience, he called (as he should) on everyone to go quietly home.[40]

However, it would be naïve to think that the Guidance Bureau ever alternated between such extremes. Its fluctuations remained within centrist boundaries, and from the beginning it operated with the logic of containment of the movement.

The Guidance Bureau acted much along the same lines with the military. It urged protesters to return home as soon as the president abdicated. Again following the military's lead,[41] it dubbed the strikes spreading throughout Egypt 'factional' (*fi'awiyya*, a contested word, which could also be translated as class-related or syndical, depending on the context). A Brotherhood leader even suggested that counter-revolutionaries were inciting the strikes![42] The Brotherhood was at the forefront of the forces that prevented the ouster of Mubarak from turning into a full-fledged revolution.[43]

---

40 Husam Tammam and Patrick Haenni, 'Egypt: Islam in the Insurrection', *Religioscope*, 22 February 2011.

41 After initial assaults on labour immediately after Mubarak's overthrow, the pro-military government issued, in June, a law banning strikes and also all other protests which would prevent the functioning of public institutions, while also promising American companies that 'the market economy' and foreign trade would keep on operating peacefully. See 'Al-Hukuuma tabda' qanun tajrim al-adrab wa tuhaddid munadhdhimi al-ihtijajat bi mawaad mukafahat al-irhab', almasryalyoum.com, 8 June 2011.

42 In spite these proclamations, when the military actually intervened to disperse the protesters in the square, the Guidance Bureau criticized this action.

43 The Guidance Bureau occasionally supported revolutionary demonstrations despite its overall stance against them following February 11, especially when the demonstrations targeted the person of Mubarak more than the old regime as a whole. See, e.g., 'al-Ikhwan tu'lin musharakatha fi Jum'a al-Tathir li al-mutalaba bi muhakama Mubarak', *al-Masry al-Youm*, 3 April 2011.

Courageously challenging their leaders, some Brotherhood members in the square collaborated with leftist and nationalist groups. They declared they supported the strikes and even announced that they were going to remain in the square until the military stepped aside. This Islamist-leftist-nationalist coalition also asked the government to raise wages, build a wider social safety net for all Egyptians and expand the freedom of unions. Such a revolt against the free market would be unthinkable within AKP ranks, a sign of the unification, discipline and professionalization of Turkish Islamic political society.[44]

There was something counter-intuitive about these developments, since until 2011 all major splits from and opposition to the Guidance Bureau (for example, the Wasat) took liberal democratic forms. In the hope that these rifts would eventually lead to neoliberal positions (as had happened in Turkey), many in Western academic and policy circles had supported the earlier splits. This was the first time that splits from and protest against the Guidance Bureau adopted a left-wing, democratic stance.

Given how earlier splits from the organization had bred only ineffective political parties, some reasoned push for a thorough change within the organization would make more sense. Based on this logic, some of these youth called for a revolution against the Guidance Bureau *within* the Brotherhood.[45] The overthrow of the Guidance Bureau, according to oppositional politicians within the Brotherhood in a Nile Delta province, would be a natural follow-up to Mubarak's overthrow.[46] Such actions could not fail to be punished, and many of the revolutionaries within the Brotherhood were soon expelled from the organization.

Shortly after the overthrow of Mubarak, the ruling military council appointed a committee of judges to make revisions to the constitution

44 These Brotherhood members also published a declaration in support of labour demands, as well as the strikes and labour protests, which the Brotherhood's Guidance Bureau had called factional. See 'Shabab al-Ikhwan yu'assisun ittihadan li tawhid juhud thuwwar 25 Yunaayir', almasryalyoum.com, 17 February 2011.

45 'Shabab al-Ikhwan yuhaddidun 17 Maris maw'id li al-thawra 'ala Maktab al-Irshad', *al-Masry al-Youm*, 27 February 2011.

46 'Fasl 4 min qiyadat al-Ikhwan bi al-Buhayrah ayyadu al-da'wa li muqata'a al-intikhabat', *al-Masry al-Youm*, 25 February 2011.

(instead of drafting a new constitution, as the revolutionary uprising demanded). One appointee to this committee was a Brotherhood member.[47] Moreover, the head of the committee was an Islamic conservative opponent of the Mubarak regime. The committee made it very clear that it would not discuss the second clause of the old constitution (which accentuated the centrality of Islamic law to legislation). Islamic law had become sacrosanct as a result of Islamist mobilization and its interactions with the Sadat–Mubarak regimes. The uprising only further reinforced these legalistic tendencies. Indeed, in July 2011 all the conservative Islamic groups returned to Tahrir Square, primarily chanting demands for an 'Islamic Egypt' and the application of Islamic law, suggesting that their coming battle would focus more on enforcing legal codes than on achieving market-led growth. Egypt's Islamists did not seem to be ready to implement the Turkish model.

This reclaiming of Cairo's central square by the Brotherhood was also significant because the Guidance Bureau had pictured the post-Mubarak Tahrir Square as a source of *fitna* (disorder).[48] They had even boycotted least-common-denominator demonstrations such as one held in early July 2011, which called for the trial of those responsible for murderers during January and February. In late July, several Islamic groups (along with the Brotherhood) organized rallies in support of the ruling Military Council (SCAF). One of the most crowded of these was dubbed the 'Friday of Stability' and was organized to counterbalance the demonstrations of the leftists and liberals on the same day (which was called the 'Friday of Determination'). This demonstration featured many classical conservative themes, such as the need to put an end to the deteriorating street-level security situation, to uphold national security and to stop attacks against the military.[49]

Throughout this period of increasing tension and the entrenchment of animosity between the liberals and the left on the one hand and the Brotherhood on the other (late February–July 2011), the organization occasionally switched its tone, both to appease its own

47 Wickham, *The Muslim Brotherhood*, 170.

48 Fitna is a central evil that the Qur'an warns against. It should be noted that in various passages, fitna may have different meanings such as temptation or lure, rather than political division or sedition.

49 '7 Harakat Tusharik al-Islamiyyin fi Jum'a al-Istiqrar', *al-Masry al-Youm*, 24 July 2011.

(revolutionary) youth and to save face. For instance, it occasionally recognized that the protesters who remained in Tahrir during these months were indeed a part of the revolution (and not counter-revolutionaries in league with the old regime, as the Guidance Bureau sometimes insisted).[50] Such fluctuations would more or less cease after the summer of 2011.

Late 2011: The Anti-military Battles and the Parliamentary Elections

The Brotherhood also stayed away from the key revolutionary battles after Mubarak's overthrow. Not only did the organization avoid the December 2011 sit-ins against the ruling military (during which another nineteen people were killed), it implied that all of the abuses and murders during these two months would be pardoned under a Brotherhood-controlled parliament.[51] The organization's leaders did not forget to dub this 'a coalition between patriotic forces' (*quwwa al-wataniyya*),[52] attesting to the Brotherhood's persistent militarist-nationalism.

The Brotherhood thus became a bulwark against anti-military activism. As the revolutionaries pushed for an end to military rule during the first anniversary of the 25 January uprising, the organization celebrated the so-called revolution as an accomplished fact. But that was not all: the organization openly argued that military rule was legitimate due to the military's role in removing Mubarak.[53] It logically followed that the revolutionaries who fought against military rule in January 2012 were actually counter-revolutionaries. The Brotherhood crowned this nonsensical conclusion with the common stock of Mubarak and Brotherhood discourse: revolutionaries were spreading fitna.[54]

---

50 See 'Al-Islamiyyun yataʿahhadun bi ʿadam al-masas bi muʿtasami al-Tahrir', *al-Masry al-Youm*, 27 June 2011.

51 For a summary of military abuses after Mubarak, see Wael Iskender, 'Year of the SCAF: A Time-Line of Mounting Repression', 11 February 2012, english.ahram.org.

52 'Ghazlan: al-Ikhwan la yumaniʿun fi manh al-ʿaskari husana takriman li muwaqafihi', 31 December 2011, youm7.com.

53 'al-Hurriyya wa al-'adala ya'udd mashru' dustur .. wa yuwakkid: Mutasikkun bi jadwal al-'askari', almasryalyoum.com, 5 February 2012.

54 'Badi: Narfud thawra thaniya didda al-'askari .. wa mayzaniyya al-jaysh sa takhdu' li riqaba al-barlaman', almasryalyoum.com, 29 January 2012.

In essence, the Brotherhood had made its peace with the emergent post-Mubarak order. While revolutionaries were fighting military rule, the organization was preparing for elections under military rule. Military dicta also made the Brotherhood's job easy: the SCAF repressed and disorganized revolutionaries, making its electoral victories a foregone conclusion in the following months. The 6 April group and other revolutionary groups lamented that the military and the Brotherhood were cooperating to liquidate them: one was arresting them while the other was declaring them to be traitors.[55]

There were wide allegations of fraud during the two-phase parliamentary elections that ran from November 2011 to January 2012. The allegations regarding workers' votes in Mahalla al-Kubra, the industrial region that remained solidly revolutionary from 2011 to 2013, are telling in terms of the military–Brotherhood compact. It was alleged that Brotherhood militia aided the military in dispersing the workers who wanted to vote outside of their working hours. The military closed the polls after their shifts and declared all attempts to vote thereafter illegal.[56]

Because the newly elected parliament was controlled largely by the Brotherhood, the military regime and parliamentary Islamic rule effectively merged. Regardless of the intentions of the activists, protests against military rule began to be perceived as protests against Islam. In early February 2012, the Brotherhood mobilized militias to scare and threaten demonstrators, foreshadowing what was to come during its rule. Anti-regime demonstrations were pictured in the Islamic (printed and online) press as pro-coup, anti-democratic and anti-revolution.[57]

The Western supporters of the Turkish model became the global proponents of the Brotherhood's framing of these events. They

55 'Shabab al-Thawra al-Masriyya yazdadun ʿazla wa al-quwwa al-siyasiyya tajahalun dawrha', *al-Sharq al-Awsat*, 24 January 2012.

56 See 'al-Hurriyya wa al-ʿadala yusaʿid al-jaysh fi fadd al-tajamhur ʿummal al-Mahalla al-mutalibun bi al-taswit', almasryalyoum.com, 3 January 2012.

57 'Shabab al-Ikhwan: Tawajjahna ila al-parlaman li himayatihi min tajammuʿat musallaha. wa iltizamna al-sabr', digital.ahram.org.eg, accessed 2 February 2012; 'Manshit al-Hurriyya wa al-ʿadala hawla 'banditta' yuthir mawja min al-sakhriyya wa al-hujum ʿala al-Ikwan', gate.ahram.org.eg, 21 January 2012.

pictured the protesters as saboteurs out on the hunt for Islamic democrats. It is indeed possible that some of the elements that joined these protests were agents provocateurs who intended to heighten tension, spread violence and prepare the scene for a coup.[58] However, the internationally current version of the events omitted three key factors. First, the major groups that initiated the revolts in January 2011 were also a part of the protests in late 2011 and early 2012. Second, the protests had an anti-military, not only an anti-Brotherhood, agenda. Finally, the Brotherhood protected the military regime (both discursively and actively) from revolutionary assaults not only during, but also before and after these events.

The Egyptian Revolt and the Structure of Islamic Political Society

The structure of the Egyptian field of Islamic politics made a Turkish-style liberalization of religion quite difficult. The January revolt further fragmented Islamic civil and political society and rendered adaptation of the Turkish model even less likely. The Brotherhood could share power with the military to keep Egyptian Islam on a law-focused path (as the constitutional committee of early 2011 signalled) while engaging in a compromise with the military regarding marketization. This could perhaps lead to a bloc as hegemonic as that in Turkey, even if more conservative than the latter. The Brotherhood's increased willingness to emulate certain aspects of the AKP experience further bolstered hopes in this direction. The Brotherhood's leadership could even take the *whole* Middle East 'from the uneven development of neoliberalization' to the regional success of a 'deepened' neoliberalism.[59] However, there were serious impediments to replicating the Turkish model.

---

58 The *New York Times* stuck to this framing in the following years as the military regime of July 2013 (quite disingenuously) advanced major court cases against the overthrown President Morsi based on the killings allegedly carried out by the Brotherhood during these months. See, e.g., 'Egypt's Ex-President Is Defiant at Murder Trial', *New York Times*, 4 November 2013.

59 Neil Brenner, Jamie Peck and Nik Theodore, 'Variegated Neoliberalization: Geographies, Modalities, Pathways', *Global Networks* 10:2 (2010): 211–16.

First of all, the workers and civil servants were situated quite differently in the two countries, not only structurally, but as a result of the processes of the previous decades. The (still evolving) regime change in Egypt came through youth action in clear solidarity with the labour movement. By contrast, the regime change in Turkey (circa 2002–07) happened *despite* workers' resistance. Left-centre labour therefore lost a lot of democratic credibility. The Turkish regime change, moreover, was not the result of a revolution and strikes. The strike wave of 1989–95 did not lead to a regime change, but was one of the factors that precipitated a terminal crisis of the old regime. The 1997 coup, which was intended to resolve the organic crisis at the expense of Islamic, Kurdish and leftist opposition, was even supported by the centre and left-wing workers' unions, if not by the civil servants' unions. This gave the new regime a strong, and to some a legitimate, excuse to crush labour in the name of democratization. The Brotherhood *leadership* (but not all of the organization's wings) was trying to portray the still vigorous strikes and workplace occupations in 2011 as in league with the old regime (a sign that they were indeed learning from Turkey), but this was not a very convincing line, given the role of labour in the preceding few years. Even Brotherhood members went against their leadership's calls to end strikes and street protests after February 2011. Mobilized workers and youth,[60] along with some public and even Brotherhood sympathy for them, made it hard for the Brotherhood government (which was a work in progress at this point) to adopt a too strict neoliberal programme. The Brotherhood's own corporatist economic inclinations were another barrier (difficulties which will be examined in the next chapter).

A second factor that endangered a Turkish-Islamic style neoliberalization was the structure of the religious and political fields, the

60 For ongoing labour mobilization in 2011 and demands that clearly could not be met within a neoliberal order (living wages, permanent contracts, medical care, return to work of the recently fired, as well as halting privatization in certain sectors), see 'Al-i'tisaamaat ta'uud min jadiid ilaa rasiif Majlis al-Vuzaraa', www.almasryalyoum.com, 25 July 2011; 'Al-aalaaf yuwasiluun al-mudhaaharaat al-fi'awiyya ihtijaajan 'ala al-rawaatib wa al-ta'miin al-sihhiii', www.almasryalyoum.com, 8 March 2011; 'Fashal safqat 'Amr Afandi wa insihaab shurakaa' min al-'ard al-jadiid bisabab 'isyaan al-'ummaal', almasryalyoum.com, 8 March 2011.

fragmentation of which was further entrenched by the revolutionary process. The Brotherhood was in constant struggle with Salafi and other radical preachers and organizations (including the Jamaa) and had to adjust its tone according to their feedback. Consequently, while Islamists, liberalized right-wing nationalists, liberalized secularists and even liberalized Marxists could easily join forces against the left and Kemalism in Turkey, Islamists in Egypt were more likely to coalesce with Salafis (and even old regime forces) against leftists and liberals (as happened during the 2011 referendum regarding constitutional amendments).

Nevertheless, the further fragmentation of the religious field throughout the uprisings made even an Islamic bloc against the left and liberals quite unsustainable. First of all, the divisions within official religion (al-Azhar and the Coptic Church) proved too explosive and unpredictable. During the initial uprising against Mubarak, low-ranking clergy and students joined the protests alongside pious Christians, despite their leaders' condemnation of the protests.[61] While the Brotherhood (and later the Salafis) would try to picture the Christians as natural allies of leftists and enemies of pious Muslims, scenes of Christians praying together with the al-Azhar crowd, which became ingrained in popular memory, discredited such simple bifurcations of the population. Second, the uprising and its aftermath witnessed the further strengthening of Salafis. The Salafi currents not only strengthened religiously, but politically as well, as attested by the electoral gains of their newly formed parties in the coming months. These currents culminated in religiously and economically anti-liberal pressures on the Brotherhood.

Moreover, the Salafi pressures on the Brotherhood turned out to be more and more unpredictable. Not all of the criticisms from this camp could be classified as 'extreme right'. For instance, one of the major parties (al-Nour) veered from the Salafi path by announcing in July that the leftists and liberals who fought for the revolution had brought Egypt freedom. To further dramatize their differences from the other Salafis, the party underlined that al-Nour was not in the

61 Husam Tammam and Patrick Haenni, 'Egypt: Islam in the Insurrection', *Religioscope*, 22 February 2011.

service of the ruling Military Council,[62] which had incited the other Islamists to declare the protesters infidels.[63]

The divisions within the Islamist camp had economic dimensions as well. Until nearly full Brotherhood empowerment within the civil bureaucracy (by mid-2012) the economic policy differences among the Islamists did not seem to be that stark, but a careful reading of parliamentary debates reveals the seeds of divisions. At this point, all Islamists emphasized the necessity of Islamic economics, which created an aura of harmony. However, some argued that the remnants of Arab socialism had to be removed in order to implement an Islamic economics. Others, most notably the al-Nour leaders, emphasized the tight link between Islamic law and social justice: their stance was different not only from Arab socialism but also from Arab neoliberalism.[64] The devil was in the details and the subtle hints, and these indicators would become crucial to the political process once the Islamists grasped power.

This fragmented religious structure in Egypt had a mutually reinforcing relation with the internal structure of the Brotherhood, which remained based on piety and moral principles rather than political calculation (as opposed to the pragmatist, pre-2013 AKP), and allowed any splinters to be characterized as immoral rather than based on political differences (a tactic which had apparently failed in Turkey during internal strife within the Virtue Party, a failure that

---

62 'Hizb al-Nour al-Salafi: Muʿtasimu al-Tahrir aʿadu lana al-hurriyya .. wa lasna khadama li Majlis al-ʿaskari', *al-Masry al-Youm*, 26 July 2011. This declaration is retrospectively ironic given the developments of July 2013, when this party sided with the military against the Brotherhood. Nevertheless, al-Nour was not consistent in its siding with the revolutionaries against the military even in this earlier stage. For instance, during the battles of January 2012, it joined other Salafi groups to declare that the anti-military protests were acts of sabotage: 'Qiyadat al-Salafiyya: Daʿwat al-hashd li 25 Yunayir sadira min qilla turid al-takhrib', almasryalyoum.com, 20 January 2012.

63 Throughout this period, another key Salafi group, Ansar al-Sunna, not only remained firmly on the side of the military, but declared that all demonstrations and other kinds of action that defied the military's authority would be religiously illicit, even if carried out by Islamists. 'al-Islamiyyun yahdharun al-Majlis al-ʿaskari min thawra thaniya bi sabab al-mabadi' fawq al-dusturiyya', *al-Masry al-Youm*, 18 August 2011.

64 'Nuwwab al-Shura yutalibun bi iʿtimad al-nidham al-iqtisadi al-Islami fi al-dustur al-jadid', almasryalyoum.com, 26 March 2012.

enabled the establishment of the AKP). Moreover, even when the Brotherhood constituted a political party (the Freedom and Justice Party), the political leaders were picked based on their religious commitment rather than their ability to build coalitions and win votes.[65] Professionalism was not on the horizon even when institutional 'opportunities' most welcomed such a development.

Many intellectuals and Western centres of power still maintained their hope in pro-liberal Islamism despite these stark differences between the Turkish and Egyptian contexts. The contrasts between the AKP and the Brotherhood might become less sharp, some reasoned, if the Brotherhood were also elected into office as a single party. Such a victory would, in this view, allow the Brotherhood to apportion the spoils of neoliberalization among its constituency. These hopes were completely misguided: all along, it was more likely that the balance of religious forces would constitute right-wing and left-wing pressures on a Brotherhood-led government, pushing it to focus more on morality, piety and *shariah* rather than on growth and consumption in order to appease the Salafis and the Jamaa, and on redistribution programmes to appease its left wing.[66]

Two more instances further demonstrate how the revolutionary process and religious fragmentation rendered the liberalization of the Brotherhood a difficult task in 2011. The Brotherhood's cold response to the ex-Islamist Turkish prime minister's message during his visit to Cairo in September 2011 that a secular state is good for pious Muslims reflected not only the Brotherhood's entrenched anti-secularism. Such ideological convictions can be downplayed over the course of a passive revolutionary process, as the experience of Turkish Islamism shows. The cold response was also a reflex shaped by the existing balance of religious power, which would have led to the further empowerment of the Salafis and the Jamaa had the Brotherhood let Erdoğan's comments pass in silence.

The way the Brotherhood and other Islamic actors approached the constitutional amendment process also demonstrated how the

65 Wickham, *The Muslim Brotherhood*, 175–6.

66 I had already pointed out these possibilities in an earlier essay: 'Fight or Acquiesce? Religion and Political Process in Turkey's and Egypt's Neoliberalizations', *Development and Change* 43:1 (2012): 23–51. Some of the Egypt–Turkey contrast throughout this book draws on the analyses in that text.

religious field tied the Brotherhood's hands. Immediately after Mubarak's deposal, old-regime leaders coalesced with the Islamists to sideline liberals and leftists and pass modest amendments to the constitution to thwart thorough revolutionary change. Forces to the right of the Brotherhood quickly framed the whole issue of voting for or against the amendments as siding with or against Islam. The Brotherhood's opponents insisted that the organization was taking the same approach on the streets, while on the international and national scene it was framing the issue in terms of democracy and freedom. It was alleged that the Brotherhood hung posters that called voting in favour of the amendments a 'religious duty'. The Brotherhood denied the claims.[67] Regardless of the truth, the spread of these posters throughout the major cities demonstrated that it would be extremely difficult in the coming months to build a broad Islamist-(neo)liberal-old regime coalition to wipe out the remnants of corporatism, as the Turkish Islamists did. Egyptian Islamism was still too exclusive and potentially repressive, which deterred liberals from considering the viability of a liberal-Islamic power bloc.

Tunisian Islamism at the Crossroads

Tunisian Islamists faced similar processes of fragmentation and revolutionary pressure. Their responses at times resembled those of the Egyptians, but at others those of the Turks. Al-Nahda, thoroughly repressed by the regime, hardly participated in the revolt, let alone led it. Still, its leaders returned from exile as soon as the dictator had been removed. Al-Nahda's return to politics precipitated an already existing polarization. Even some of the leftist politicians and parties that had opposed Bourguiba's and Ben Ali's repression of al-Nahda were now alarmed by what they saw as an Islamic–Salafi invasion of the public sphere in the guise of a moderate party.[68] The international push for the application of the Turkish model in Tunisia contributed to this secular-Islamist polarization and its increasing marginalization of other axes of politics.

67 'Ikhwan Iskandariyya yanfun ʿalaqatha bi lafitat tuwayyid taʿdil al-dustur liannaha wajib sharʿi', *al-Masry al-Youm*, 15 March 2011. Also see Wickham, *The Muslim Brotherhood*, 171–2, for partial acceptance and remorse.

68 Laryssa Chomiak, 'The Making of a Revolution in Tunisia', *Middle East Law and Governance* 3 (2011): 68–83.

After the removal of the relatively more secularist Tunisian old regime, veiling, Islamic facial hair, charitable activities, Islamic schooling and construction of new mosques quickly spread throughout the country.[69] Though experienced as an era of freedom by many, this novel display of organized religiosity threatened others. Shortly before the first nationwide elections after Ben Ali's ouster, throngs occupied Tunisian streets in protest of the director of *Persepolis*, an animated film critical of the Iranian revolution. The motivation of the protesters, however, was not the film's political stance, but its depiction of God as a wise, elderly man.

Two decades of scholarship had emphasized how al-Nahda was completely repressed and disorganized. No one seriously predicted a sweeping Islamist victory at the polls, but it happened: the party got more than 40 per cent of the votes, while its closest competitor got 8 per cent. At this point, analysts claimed that the party was successful because it had organized successfully underground and in the prisons during the decades of repression; because it stood out as a symbol of resistance to the dictatorship; and because it carried out a successful campaign, especially in the countryside where leftist parties were nearly absent.[70] However, all of these explanations are problematic, since the same can be said about at least some of the leftist parties (organization underground and in prisons, resistance against the dictatorship, and some outreach in the countryside).[71] While a full explanation of al-Nahda's electoral victory requires more research, one factor that united close to half the population seems to be the

---

69 Teije Hidde Donker, 'Re-emerging Islamism in Tunisia: Repositioning Religion in Politics and Society', *Mediterranean Politics* 18:2 (2013): 207–24.

70 Erik Churchill, 'Tunisia's Electoral Lesson: The Importance of Campaign Strategy', *Sada*, 27 October 2011.

71 Haugbølle and Cavatorta, for example, base their alternative explanation on levels of religiosity and charitable activity that had been rising during the last two decades as a reaction to the regime's immorality, inegalitarianism and imposition of secularism. It is, however, problematic to assume that these grievances are then quasi-naturally translated into political Islam (especially of the liberalized variety), since they could have been framed and voiced in many different ways. Rikke Hostrup Haugbølle and Francesco Cavatorta, 'Beyond Ghannouchi: Islamism and Social Change in Tunisia', *Middle East Report* 262 (Spring 2012): 20–5. For a criticism of the assumption that political forces reflect social forces, see Cedric de Leon, *Party and Society: Reconstructing a Sociology of Democratic Party Politics*, Cambridge: Polity, 2014.

mirage of the Turkish model, which had kept the region under its spell for the previous decade: under its influence, some Tunisians were craving a Turkish-style combination of religiosity, economic success and global acceptability.

After claiming 40 per cent of the seats in the first elections, al-Nahda was sure to control the fate of Tunisia. It could perhaps lead the country in a neoliberal Islamic direction. What appeared especially promising in this regard was the unification of most Islamic forces (including the so-called Salafis) under the leadership of this moderate Islamic party. It seemed that divisions internal to the movement could be absorbed and postponed (as had happened in Turkey) to build a strong liberal, democratic and Islamic regime. Even though the unification was partially due to the legal exclusion of two Salafi parties, opinion polls showed that in any case they had extremely weak support. In short, Tunisia seemed like a strong candidate for the application of the Turkish model in 2011.

Turkey and the 2011 Revolt

The first part of this book argued that Egypt's religious and political structures were not favourable to the Turkish model of liberal Islamization. The barriers to following that path were further exacerbated by the 2011 uprising. Nevertheless, it was still possible for Islamists throughout the region to make use of the Western/global push for 'moderate Islam', especially post-2011: perhaps regional-global hegemonic forces could outweigh national hegemonic forces, as well as institutional and sociological realities. Tunisia provides an example of such a possibility.

Nevertheless, whether global hegemony could have this effect also depended on the way each (actual and potential) hegemon in the region acted – and most important was the stance and strategy of the emerging regional hegemon, Turkey. A clear, distinctly liberal Islamic and consistent Turkish involvement (when coupled with global hopes and interventions) could counterbalance (if not annul) the significance of national legacies.

However, the Arab uprisings actually dynamited the political liberalism of the Turkish model itself, if not (as yet) its economic liberalism. As the uprisings and regime changes unfolded, Turkey shifted further and further to the political and religious right (and to plain sectarianism), even if in an inconsistent way. Like its mentor the United States, Ankara sent mixed and contradictory messages throughout the Arab Spring, a deadly turn for a hegemonic model.

The Suicidal Right-Wing Diplomatic Shift[72]

Along with the US and most of the EU, the Turkey remained silent in January 2011 as protests against the Ben Ali regime mounted in Tunisia, in contrast to the immediate support for the movement offered, for different reasons, by Qatar, Iran and Hezbollah. Erdoğan made a more notable intervention on Egypt. Speaking on Turkish TV on 1 February 2011, a week after the first 'day of rage', he advised Mubarak to 'meet the people's desire for change with no hesitation': 'you must be first to take a step for Egypt's peace, security and stability, without allowing exploiters, dirty circles and circles that have dark scenarios for Egypt to take the initiative.' This was broadly in line with the Obama administration's call on 30 January for an 'orderly transition', and indeed followed Mubarak's announcement that he would not stand in the scheduled September 2011 presidential election.

Like Washington, Ankara was again silent as protests erupted in Bahrain in mid-February and turned a blind eye as demonstrators were shot and gassed at Pearl Roundabout. On 20 March, just a week after Saudi tanks rolled down the causeway to crush the democracy protesters, Erdoğan announced that Turkey and Saudi Arabia 'provide an important contribution to regional peace and stability, and exhibit a model cooperation'. Indeed, Erdoğan and Davutoğlu moved to consolidate Turkish relations with Saudi Arabia as the Arab Spring wore on, serving to strengthen the sectarianization – Sunni versus Shia and Alawi – of the region. Ankara was prudently silent about the uprising in Yemen as well, where Saudi and American interests might have been endangered had demands for jobs, living standards and democratization been satisfied. As repression took its toll, the divisions within the ruling tribal elite took on greater salience, eventually pitching tribe against tribe, rather than activists against the

---

72 Parts of this analysis on Turkey's involvement have been previously published as Cihan Tuğal, 'Democratic Janissaries? Turkey's Role in the Arab Spring', *New Left Review* 76 (2012): 5–24.

dictatorship. Tribal brokerage ultimately led to the removal of President Saleh without any major change in the state apparatus, which was still fit for purpose as far as the Saudis and the Obama administration were concerned. This retribalization of Yemen reached its apex with the declaration of a federation in 2014.

The politics of the Arab Spring underwent a decisive change with the militarization of the Libyan uprising, under the auspices of the NATO powers. On 17 March 2011, the 'international community' authorized itself to impose a no-fly zone – in effect, aerial warfare against the Gaddafi regime. The Erdoğan government was torn on this point. At first Erdoğan himself had been opposed to NATO intervention. On 15 March he announced in a TV interview that he had personally telephoned Muammar Gaddafi and advised him to listen to the people and appoint a new president. A lot of swerving followed, once the NATO operation was under way. On 25 March, a Turkish naval force was sent to enforce the blockade of Gaddafi-held ports. The Turkish parliament approved the dispatch of further forces, including troops if necessary. Turkish officials protested at France's Operation Harmattan stealing a march on the combined action of NATO powers, and the airbase at Izmir was offered as a base for the bombardment. The French countered that Erdoğan and Davutoğlu were piqued at not having been invited to the summit President Sarkozy had called. Sarkozy moved to block a leading Turkish role in the assault – which was not difficult, given the mixed feelings and internal divisions among pro-government forces in Turkey. Erdoğan and Amet Davutoğlu grudgingly settled for giving logistical support to NATO. In early July 2011 Davutoğlu flew to Benghazi to meet the Transitional National Council leaders and announce Turkey's recognition of the National Transitional Council as the legitimate representative of the Libyan people.

These inconsistencies were in good part caused by the difficulties of reconciling Davutoğlu's 'zero problem' approach with the realities of Turkey's Western alliances. Along with the US and other major Western states, Turkey had developed good business as well as diplomatic relations with Gaddafi, profiting in particular from the post-2009 Libyan construction boom. It was not clear that the violent overthrow of the regime would benefit Turkey, whereas the Western powers, who were more in control of the transition, could count on their ability to divide and manipulate the new Libyan powerholders. But the Turkish government's lurches had another source: the ideologues and activists from Islamist backgrounds, who still formed the ideological vertebrae of the AKP, had fought dictatorships – but they had also opposed Western military action in the region, which since 1990 had adopted, however selectively, the agenda of toppling dictators. Many of these AKP supporters were now making their peace with Turkey's sub-imperial role in the region as a bulwark of the NATO order. This has been the diplomatic and geopolitical dimension of the larger process of absorption that I described as a 'passive revolution' in the first part of this book. In May 2011 – a month in which over seven hundred Libyan civilians were killed by NATO airstrikes, according to Tripoli – Davutoğlu summarized the position of these former Islamist anti-imperialists with respect to the radical upheavals of the Arab Spring:

> A revolutionary spirit, a culture of rebellion has developed in this region . . . If I were not in this post, or if I were young, I would chant, 'Long live the revolution'. But as the big power [*büyük devlet*] that guards stability in the region, we have to make sure that the people are harmed as little as possible.[73]

A mature, 'disenchanted' empathy with youth and rebellion combined with a eulogy of order and stability; an 'ethics of responsibility' that upholds the state as the protector of powerless populations, even as its missiles rain down upon them; such are the achievements of the AKP's Turkish model.

In sum, by the summer of 2011, Turkey's interventions in the uprisings were being shaped by two major factors: political economy and ideological heritage. Given Turkey's growing capitalist orientation and its search for new markets and cheap labour, it was not clear which policies would help best in its competition with Western businesses. Ideologically, given how little Islamization the AKP had achieved in ten years, its ideologues and activists now saw the uprisings as the perfect opportunity for flexing their Islamic muscles. Two

73 Aslı Aydıntaşbaş, 'Davutoğlu'yla zor sohbet', *Milliyet*, 5 May 2011.

other factors interacted: with the slowing of growth after 2008, the AKP had ratcheted up Islamization at home to retain the popular fervour in support of the government. The uprising now, if rightly used, gave the AKP the opportunity to consolidate both its capitalist and its ideological credentials. However, during the summer of 2011, a third factor began to drive Turkey's foreign policy profile (which had experienced ups and downs in the first half of the year) in a new direction.

The Syrian Engagement: Turkey's Unintended Descent into Sectarianism

In Syria, the same free market policies that Erdoğan and Davutoğlu had been promoting through the regional Economic and Trade Association had helped to worsen the plight of youth in the country's run-down agricultural towns, from Daraa in the south to Homs, Hama and Idlib, which would be the centre of the revolt, while a tiny elite had grown spectacularly rich. Initially, in late March and April 2011, as Damascus met demonstrations with tear gas and water cannons, Erdoğan again tried to position himself as a mediator, attempting to persuade President Assad to negotiate with the Syrian Muslim Brotherhood and schedule elections. Even as Turkish naval ships were readied for the NATO operation against Gaddafi, Erdoğan was informing the international press that he had urged Assad to take 'a positive, reformist' approach: 'It is our heartfelt wish that there should be no painful events here as in Libya'. Ankara's aim was a managed democratic transition that would broaden the base of the Assad regime – a strategy of passive revolution which recognized that, if things were to stay the same, things would have to change. This would also be best for Turkey's economic interests: a peaceful, democratized environment, in which marketization could be pursued aggressively, would be beneficial to Turkish business as well.

This was in stark contrast to Riyadh's line, as conveyed to a former US State Department operative by a 'senior Saudi official', who noted that 'from the beginning of the Syrian upheaval, the King has believed that regime change would be highly beneficial to Saudi interests, particularly vis-à-vis the Iranian threat. The King knows that other than the collapse of the Islamic Republic itself, nothing would weaken

Iran more than losing Syria'.[74] The Iranian spectre kept on haunting the region in the most destructive way. As the Saudi position gained traction in Washington, the Turkish line also began to change. While maintaining contact with the Assad regime, the Erdoğan government in May 2011 allowed the leader of the military wing of the Syrian Muslim Brotherhood to give a press conference in Istanbul; in June 2011 Turkey organized a conference of the Syrian opposition. In July 2011 the Free Syrian Army (FSA), aiming at the military overthrow of the Assad regime, was established in the southern Turkish province of Hatay, with US logistical support and Saudi money and arms; FSA leaders were given the protection of the Turkish police. This could only serve to confirm Assad's fatally destructive decision, based on the Baath view of Syrian Sunni Islamists as owing allegiance to Gulf powers, to attempt to shore up the existing order by force. The principal demand of the FSA was for a no-fly zone – in effect, Western bombardment of Syrian defences. Its campaigns, focused mainly in the vicinity of Homs, were waged with one eye on the Western media embedded in its ranks; the greater the atrocity, the more likely it would be to create international pressure for US airstrikes. The death toll duly rose as Syrian forces shelled FSA positions in residential areas, and sectarian militias, both Alawi and Sunni, looted and killed amid the destruction.

In Turkey, the jingoism of the liberal and conservative press rose to a crescendo by early 2012. Calls for Turkish intervention also came from conservative forces in the Arab world, not least the London-based daily *Sharq al-Awsat*, whose main precondition was that there should be Western approval beforehand. The Muslim Brotherhood and other Islamist forces were happy to play the anti-imperialist card themselves when Erdoğan spoke of separating religion from the state, but they played the humanitarian intervention card when they wanted to get rid of a regime.

Turkey did not lead, but followed. The AKP's Westernist wing mimicked American initiatives, while the party centre came to adopt a cleaned-up version of Riyadh's line. Gül still paid special attention to appearing to be committed to the international (that is, the

74 John Hannah, 'Syria: The King's Statement, the President's Hesitation', *Foreign Policy* blog, 9 August 2011.

Washington) line. While both the prime minister and minister of foreign affairs gave bellicose speeches, he emphasized that Turkey was not interested in waging war, though at the same time vaguely claiming that this was the official position.[75] Erdoğan and his circle, however, became much more pro-intervention throughout 2013, frequently protesting the evermore sluggish moves of the 'international community', especially in the aftermath of Rouhani's presidency in Iran and the pending US–Iranian thaw. The AKP's lack of hegemonic initiative in Syria plunged the Turkish model into a coma: it got stuck between following Riyadh and following Washington, with disastrous domestic consequences. After this, the Turkish model continued in a vegetative state until its official death in June 2013.

Erdoğan's relatively more sectarian stance was reinforced by internal (social and intellectual) dynamics. Overall, the Islamic Turkish press was much warmer to the idea of intervention in Syria than in Libya, and for the worst of reasons. In addition to the sympathy for the Muslim Brotherhood and other Islamist forces in Syria, heavily targeted historically by the Baath regime, Islamists identify with Syrian Sunnis against the Shia (though neither sympathy had prevented the AKP from developing close ties with Assad). Although Turkey's marginalized and impoverished Alevis have different religious practices from those of the Syrian Alawis, and very few ties with them, the Syrian Sunni hatred of the ruling Alawite minority in Damascus was reproduced against them. The Turkish Islamist movement has been led, staffed and overwhelmingly supported by Sunnis, despite the existence in the country of this sizeable Muslim sectarian minority. In 2012, Turkish Alevis once again found chalk marks on their doors, reminiscent of those of the 1970s when Sunni mobs – led by the right-wing nationalist Grey Wolves, but drawing in conservatives and Islamists – carried out sectarian massacres. This ideological climate paved the way for sectarian killings by the Turkish police in 2013 and (later) Turkey's alleged support for the Islamic State of Iraq and al-Sham (ISIS).

75 Cumhurbaşkanı Gül'den önemli açıklamalar: 'Türkiye'nin savaş arzusu yoktur', zaman.com.tr, 20 September 2013.

The emergent Kurdish statelet further complicated Turkey's involvement. In northern Syria, the Party of the Democratic Union (PYD), the Syrian wing of the PKK, was the best implanted and most tightly organized of the Kurdish forces. In the summer of 2011, as the Erdoğan government gave its support to the FSA, Assad offered a citizenship deal to Syrian Kurds and stopped sharing intelligence on the PKK with Turkey. Ankara tried to get Masoud Barzani, the ruler of Iraqi Kurdistan, to impose his hegemony on the Syrian Kurds but the results were short-lived. When Assad pulled back his forces from the northern and southern borders to drive the FSA out of Aleppo in July 2012, the PYD was left in control of a string of Kurdish border towns: Ayn al Arab (Kobanê) and parts of Qamishli, Efrin and Amude. This move led to the gradual formation of an autonomous Western Kurdistan (Rojava) in 2013–14. Growing Kurdish autonomy was thus one of the dynamics that led to the end of the Turkish model, with the Turkish state eventually becoming more aggressive against both the Syrian Kurds and its own Kurds, and developing shady relations with ISIS.

Reigniting the Ashes of Imperial Rivalry

Finally, any revision of Turkey's relations with Syria would also mean a redefinition of relations with Iran. In the years leading up to the Arab Spring there had been a significant rapprochement between Ankara and Tehran, despite American (and Israeli) scepticism. The emergence of Iraqi Kurdistan helped the rulers of both countries converge in fighting Kurdish insurgency. Bilateral trade had increased significantly in the previous ten years; by 2012 Iran was Turkey's second-largest supplier of natural gas, after Russia. In May 2010, Turkey and Brazil brokered a low-level uranium-processing deal with Iran, both apparently thinking they had Washington's green light for it. By September 2011, however, Turkey had agreed to site a NATO missile-defence radar system near its border with Iran, though pleading that there should be no mention of Iran's nuclear programme as a rationale. Joost Lagendijk, former co-chair of the Turkey–EU Parliamentarians delegation, suggested that the US 'needs Turkey' not just to topple Assad, but also to contain Iran. Ruling out bombings and pointing out the ineffectiveness of sanctions, Lagendijk insisted on the centrality of diplomacy in the containment effort. He followed this thought with an emphasis on Turkish involvement:

> And there Turkey comes in . . . Because of Syria and the NATO missile shield, relations between Ankara and Tehran are not that cosy anymore. The US needs Turkey to bring down Syrian mass murderer Bashar al-Assad and to counter Iranian dominance in Iraq. Now is a good moment to reflect upon the most effective strategy on Iran that could avoid an Israeli attack that both Obama and Prime Minister Erdoğan don't want. . . . Above all, the US and the EU should accept the crucial role in new negotiations of emerging, non-traditional powers, such as Turkey, Brazil and South Africa, that are more trusted by Iran.[76]

In 2012, the (perceived) Iranian threat was still central in reproducing the Turkish model.

In the aftermath of the US occupation of Iraq, Israel's long-standing campaign to maintain its nuclear monopoly in the region coalesced with Saudi hostility to Iran and to the 'Shia crescent' that Riyadh sees extending from Iran, through Maliki's Iraq, to Syria and Hezbollah-run southern Lebanon. With the growing sectarianization, Turkey played an increasingly open part in a Western-backed Sunni coalition whose ultimate target during 2011–12 was Iran. If there were rumblings of discontent in the US, and among secular as well as conservative circles in Turkey, that Ankara was getting too cosy with Iran and even Ahmadinejad himself in 2009–10, the pendulum swung back, gaining added momentum from the Sunni background of the AKP and the broader Islamist movement. There was growing talk of a possible war with Iran, especially if Turkey decided to send troops into Syria. Simultaneously, the Sunni Arab press celebrated, with some caution, the arrival of 'Sunni Turkey'. Arab commentators, and some of their Turkish counterparts, invoked the historical rivalries between the Ottoman and Persian empires, as if the AKP regime needed any inflation of its imperial pretensions. Some Islamist intellectuals asserted that there was already a sectarian war going on, and that Iran, Iraq and Syria had started it. They jumped on the bandwagon of sectarianization, claiming that Turks could not ignore this 'fact' and that Turkey should be preparing to fight this out as a Sunni–Shia war.

---

76 Joost Lagendijk, 'Using Turkey's expertise to deal with Iran', *Today's Zaman*, 29 February 2012.

In Iraq, it was suggested, this could mean a coalition of Iraqi Sunni and Kurdish forces, with broader Arab and Turkish Sunni backing, aligned against Maliki's Shia-dominated government in Baghdad. There was a hint of this in April 2012, when the (Sunni) vice president of Iraq, Tariq Hashemi, took shelter in Turkey after first escaping to Qatar and Saudi Arabia, after the Maliki regime had issued an arrest warrant for him. The Iraqi government responded with a verbal attack, and Turkey retaliated in kind. In the middle of this cross-border shouting match, Massoud Barzani chose to visit Turkey and tensions rose still further. There was no doubt that the AKP government descended from its self-appointed throne of supra-sectarianism when it decided to harbour a high-profile figure internationally accused of sectarian massacres, even if some of the charges were fabricated (and others might be laid at Maliki's door). The regime confirmed, once again, the Sunni self-identification of the Turkish state. A couple of years later, Hashemi perhaps shaped the strategic thinking of his host when he characterized the rise of ISIS as a 'revolution of the oppressed, downtrodden and marginalized people'.[77]

Tensions with Iraq persisted in 2013, despite Davudoğlu's visit to Shia centres in Iraq to 'normalize' relations. His talks with the Iraqi foreign minister Zabari circumvented the primary diplomatic wound (the Hashemi affair).[78] Meanwhile, both the Arabophone and the Anglophone press were expressing amazement at Turkey's deepening relations with Iraqi Kurdistan and its apparent encouragement of further Kurdish independence in that country,[79] while its relations with its own Kurds worsened.

The Crumbling of Regional Leadership Hopes

Internationally, proponents of a Turkish model for the Islamic world often counterpose it to the examples of Iran or Saudi Arabia, set at

77 'Iraqi Kurds Maneuver between Maliki and Mosul', al-monitor.com, 13 June 2014.

78 'Davudoghlu yaksir jumud al-ʿalaqat al-ʿiraqiyya al-Turkiyya .. wa yahdhur min takrar ma'asa al-madi', *Al-Sharq al-Awsat*, 11 November 2013.

79 'Iraq's Kurdish Region Pursues Ties with Turkey – for Energy Revenue and Independence', *Washington Post*, 9 November 2013; 'Kurdistan al-ʿIraq tajid fi Turkiyya halifan ghayr mutawaqqaʿ fi saʿiha min ajl al-istiqlal', *al-Sharq al-Awsat*, 11 November 2013.

the opposite end of the spectrum. The developments of 2011–12 suggested a different picture. The main lines of demarcation in the region were becoming less ideological and were no longer drawn between the 'moderate Islamists' and the conservatives. The exacerbation of the Syrian conflict began to crystallize supposedly 'primordial' sectarian differences. Unlike as they may be in some respects, Saudi Arabia and Turkey now found themselves in the same camp, with Iran as the common enemy.

But though the situation changed (especially after July 2013), Saudi Arabia, with barely a third of Turkey's population, had the greatest success in shaping the current political flux in its own interests. Not a murmur was raised by the 'international community' when it subjected its own Shia population to the same treatment that Assad meted out to Syrian protesters. Erdoğan made a big show of his September 2011 tour of the Egyptian, Tunisian and Libyan capitals, accompanied by 280 Turkish businessmen ready to tap into cheap supplies of labour and declaring his intention to triple Turkish investment. The trip again underlined the inseparability of Turkish diplomacy throughout the Arab uprisings and the interests of Turkey's business class.

The visit also demonstrated the limits of Turkish influence. The Muslim Brotherhood had no objection to citing AKP Turkey as an economic model, but Erdoğan's call for a secular state incited a bitter 'anti-imperialist' response from the Brothers: the organization told him not to meddle in Egypt's internal affairs. Meanwhile President Morsi's first foreign visit was to Riyadh. The Saudi success was further corroborated by the July 2013 coup in Egypt, when a pro-Gulf general kicked the (Erdoğan-supported) Muslim Brotherhood out of power.

Turkey's willingness to put sectarianism before the principles of democratization and self-determination reached a dramatic apex in the Gulf. Bahrain, with its Shiite majority and Sunni autocratic monarchy, served as a litmus test. Not only did Turkey turn a blind eye when the monarchy violently crushed the protests; in the first months of 2012, as a prelude to increasing cooperation with the Gulf regimes, Gül visited the United Arab Emirates and demanded democracy for Syria during his friendly meetings with the autocrats there. Nothing could better illustrate the nature of Ankara's commitments to democracy and non-intervention in the region. Throughout 2011–12, Turkey only solidified its relations with the Saudis. The embarrassment in 2013 was more internationally visible. Turkey became more and more isolated, with Qatar and Turkey the only regional regimes to vociferously oppose the Saudi- and Gulf-backed coup in Egypt and side with the Egyptian Muslim Brotherhood. By early 2015, Ankara broke this isolation only by becoming a follower of the Saudi-led campaign against the Shia upheaval in Yemen and once again reinforcing the region's sectarianization. The consolidation of Saudi moral authority was sealed, as the AKP gradually fell silent regarding the Riyadh-backed Egyptian junta.

After the slight rapprochement between Washington and Tehran – as evidenced, among other things, by Maliki's cordial visit to the former – Ankara also sought better relations with Iraq and Iran. Some hopeful liberal analysts were even encouraged to exaggerate and declare that the AKP's foreign-policy was being 'reset'. Gül invited Rouhani to Turkey and Davutoğlu and Iran's new foreign minister met in a positive environment; the Turkish foreign minister visited Shia shrines in Iraq; and the prime minister started to verbally attack al-Qaeda after a long lapse.[80] In short, despite increasing tensions between Turkey and the United States, the new regime was still willing to take cues from the global hegemon to reshape its regional policy, but again, not necessarily in consistent ways: Ankara kept on pushing for the sectarianization of the Syrian conflict and sought military intervention, while differentiating between a good al-Qaeda and a bad one and apparently shipping arms to (at least) one of them. In Syria and within Turkey, the regime became more publicly anti-Alawi and anti-Alevi in 2013, but at the same time Iran was again declared a friend.

Instead of being the indicators of a 'reset', these contradictory moves demonstrated that Ankara was slowly losing its potential to be a regional hegemon. The June 2013 revolt in Turkey further undermined the calm self-confidence of the Islamic neoliberals. But they had been already led astray by the developments of the previous two years. By early 2014, there wasn't a trace of the imperial grandeur

80 Cengiz Çandar, 'Dış politikaya 'reset', bir tür 'Türk-Kürt ittifakı', bir tür 'Kürt bölünmesi', *Radikal*, 13 November 2013.

that had marked the speeches and appearances of the Turkish leaders.

What theoretical lessons can we draw from Turkish involvement in the Arab Spring? First, neither global nor regional hegemony is a given fact. It has to be constituted and reproduced. Hegemonic messages do not travel from Washington, DC, to Cairo in unmediated ways. Without the constant strategizing of hegemonic actors at multiple levels, consent cannot be built. Second, the blocs, civil societies and political societies of individual nations can be redone or undone by regional and global hegemons. Turkish involvement aborted the Syrian revolution (by militarizing it); but the lessons and hopes drawn from Turkey inspired and solidified the emergent Tunisian leadership. Third, attempts at regional hegemony are deeply shaped by internal dynamics. Turkey's political economy, the AKP's ideological heritage, and certain national specificities (the Alevi and Kurdish questions) both enabled and seriously restricted the country's temporary rise to regional hegemony.

Iran and the Arab Uprising

The protests in Iran predated the Arab uprising, but it is useful to take a closer look at them here, since they shaped the way the Iranian regime responded to 2011 and consequently impacted the regional hegemonic potential of this country. Analysing the 2009 protests in the context of 2011 also suggests both potentials for opposition and their limits in Iran.

The protests in Iran were in line with mainstream global hopes.[81] Perhaps the protestors there had even better reasons to look to the Turkish model than did their Arab counterparts. The wave of protest that began in Iran in 2009 brought to the fore the issue of freedom, but not that of social justice. It thus exhibited parallels to the wave of revolt covered in this book (as a response to the police state and

81 One scholar summarizes the goal of the protests as follows: 'political rights, greater cultural openness in the face of a strict Islamic code of conduct, less ideological/religious screening for jobs, better governance and political accountability, negotiated accommodation with the global order, and an end to cliquish corruption'. Farideh Farhi, 'Tehran's Delayed Spring?' *Globalizations* 8:5 (2011): 618.

authoritarianism), but was quite dissimilar in its lack of concern with commodification and other social issues. This is far from being a paradox, given that revolutionized corporatism had decommodified large swathes of social life.

Even the Iranian attack against authoritarianism was of a different mould. The Tunisian and Egyptian revolts overthrew dictators, but they were not content with the parliamentary democracy that replaced them. In Egypt, activists dubbed formal democracy 'sanduqocracy': the idolatry of the ballot box (literally, the power of the ballot box). They emphasized that in a country where most people did not vote and the remainder could not get organized except through either the old regime or Islamist parties, the ballot box did not necessarily reflect the power of the people. But their criticisms went beyond this problem and touched on the same issues that protesters brought to the fore in many places throughout the globe: the corruption of the existing parties, their unwillingness and incapacity to represent the people, and their manipulation by established elites. Indeed, the 2009–13 revolt was an uprising against the limits of representative democracy everywhere (including 'the West').

Except in Iran. Unlike even the Arab countries, there was a real craving for the basics of formal, procedural democracy in Iran. The protesters alleged that the clerics rigged the vote consistently, but did so even more maliciously during the 2009 presidential elections. Sticking to the rulebook of formal democratization would seem to bring serious advances in such a context.

Moreover, since the regime had spoken in the name of social justice for decades there was weariness with such rhetoric and the protesters did not resort to it. To the contrary, some of them wanted the development that commodification could bring. Turkey remained a model for some of the protesters in this sense, too. A part of the agenda of the protesters was support for the officially defeated candidates, Mir-Hossein Mousavi and Mehdi Karroubi, both veterans of the Islamic left who had turned their backs on anti-capitalism and become (Islamic) liberal democrats. Amazingly, relative isolation from the Western world brought about the type of social movements that Western pundits desired to see everywhere. Unlike their Tunisian, Egyptian, Turkish, Brazilian, Greek, Spanish and US counterparts, the Iranian protesters wanted liberal democracy. It appears that Western goods become truly desirable only in their absence.

This overall contextual difference gave rise to the middle-class revolt anticipated by modernization theory.[82] Professionals, whose mobility and expectations of a better life were blocked, revolted against the system. What modernization theorists have failed to note, however, is that these middle classes and their expectations (not only their frustrations) were the products of an expansive welfare system (and not a rentier state).[83]

Still, the protests exhibited some parallels to those in the Arab Spring and Turkey: the (apparent) absence of formal leaders, the heavy use of virtual technology, and the networked (rather than solidly organized) nature of the participants. But these formal similarities should not obscure the stark difference: as protests under a regime that at least officially resisted the neoliberal world order, the Iranian uprisings did not call into question the basic parameters of that order.

Still, the liberalism of these protests and their alignment with the new world order should not be exaggerated, since, after all, the activists were shouting 'Allah-u Akbar' from the rooftops. Despite their militancy, it is questionable whether a majority of the protestors had radical demands. How many desired an overthrow of the regime? How many desired liberalization within an Islamic and independent republic? We don't know the answers to these questions, but the main arguments in the public sphere (which is highly restricted in Iran) were in favour of liberalization within the regime.

Regime Response and the Contest over Claiming the Street

The brutal repression of the massive protests was much more successful when compared to the Arab revolt, despite the smaller death toll than the Arab cases (around seventy in Iran versus close to 1,000 in Egypt in only the three weeks that led to Mubarak's overthrow). This might partly reflect the more exclusively middle-class nature of the

---

82 Farhi, 'Tehran's Delayed Spring?', 619.

83 Kevan Harris, 'The Brokered Exuberance of the Middle Class: An Ethnographic Analysis of Iran's 2009 Green Movement', *Mobilization* 17:4 (2012): 435–55.

Iranian movement. But the intensity and depth of the repressive apparatus in Iran should not be neglected. Unlike in Mubarak's Egypt, Iran's paramilitaries and even the official repressive apparatus are the offspring of revolutionary mobilization. They therefore know how to assess the mood on the street and control it. It is extremely difficult to win even partial concessions through an uprising when your enemies are ex-revolutionaries. After a few demonstrations that numbered in the millions, the police and the paramilitaries gave smaller crowds very little chance to regroup and sustain protest. In February 2011, demonstrations flared up again in support of the Tunisian and Egyptian uprisings. This time, the repressive apparatus moved in much more quickly and prevented a 2009-scale uprising.

The Internet both helped mobilize and repress dissent. While public attention mostly focused on how Twitter and Facebook facilitated the Green Movement,[84] the regime also used the Internet in quite sophisticated ways.[85] According to one account, there were less than 20,000 Twitter users throughout the country at that time; it was Mousavi's circles and not the Twitter networks that organized the protests.[86] Moreover, the regime not only filtered, controlled, shut down and hijacked opposition websites, it also manipulated them to spread disinformation and channel protesters into self-destructive venues. The regime in addition sent threatening emails to protesters and published pictures and films of protesters online. The paramilitary *Basij* too used the Internet as a mobilizing tool. The regime even provided Internet-oriented lessons to the paramilitary to equip them with the latest technology in blogging, social networking and online spying.

To add to all of this, the Iranian 'Green Movement' also faced an arguably stronger (and multiclass) counter-movement. Ahmedinejad's factory shares distributing populism and anti-imperialist rhetoric

84 M. Hadi Sohrabi-Haghighat and Shohre Mansouri, '"Where Is My Vote?": ICT Politics in the Aftermath of Iran's Presidential Election', *International Journal of Emerging Technologies and Society* 8:1 (2010): 24–41.

85 Saeid Golkar, 'Liberation or Suppression Technologies? The Internet, the Green Movement and the Regime in Iran', *International Journal of Emerging Technologies and Society* 9:1 (2011): 50–70.

86 Evgeny Morozov, 'Iran: Downside to the "Twitter Revolution', *Dissent* 56:4 (2009): 10–14.

were backed by clerical, middle-class, Basiji and Revolutionary Guard mobilization.[87] Ultimately, the movement could not become the vehicle through which new blocs could be forged. The old (im)balances were reproduced.

Both the regime and the protestors claimed that the Arab Spring fulfilled their own desires. While the protestors saw direct continuity between themselves and the Arab protestors, the regime declared the final, regionalized victory of the 1979 revolution. However, the regime's interventions in Bahrain, Syria, Yemen and Saudi Arabia did not help its cause. In all of these cases, the Iranian regime was perceived as playing a sectarian card in order to expand its regional control, rather than pushing for dignity and social justice (let alone freedom).

Iran significantly contributed to militarization in Syria. Unapologetically siding with its ally, the regime not only gave a blank check to Assad but provided many resources. One consequence was the cessation of military cooperation between Hamas and Iran.[88] For Iran, this meant more than simply losing a key ally in the region. The Hamas–Iran alliance had allowed the regime to present its regional policy as one of resistance rather than sectarianism. Its leaders argued that they were building an 'Axis of Resistance', not a 'Shia Crescent', as the Western pundits and Saudi Arabia argued. When the relationship soured, the Axis of Resistance came more to look like a Shia Crescent (a good example of a self-fulfilling prophecy). In short, the Arab revolt had comparable results for Turkey and Iran. Both regimes saw an ideal opening to expand their regional hegemony, but they further delegitimized themselves in the process.

Approaching the End of Islamic Liberalism

The 2011 uprisings put the Turkish model more solidly on the mental and strategic map. While the old regimes were intact, a gradual transition to liberal Islam was next to impossible. The uprisings were ideal from this angle, in that they aborted the old regimes *without*

87 Farhi, 'Tehran's Delayed Spring?', 619–20.

88 Robert Tait, 'Iran Cuts Hamas Funding over Syria', *Daily Telegraph*, 31 May 2013.

offering anything new; they thereby brought to the centre of the strategic table the only serious alternative that had been on everyone's mind for a while, the Turkish model. In 2011, Ali al-Bayanouni (the Syrian Muslim Brotherhood's leader between 1996 and 2010) stated: 'The AKP is neutral in the area of religion – neither does it impose religion upon Turkish citizens nor does it seek to fight religion, and for this reason we find [it] to be an excellent model'.[89] In early 2012, the leader of Libya's National Transitional Council, Mustafa Abdul Jalil, also endorsed the Turkish model without any reservations:

> Turkey's democratic structure is an example for Libya and other countries that experienced the Arab Spring. Libya will take Turkey as a model for its own political and democratic structure. And our friendly relations will be much more powerful in the new era.[90]

Egyptian and Tunisian Islamists similarly endorsed the Turkish model.

As this chapter has demonstrated, however, the moves of the Turkish *state* did not help the cause of the Turkish *model* in the aftermath of the uprisings. The next chapter will analyze how the internal dynamics in Egypt completed the work the Turkish leaders started and thereby sealed the fate of Islamic liberalism in the Arab context.

---

89 'Islamic Evolution: How Turkey Taught the Syrian Muslim Brotherhood to Reconcile Faith and Democracy', *Foreign Policy*, 11 August 2011.

90 'Turkey Model for Countries of Arab Spring', *Anadolu Agency*, 13 February 2012.

CHAPTER 5

The Attempt at Passive Revolution

The Turkish model, an Islamic passive revolution, seemed a distant possibility for the Arab countries before 2011. The revolts boosted hopes that it could now be exported, but this was simply wishful thinking – the uprisings had actually made adoption of the Turkish model even harder. The Muslim Brotherhood's various passive revolutionary moves further undermined the basis for the replication of the Turkish scenario across the Arab world.

Yet failure of the Arab passive revolution was nothing to celebrate. Revolutionary action did not take Egypt in a productive direction. In interaction with the Brotherhood's clumsy passive revolution, it rather prepared the way for restoration. The failed passive revolution even led to the further empowerment of oil monarchies throughout the region. These unintended consequences of both revolutionary and passive revolutionary activity call for a rethinking of political action, which I take up at the end of this chapter with some preliminary notes on the theory of revolution.

Brotherhood Control over the State

Egyptian revolutionaries returned to the streets eighteen months after the ouster of Hosni Mubarak, and 2012 was a hot year in Egypt.[1] While the polarization of the country's political society across the Islamist–secularist divide was evident by this point, interpreting the dynamics of Egyptian politics through the prism of this divide would be highly limiting. More than just a struggle between Islamists and secularists, the new Egypt reflected a threefold division between partisans of the revolution, counter-revolutionaries and passive revolutionaries. The weakness of the organizational capacity (and anarchistic-autonomist tendencies) of Egypt's revolutionary camp

1 The pre-election parts of this chapter draw on a previously published essay, 'Egypt's Passive Revolution', jadaliyya.com.

contributed to the (still shaky) triumph of the country's passive revolutionaries in 2012, as evidenced by the Muslim Brotherhood's success in the presidential election.

The Footsteps of the Passive Revolution

The division between the three camps was marked by their commitment to revolutionary goals (or lack thereof), rather than pure ideological or religious principles. In other words, the role of Islam in the new Egypt was by no means the major question defining the country's emergent political arena. In fact, all three camps encompassed individuals and groups desiring a more Islamic Egypt. The passive revolution was gaining momentum in Egypt because the old regime had faded, but its challengers proposed only vaguely defined promises (for example, 'liberty' and 'social justice'), without giving meaning to these broad promises or mobilizing popular support behind *concrete demands*. The Islamic–secular divide, then, was one factor among many in this process and not yet the defining one.

The leading actor in the passive revolution in Egypt was no doubt the Muslim Brotherhood – 'Mubaraks with beards', as one (Islamic) opposition figure described them to me. Conventional western perceptions of the Brotherhood, oscillating between the image of a dangerous theocratic force and, more sympathetically, an agent of democratic change, ignored the group's most striking feature. Specifically, many local observers in Egypt saw the challenge of the Brotherhood's growing power not in a threat of building an Islamic regime but rather in the group's unilateralism and tendency to monopolize power. Thus, many feared that the Brotherhood could exploit revolutionary momentum and discourse to advance goals that were inconsistent with the basic demands of this revolution – such as the group's interest in deepening the neoliberal project in Egypt.

The lines between the three camps were not static but were instead a set of dynamic political boundaries that could be modified or undermined by other dimensions of political conflict. For example, while the breakdown of Egypt into three camps was apparent during the lead-up to the 2012 presidential election when candidates positioned themselves vis-à-vis the revolution and its goals, these same divisions were largely orthogonal to the political battles surrounding the constitution-drafting process. During this process, conflict revolved around spats over the role of Islamic principles in the new political system, thereby crowding out conflicts between partisans of the revolution and their adversaries.

It is therefore not surprising that revolutionary movements failed to have much impact over the constitution-drafting process. Lacking political organization, leadership and experience, the revolutionaries could only attack the military-managed transition from outside that process. Meanwhile, the Islamists and the 'civil forces' (*madaniyin*) bickered under the shadow of the military, fighting over the balance of representation between Islamists and secularists inside the Constituent Assembly rather than over the extent to which those selected to write the country's next constitution would uphold the revolution's demands of liberty, dignity and social justice.

Leaderless Revolts or Disorganized Leaders?

This brings us to the crux of the problem that faced Egypt's revolutionary process from 2011 to July 2013, namely the inability of the revolutionaries to participate meaningfully in *institution-building* processes due to their lack of organization, experience and programmatic vision. This shortcoming kept the field wide open for passive revolutionaries and those who wanted to appropriate revolutionary discourse and goals for the purpose of advancing narrow agendas. This is not to say that the revolutionaries did not see the importance of the battles shaping Egypt's new political institutions. Revolutionary movements frequently issued statements discussing the flaws of the constitution-writing process and criticized politicians for bickering over seats in the Constituent Assembly rather than advancing the goals of the revolution. Such statements, however, made no lasting impact. The problem was not that revolutionary activists overlooked battles over institution-building, but rather that no one would lend them an ear among the players engaged in these elite-driven conflicts. The absence of revolutionary political organization in effect shielded the process of institution-building from the demands of the revolution.

This is precisely the weakness of the 'leaderless revolution'. It is perhaps possible to overthrow a dictator even in the absence of leaders, experience and programme. But building institutions and formulating and executing policies and platforms are impossible without leaders to shoulder these burdens.

The disorganization of activists in Egypt was not a conscious choice, as was the case with many Western-based protest movements post-2009, but rather a limitation imposed by the legacy of the old regime. The late president Anwar al-Sadat and his successor Hosni Mubarak had destroyed all political organization in Egypt save the Islamists and a few loyal opposition parties. The remnants of the old regime, including the country's post-Mubarak military rulers, harassed, tortured and killed revolutionary activists. They also collaborated with passive revolutionaries to limit their role in shaping Egypt's emergent political institutions, including its new constitution.

Furthermore, disorganization among revolutionary forces was reflected in the ambiguity surrounding their calls for social justice and their failure to define this goal in concrete terms. The 'professional capacity' necessary to build such a vision (and then weave class and other forces into a sociopolitical bloc in support of that vision) takes more than the well-meaning efforts of bright individuals. It demands the concerted effort of leaders, cadres, intellectuals and experts over the course of years, if not decades – not just of those that might appear in the heat of a revolutionary moment.

As a result of the disorganization of revolutionary forces, supporters of the revolution had to settle for presidential candidates hailing from Egypt's traditional class of political elites, who failed to offer a coherent vision of how to advance the revolution's calls for freedom and social justice. These candidates included Abdel Moneim Abul Futouh and Hamdeen Sabbahi. In the second round of the vote, the choice that revolutionaries faced was even worse, specifically one between the counter-revolution and the passive revolution, namely Mubarak's last prime minister, Ahmed Shafik, and the Muslim Brotherhood's candidate, Mohammed Morsi. In this context, partisans of the revolution could not find an alternative on the ballot who truly represented them. They could either vote for Morsi, the lesser evil when compared to Shafik, who was the candidate of the old regime, or they could boycott the presidential election altogether. With some reluctant revolutionary support behind him, Morsi won the presidential race.

The Egyptian experience offers lessons for political activists worldwide. Passive revolutionaries are most likely to carry the day if revolutionary situations emerge in the absence of a transitional programme and an organization with mass ties to mobilize support behind a revolutionary vision. As demonstrated by post-Mubarak Egypt, in such a scenario, passive revolutionaries may emerge as the only viable alternative to counter-revolutionaries – but obviously, they are not 'alternatives' in a robust sense.

The Old Regime and the Brotherhood: From Convergence to Clash

The military first seemed to resist recognizing the results of the 2012 presidential elections. There was high drama as the Brotherhood supporters occupied town squares and declared that they would not leave until the results were officially recognized. However, the press revealed that the military and the Brotherhood were in fact bargaining behind the scenes.[2] The military was simply pressing for the preservation of its privileges in return for allowing a Brotherhood candidate take over the presidency.

The Brotherhood now combined the power of the presidency with that of the parliament. According to the Arabic Network for Human Rights Information, the first couple of months of the new presidency saw the deaths of around 100 activists.[3] The Brotherhood regime also curbed the independent press. The culmination of the new regime's pressure on the liberal press came towards the end of its rule: *Egypt Independent*'s weekly edition was banned from going to press in the spring of 2013. Nevertheless, the adaptation of old regime techniques by the new regime was far from smooth. Unlike Turkey, the changes within the religious field, ongoing protests and the resulting feebleness of neoliberal direction rendered the old regime–new regime convergence troublesome.

The Reconfiguration of Islamic Political Society

Right after the elections, the Islamists seemed to constitute one united front against the secular forces, yet they soon turned against each other.

---

2 'Egypt Army, Islamists in Talks to Resolve Impasse', reuters.com, 23 June 2012.

3 'Reach of Turmoil in Egypt Extends into Countryside', *New York Times*, 15 September 2013.

The rifts were widespread, though those between the Nour Party and the Brotherhood seemed sharpest. Even the Brotherhood's staunchest ally throughout the process, Jamaa Islamiyya, criticized the organization on issues of social justice and poverty. Though it reserved its more serious criticism for the left and the liberals, it held the Brotherhood partly responsible for the worsening economic situation.[4] Jamaa insisted that the Brotherhood was not doing enough to promote social justice and to make a clean break with Mubarak-era economic policies.[5]

The Nour Party had much harsher criticisms of the Brotherhood. It shared with the Jamaa criticism of the Brotherhood's weakness on social justice issues. The vice president of al-Da'wa al-Salafiyya (the mother organization of Nour) accused the Brotherhood of working with the United States, which served local and foreign businessmen rather than the poor.[6] For several months, the party also attacked the Brotherhood as a monopolizer of power. As early as January 2013, it held behind-the-scenes meetings with the Salvation Front (the coalition of liberal and old regime forces). At the end of that month, these meetings came out into the open and the party called for a unity government that would include secular forces.[7] The party defended its negotiations with secular forces on the grounds that all means were legitimate in the effort to promote national unity and dialogue (which the Brotherhood had undermined through its lack of cooperation with non-Brotherhood forces).[8] The Brotherhood soon fired back. Morsi dismissed one of his aides, a member of the Nour Party, which caused even more anti-Brotherhood mobilization among the Nour's ranks.[9] While Islamic neoliberalism had also faced much

4 'Mutashaddidun Islamiyyun yattahimun Jabhat al-Inqadh bi tabanni al-'unf qabil mudhaharat siyasiyya al-yawm', *al-Sharq al-Awsat*, 15 February 2013.

5 'Al-Mutahaddith bi ism al-Gama'a al-Islamiyya: Morsi ahamma Shar'iyya . . . wa tathir al-muassasat lam yatahaqqaq ba'ad', almasryalyoum.com, 17 January 2013.

6 'Barhami: al-Gharb yahsal 'ala amwalna thumma yuhasirna biha', almasryalyoum.com, 11 January 2013.

7 'Egypt Rivals Hold Rare Meeting and Call for Dialogue', *New York Times*, 31 January 2013.

8 'al-Islamiyyun yuwajihun salbiyyaat al-Ikhwan li al-istimrar fi al-hukm', *al-Sharq al-Awsat*, 4 February 2013.

9 'Mustashar al-Riasa al-Masriyya al-Muqal li al-Sharq al-Awsat: al-Ikhwan yaghraqun . . . hawalna inqadhhum wa rafadu', *al-Sharq al-Awsat*, 19 February 2013.

Islamic criticism in Turkey for over ten years, this opposition was mostly outside of parliament and the major institutions of the state. The fragmented Islamic political society in Egypt carried these religiously motivated disturbances to the heart of the attempted passive revolution, seriously interrupting it.

Two factors stopped the Brotherhood regime from immediately imploding: the still-intact internal discipline of the Brotherhood and the paramilitary support of Jamaa Islamiyya (which, it turned out, was a mixed blessing, not least because it fostered popular sympathy for anti-Brotherhood military violence). One important factor that reinforced unity among Islamists was the confusing condition of the police forces. On the one hand, most of the police forces were still boycotting the post-revolutionary situation by simply staying off the streets. On the other hand, there were frequent reports in liberal as well as in old regime media that the Brotherhood was also infiltrating the security forces (claims which the Brotherhood adamantly denied). While the tensions between the Brotherhood and the police mounted, there was greater concern in the mainstream that the intensifying street protests, crime and chaotic traffic could get completely out of hand in the absence of the police. In March, the Jamaa rushed to the help of the Brotherhood by threatening the protesters (and the larger public): they would enforce order if the police forces failed.[10]

In the following months, there were more and more reports of Islamic groups and individuals (possibly connected to the Jamaa) 'enforcing order' based on Islamic precepts. Paramilitaries not only started to control the streets but also began terrorizing protesters. Some factions of the Islamic movement were gradually returning to the militarized strategy of the early 1990s, but now targeting revolutionaries more than the security forces.

Economic Impasse

Throughout its attempted merger with the state, the Brotherhood not only followed the Turkish model from a distance, but sent delegations of politicians and bureaucrats to Turkey to actively learn from Turkish practice. These teams systematically travelled to Turkey and

10 'Safwat ʿabd al-Ghani: al-Gamaʿa al-Islamiyya lan tanzil li himaya al-munshat illa law insahaba al-aman', almasryalyoum.com, 9 March 2013.

attended programmes that consisted of fifteen to twenty lessons on the banking system, social security, health care and education. They also met and talked with government ministers. Tunisians and Yemenis also participated in these programmes.[11] There was no public information on the contents of these lessons, but we can get a glimpse of what the Brotherhood learned from the Turkish model by studying its policies during its year in power.

Developmental Policy

Overall, both the transition military regime and Brotherhood rule continued Mubarak's liberal development policies. An unimaginative Egyptian neoliberalism remained dependent on oil, gas, tourism, Suez Canal revenues and foreign direct investment. Partly due to political instability, the revenues from these sectors proved unstable in the months following 25 January 2011. As a result, the budget deficit increased, and so did external debt, which became Egypt's main method of covering its deficit (followed by foreign aid). The external debt reached as high as 30 per cent of the budget in January 2013.

Throughout the crisis, the main policy recommendations circulating in the corridors of power and the international press emphasized attracting foreign investment (inevitably scared off by the turmoil), rather than strengthening either local businesses or the government sector. Even though modern Islamist economic ideology enshrines small and medium-sized business, the Brotherhood continued their marginalization in favour of foreign companies, their subsidiaries and other local big businesses.[12]

In 2012, pro-Brotherhood businessmen established a business association following the example of the Turkish Islamist business association MÜSİAD. In their official platform, these businessmen

---

11 'Bürokratlar ders alamamış', *Taraf*, 8 July 2013. Even though we don't know whether these lessons included information on how to fight the remnants of the old regime, the pro-passive revolution liberal Turkish newspaper *Taraf* subtly implied (through a title that had nothing to do with the content of its news on these lessons ('The Bureaucrats Were Not Able to Learn Their Lessons') that the Egyptians were not able to draw the right *political* lessons from these programmes. The paper thereby suggested that not imitating Turkey thoroughly enough was the cause behind the coup in July 2013.

12 'Today, like Yesterday: Policies of the Former Regime Linger, Much to Detriment of the Economy', *Egypt Independent* 50, 25 April 2013.

argued that MÜSİAD had aided the decentralization of Turkey's economy and the development of small and medium-sized businesses, neglecting research that demonstrated the strength of opposite tendencies (see chapter 3). Their association would, they argued, rechannel the focus of Egyptian businesses from speculation and cronyism to productive development.[13] Their role models, the AKP and the MÜSİAD, had also used the same rhetoric while at the same time actually reinforcing business–state interdependence, financialization and speculative growth in Turkey.

Meanwhile, the Brotherhood emphasized its pro-business credentials and even attempted to woo back Mubarak-era businessmen who had fled Egypt out of fear of persecution due to their links with the old regime. In other words, the Brotherhood desired continuity not only with Mubarak-era policies but with the Mubarak-era dominant class as well. The sly businessmen did not rush back.[14]

However, the overall promises of the Brotherhood regime were not that consistent. The organization's website still reflected many unresolved issues. For instance, in early 2012 Morsi published a piece that promised more business promotion and wage controls. Typically, the exact tools for accomplishing either remained unspecified, despite the length of the article.[15] In the meantime, the Brotherhood promised to American audiences an unregulated market, while promising to workers at home high wages and unionization.[16]

These policy debates and moves left very little room for considerations of social justice, one of the four fundamental themes of the Arab Spring, and the implementation of maximum and minimum wages, the only solid demand that emanated from this theme. Implementation got stuck in the bureaucracy, and this theme was mostly used for purposes of political legitimation rather than serious

---

13 'Brotherhood Businessman Urges Business to Play Role in Development', 15 April 2012, egyptindependent.com.

14 David J. Lynch, 'Egypt's Islamists Woo Mubarak Tycoons as Mursi Seeks Funds', 14 February 2013, bloomberg.com.

15 Mohamed Morsi, 'FJP Chair: FJP Visions for Egypt's Future', ikhwanweb.com, 1 January 2012.

16 See the contrast of tone and content in the Anglophone and the local press for this dual strategy: 'Overtures to Egypt's Islamist's Reverse Longtime US Policy', *New York Times*, 3 January 2012; 'al-Tahaluf al-Damoqratii yajtami'li munaqasha ajandathu al-tashri'iyya', almasryalyoum.com, 6 January 2012.

discussion. Economists also mobilized to oppose the measure. Some Salafis pushed for it, but ran up against the Brotherhood's opposition (a factor which fed into the fragmentation of Islamic political society). Labour activists were highly critical because the actual steps remained vague. For example, proposed laws did not specify whether the requirement of minimum and maximum wages applied to the private as well as the public sector.[17] While the more neoliberal parties, such as the Free Egyptians, opposed minimum and maximum wages generally, the Brotherhood occasionally tried to find a middle path between strict deregulation and the demands of the revolution. For instance, during parliamentary proceedings its leaders granted that the private sector should be left to its own devices when setting wages, while some controls could be established in the public sector.[18]

Left-wing economists also voiced demands for more progressive tax policies that would both redistribute income and help reduce the budget deficit, even though this did not become a programmatic demand of the revolt. The Brotherhood systematically avoided steps in such directions. Nevertheless, its tax and revenue policies did not satisfy orthodox economists either, since the organization did not completely play by the rulebook of neoliberal economics. For example, the Brotherhood regime applied higher taxes to foreign cigarettes, raising eyebrows among 'experts'.[19] The experts also kept on pressing for quick acceptance of the IMF programme (and especially its cuts in subsidies),[20] to no avail.

In short, there was very little economic debate and legislation after February 2011 that could appease the popular classes *or* unite the regime, the dominant classes and the experts to help them weather the revolutionary storm. The emergence of mass protests became unavoidable.

17 'Maximum and Minimum Wage Law Lacks Details, Faces Obstacles in Implementation', egyptindependent.com, 25 February 2013.

18 'Al-Sha'ab yuwafiq 'ala tahdid 135 alf ginih ka had aqsa li al-ujur', almasryalyoum.com, 23 April 2012.

19 'Rais al-Dara'ib: Hazin li diya' hasila maliyya bi sabab iyqaf ta'dilat al-dara'ib', almasryalyoum.com, 10 January 2013.

20 Niveen Wahish, 'Telling It Like It Is', *al-Ahram Weekly*, 10 January 2013.

Protests

Port Sa'id exploded in late January 2013 as a reaction to murderous police brutality against soccer fans. The core demand was political and economic independence from the 'Brotherhood state' (the protestors' own words). This was a multiclass revolt with businessmen and professionals participating as much as the labour unions. Consequently, the demands were disparate, including government non-interference in the economy, the establishment of free trade zones and a generous minimum wage. This Suez Canal town witnessed a general strike in February; the ideological atmosphere reinforced by the strike, though, resembled American libertarianism more than revolutionary syndicalism.[21] This was, in a sense, the Egyptian Revolution's Kronstadt: rather than attacking the platform of the Brotherhood as such, the revolt's main impact was weakening the government and pushing it to heavy-handed violence, thereby rendering neoliberal peace impossible (just as the Kronstadt rebellion had undermined the consent-building capacity of the young Soviet regime by using Soviet slogans and pushed the regime to adopt a dictatorial position).

The Port Sa'id rebellion resulted in a mini-military takeover. Anticipating what was to come in a few months, some local residents cheered the arrival of the military and the restoration of order. A few of the protestors even invited the generals to take over the whole country, though others shouted that they wanted to rip the soldiers apart as well, not just the much-hated police.[22] Port Sa'id was a rehearsal for the July coup.

Even though the initial Port Sa'id push was libertarian, the strike incited more pro-labour protests in Egypt's industrial zones. Workers in the Nile Delta towns of Mahalla and Mansura struck and blocked roads in February. They also called for acts of civil disobedience such as refusing to pay electricity bills.[23] Egypt was thus still marked by

21 I would like to thank to Nezar al-Sayyad for drawing my attention to this point. Still, much research remains to be done to ascertain the exact character of this turning point in recent Egyptian history.

22 'As Crisis Deepens in Egypt after Ruling on Riot, Calls for a Military Coup', *New York Times*, 9 March 2013.

23 'Civil Disobedience Launches in Egyptian Nile Delta Cities of Mansoura and Mahalla', *Ahram Online*, 24 February 2013.

dynamics that were the reverse of the Turkish case, where neoliberalism was predominant (up until June 2013). Instead of all protests being converted to a liberal language, as in Turkey, even potentially pro-neoliberal and proto-libertarian protests incited dynamics and protests that put neoliberalism at risk.

Meanwhile, other types of socio-economic protest (which had been waxing and waning ever since February 2011) intensified during early 2013. There were several demonstrations and marches against unemployment. Consumer associations and street mobilizations also drew attention to price hikes.[24] Still, as throughout the Arab Spring, the political representation of these protests remained weak or problematic. Even during the anniversary of the establishment of the 6 April Youth Movement, the focus was squarely on political issues and rights. The commemorations expressed only symbolic solidarity with the workers and their demands.[25]

The IMF Package

Global capitalist dynamics were as decisive in undermining Egypt's passive revolution. The IMF's involvement in the process is a clear example of this global–national interaction. The Brotherhood sent mixed messages regarding its position on the IMF package, stretching from the days when it was not in full power to the months following the presidential elections. This suggests that there was a lot of unpublicized push and pull within the organization, since Morsi and others made proclamations now sympathetic to, now distrustful of the IMF. For instance, in the middle of ongoing negotiations with the IMF (carried out by a government which was not yet under full Brotherhood control), Morsi announced that they were not against the IMF, but that this institution was not helping the Egyptian people: neither the IMF nor the government were transparent regarding the loan proposed in early 2012, which was likely to increase the debt burden on the Egyptians rather than help them develop. Under these conditions, the Brotherhood would have to seek other resources (a subtle

24 'Harakat ijtimaʿiyya tu'ajjij mashaʿir al-ghadab didda al-nidham', 26 March 2013.

25 '6 Abril tuwajjih indharan akhiran li Morsi wa al-Ikhwan fi Yawm al-Ghadab', 7 April 2013.

hint at Gulf money, the possibility of which the organization used as leverage in its negotiations with the IMF after July 2012).[26]

Early in March 2012, Brotherhood leaders trumpeted to the Western press that they 'did not have any difficulty with the Monetary Fund'.[27] This turned out to be an overstatement. The IMF representatives would soon leave Egypt and point to the discord between Islamists and government officials to account for the failure of the negotiations.[28] They had reached an agreement with the government, the IMF representatives explained, but parties in the parliament (including the Brotherhood) as well as the ongoing strikes throughout the country prevented the deal from materializing.

After coming to power, the Morsi government promised several times that it would follow 'economic logic' in its policies. The regime faltered, however, on the heels of the anti-austerity protests of early 2013. Tax increases and subsidy cuts that had been announced as imminent were again suspended in March 2013. Since the IMF loan the government so badly needed was dependent on these measures, this step back threw IMF–Brotherhood relations into disarray. How could the Brotherhood's neoliberals implement such measures when faced with a striking, road-blocking disobedient citizenry without further resort to force? The Brotherhood proved inept in its economic management, in contrast to the Turkish Islamists' smooth implementation of an IMF programme in the early 2000s.

The following weeks and months also witnessed riots by several groups regarding the IMF package. In response to the regime's attempts to liberalize bread prices and desubsidize bread, bakery owners from all over Egypt gathered in Cairo to block streets. They also prevented the distribution of flour to bakeries. Even though these actions were militant, protesting bakery owners spoke the regime's language of liberalization and contested the details of the policy

26 'Al-Hurriyya wa al-ʿadala yaltaqi Wafd al-Naqd al-Duwali . . . wa yu'akkid ghiyab al-maʿlumat ʿan ihtiyajat al-muwazana', almasryalyoum.com, 19 March 2012.

27 'Reuters: al-Ikhwan yamilun li qabul qard Sanduq al-Naqd', almasryalyoum.com, 8 March 2012.

28 'Bloomberg: Baʿtha al-Naqd ghadarat al-Qahira dun taqaddum bi sabab khilafat al-Islamiyyin wa al-hukuma', almasryalyoum.com, 22 March 2012.

rather than its spirit.[29] At the same time, however, labour action featuring anti-neoliberal demands persisted. Fuel shortages, soaring food prices and electricity blackouts became more intense as March turned to April. The government's ongoing negotiations with the IMF under these conditions led to further protests in April.[30]

Moreover, the Brotherhood did not encounter difficulties only on the streets. Islamists were divided among themselves when it came to the IMF package. The Nour Party, especially, fought militantly to block acceptance of the IMF programme. Its criticism was not based on social justice concerns alone: the party questioned whether the package conformed to Islamic precepts (especially on the issue of usurious interest).[31] Seeking to push Egypt towards a more clerically controlled regime, al-Nour also held that the ulama had to be consulted on issues of foreign debt, to which the Brotherhood responded pragmatically and liberally: the source of power in democracies was the people, and the parliament would be of no use if the clerics decided everything![32] The Brotherhood was able to block such theocratic attempts this time around (in February 2013), but the regime it was building paved the way for more to come. The revolutionary process, the street protests and the balance of Islamic forces rendered the situation in Egypt much more complex than it had been in Turkey, where the AKP's passive revolutionaries never encountered such Islamic law–based *economic* resistance to their policies.

Neither willing to perpetuate Mubarak's corrupt crony neoliberalism, nor able to purify it, the Brotherhood regime ended up in frustrating stagnation. By May 2013, unemployment had risen to 13 per cent and growth was hovering at around 2 per cent annually (compared with 9 per cent and 5.5 per cent, respectively, under Mubarak). Faced with ever more shortages, the Brotherhood maintained that there were enough oil and food, but certain people were

29 'Differences over Bread', *al-Ahram Weekly*, 21 March 2013.

30 'Wafqa ihtijajiyya amaam 'Dar al-Qada', didda Qard Sanduq al-Naqd al-Duwali', *al-Masry al-Yawm*, 3 April 2013.

31 'Al-Nour: Qard al-Naqd yajib an yahsal ʿala muwafaqa kubbar al-ʿulama', almasryalyoum.com, 12 February 2013.

32 'Salafiyyu al-Shura yarfudun qardan Awrubiyyan li shubha al-riba . . . wa al-Ikhwan: al-fuqara yahtajunhu', *al-Masry al-Youm*, 10 February 2013.

hoarding, stealing and causing panic, both in pursuit of egotistic economic gain and to destabilize the regime. This Brotherhood analysis was mimicked by the *New York Times* after the July 2013 coup: old regime forces had created a false shortage. However, the reality was more complex. In the ever-vibrant political scene in post-Mubarak Egypt, consumer activism was on the rise. As a part of this activism, a group of associations frequently drew attention to the multiple causes behind the persistent shortages. They partially agreed with the Brotherhood's analysis: some hoarders were maximizing profits in the black markets. However, they criticized the Brotherhood for allowing most of this activity and actually participating in some of it.[33] Old regime conspiracies, to the degree they existed, only reinforced the economic, religious and political structures which were already unconducive to a passive revolution. Prominent analyses of the July coup, which focus either on conspiracies or simply the Islamic–secularist divide, ignore these global capitalist dynamics and their interaction with the labour and Islamic scene in Egypt.

July 2013: Restoration

This overall context prepared the ground for what some naïvely called the second revolution. Millions mobilized to topple the Brotherhood, but their actions ultimately led to a military–judiciary seizure of power, with the support of centrist politicians and clerics.[34] The result was 'popularly supported military rule', by more or less the same military-police-judicial-business elements who had been in power during Mubarak's reign and who had struck a (shaky and incomplete) coalition deal with the Muslim Brotherhood.

The Reassertion of Elite Rule

Tamarod, an unprecedented grassroots campaign, collected millions of signatures and called for President Morsi to step down. Huge crowds gathered all around Egypt on 30 June 2013, in order to reinforce the campaign's demand. The main mood among the Tahrir

33 'Jamaʿiyyat al-Mustahlikin: azmat al-solar sababha al-suq al-sawda' wa al-tahrib', almasryalyoum, 18 January 2013.

34 Parts of the analysis of the July 2013 coup in this section were previously published as 'The End of the "Leaderless" Revolution', 10 July 2013, counterpunch.org.

Square protesters seemed to be pro-military. There were even groups that openly called for a military intervention. Not only pro-Mubarak civilians, but also thugs and Mubarak-era security personnel came to the square in their uniforms. During the month of June, it had become increasingly clear that the military intended to use the rebellion as an opportunity to intervene.

There were calls for a general strike during the protests of 30 June, alongside louder calls for military involvement. In fact, the national situation that set the scene for Tamarod had a labour dimension, though it was not articulated firmly as a part of Tamarod's platform. Moreover, some of the left-leaning groups in Tahrir (6 April, Strong Egypt Party, Revolutionary Socialists) protested openly against the military, not just the Brotherhood.

When the military intervened, a few anti-coup speeches and slogans were drowned by the overall pro-military atmosphere in Tahrir. The unfounded optimism that anti-militarist forces would remain in Tahrir Square until the military left did not change the main dynamics. Nobody mobilized Tahrir to fight their erstwhile torturers. Ultimately, July 2013 witnessed not only the removal of an unpopular president but the making of a full-fledged dictatorial regime: a hasty crackdown rounded up hundreds of Brotherhood and non-Brotherhood Islamists. Many television channels were closed down. The military appointed an old regime judiciary figure to replace the president. The massacres that followed were the necessary ingredients that accompanied any military takeover: the new/old regime brutally murdered hundreds, perhaps thousands of Brotherhood members.

A few months after Tamarod's 'success', some of its primary organizers turned against its top leaders, who kept on siding with the military well into 2014. They declared to the press that they had been tricked into a coup and that a coup had not been their goal.[35] This naïveté was a product of not only the national Egyptian context, but the post-1980 overall global atmosphere, in which revolutionary organization and strategizing were looked down upon or even ridiculed. Revolutionary uprisings, in the current context, are supposed

35 'Stuck between Two Revolutions: A Conversation with a Former Member of the Tamarod Campaign', madamasr.com, 25 January 2014.

to proceed without well-trained organizers and strategizers – giving a free ride to conspirators.

The success of the coup consisted not only in deposing the Brotherhood, but in pushing civil and political forces to the side of restoration. Once-independent journalists came to be backers of military dictatorship. So did many political leaders of what I called the 'Official Revolution' in the previous chapter. What remained of Nasserism, as represented by Sabbahi, embraced the coup's leader (General Abdel Fattah al-Sisi) and declared him a hero. Sabbahi still dragged his feet while following the steps of the dictator, as when he announced, during an interview on TV, that al-Sisi's decision to run for presidency was wrong while still insisting that the general had 'saved' Egypt.[36]

Liberal and Radical Misinterpretations

Most of the initial responses to the military intervention missed the crucial point: under the Brotherhood–military coalition, Egypt was quickly moving from popularly supported authoritarian rule to popularly supported totalitarian rule. Tahrir activists exhibited the will to slow down this transformation, but not the tools to stop it without the military's pernicious 'aid'. Procedure-focused liberal critics of the military intervention completely ignored that under certain conditions, an elected president can help build a totalitarian regime that will render all future elections simple plebiscites. The street needed to act to defend the Egyptian revolution and perhaps even to recall the president. Liberal accounts, with their pronounced fear of the mob,[37] ruled out not only such risky moves, but all other forms of participatory democracy.

As dangerous were the accounts that listed the abuses of the Brotherhood–military regime but stopped short of discussing the calamities a non-Brotherhood military regime could produce (and did indeed produce in the coming months). Those who called the military coup a 'second revolution' pointed out all the autocratic

36 'Bi al-Fidyo: Madha Qala Murash'shihu al-Riasa al-Sabiqun 'an a-Sisi', shorouknews.com, 29 January 2014.

37 Noah Feldman, 'Democracy Loses in Egypt and Beyond', bloombergview.com, 3 July 2013.

moves of the Brotherhood regime,[38] but they did not explain in what sense the military junta that replaced it had democratic potential. (A broader circle of pro-Tamarod intellectuals focused on the illegitimate moves of the toppled president without going into whether or how these legitimized the moves of the military and the judiciary after he was deposed.)[39]

The assertion, frequently seen in both the English and Arabic newspaper commentaries, that 'all the factors that rendered 25 January a revolution also legitimized calling June 30 the second revolution' ignored one blatant fact (along many others): 2013 was not 2011.[40] The two years that had passed had led to different social and political possibilities. During these two years, the priority could have been organizing popular power, alternative institutions and revolutionary leadership in order to prevent (or at least slow down) the increasing authoritarianism of those in power rather than hastily toppling them to open the way for the revolution's previous enemies.

These misinterpretations can actually be mapped onto the general theoretical and political tendencies of the day regarding not only the Middle East but global politics as well. On one end of the spectrum, we find liberal analysts who expect democratization from reforms to existing institutions. They have lamented the July coup and pictured a victimized Brotherhood as the main hero of Egyptian democracy, and Morsi as an Egyptian version of Salvador Allende. On the other end of the spectrum are most of the radicals, even though we find some left-wing liberals there as well. On that end, the coup was met first with denial, then mostly silence.

Liberal scholars and journalists compared the coups against Morsi and Allende, and after an article in the *New Yorker* to that effect the comparison went viral. Morsi can one day come to occupy a place in the pedestal of democratic consciousness as a vanquished hero. However, given the Brotherhood's and Morsi's generous cooperation

---

38 Hani Shukrallah, 'Egypt's Second Revolution: Questions of Legitimacy', english.ahram.org.eg, 4 July 2013.

39 Khaled Fahmi, 'al-shar'iyya wa al-thawra', shorouknews.com, 5 July 2013.

40 Ahmad al-Sawi, 'thawratan aw inqilaban', shorouknews.com, 5 July 2013.

with the military during their tenure, the two situations are far from comparable (and not just because the ideologies of the two leaders are quite different, as is usually and quickly noted). Allende didn't have an inkling of what the Chilean military was capable of: the latter was mostly a hands-off institution. Likewise, there is no indication that Allende knew much about General Pinochet when he appointed him. By contrast, the military had ruled Egypt brutally and repressively for several decades. The Brotherhood knew the military's capacities and intentions very well. It openly played with fire, knowingly slept with the enemy. The coup's leader, al-Sisi, was on record for his humiliating handling of revolutionaries and the rounds of torture he had orchestrated.

It is possible that the Brotherhood was again following the famous Turkish model: it was only apparently coordinating with the military, but its real, hidden goal was removing, even prosecuting and persecuting the murderers. This is possible – yet it should be noted that, unlike Turkey, there were active street battles and nationwide campaigns against military rule following February 2011. The Brotherhood took no part in these struggles, and it occasionally resisted and condemned them. Even if the Brotherhood stealthily aimed to liquidate the generals (which is quite doubtful), it wanted to do so *without the aid of and in the absence of revolutionaries*. It wanted to make sure that these fitna-makers were out of the picture first. In stark contrast to Allende, then, Morsi cooperated with the military regime in order to suppress dissent. The Brotherhood (or at any rate, some of its leaders) chose to work with the counter-revolutionaries against the revolutionaries, rather than vice versa. It was later to pay dearly for this choice.

In a mirror image of the liberals, radical commentators insisted that neither the military nor the National Salvation Front (the coalition of anti-Brotherhood centrist politicians) represented the masses in Tahrir, whose real demand was democracy and early elections. This disclaimer on behalf of the apparently pro-military millions does not alter one of the rules of thumb of politics: those who cannot represent themselves will be represented.[41]

---

41 'They cannot represent themselves, they must be represented.' Karl Marx, *The Eighteenth Brumaire of Louis Bonaparte*, 1852.

This old statement regarding the nineteenth-century French peasantry warns us against the beautification of unorganized masses, a romanticization now in high fashion. Multiple anti-representation theses from rival ideological corners (anarchist, liberal, autonomist, postmodernist and so on) all boil down to the following assumption: when there is no meta-discourse and no leadership, plurality will win. This might sometimes be true in the short run. Indeed, in the case of Egypt, the anonymity of Tamarod's spokespersons initially helped. The 'spokespersons' (who were not leaders, it is held) could not Ube vilified or demonized as partisan populists. Moreover, thanks to uniting people only through their negative identity (being anti-Brotherhood), as well as to its innovative tactics, Tamarod mobilized people of all kinds. Nevertheless, the mobilized people fell prey to the only existing option: the old regime!

When the revolutionaries do not produce ideology, demands and leaders, it does not mean that their revolt will have no ideology, demands and leaders. In fact, Tamarod's spontaneous ideology turned out to be militarist nationalism, its demand a postmodern coup, its leader the *feloul* (remnants of the old regime). This is the danger that awaits any allegedly leaderless (we should instead call it disorganized) revolt: appropriation by the main institutional alternatives of the institutions they are fighting against.

The folk belief (or more precisely, the propaganda) that Tamarod had no leaders also deserves closer scrutiny. The movement indeed had identifiable, though young and inexperienced, leaders. These leaders were strongly pro-military, even though some of them had fought military rule earlier in the uprising. As late as August 2013, after all the bloody massacres, this mixed prehistory of the movement bred false hopes among the intelligentsia of a possible fallout between the movement and the military.[42]

The misinterpretations of the coup, in sum, were not only analytically fallacious but politically devastating. They either summoned the passive revolutionaries to protect the Egyptian revolution or postponed, in many circles, the realization that a thorough restoration was taking hold of Egypt.

---

42 'Egypt's Rebels Who Lost Their Cause?', huffingtonpost.com, 30 August 2013.

Economic Measures

Though I have described Egypt's top military leaders as counter-revolutionaries, their post-coup performance demonstrated that they had learned from the Brotherhood, and perhaps from other cases of passive revolution as well. The lines between passive revolution and counter-revolution can in fact be quite blurred.

One of the post-July military regime's policies was buying off the opposition based on revolutionary promises. In early October 2013, the regime increased the minimum wage, though it failed to specify where the funding for this increase would come from. No maximum wage was stipulated. The legislation was quite haphazard. For instance, the law did not restructure the pay scale at the bottom of the wage hierarchy (let alone at the higher scales).

At the same time, the military regime continued the anti-union policies of the Brotherhood (which in turn had only extended the anti-union policies of Mubarak and Sadat). The pro-military constitutional committee simply retained the former (Brotherhood-written) constitution's wording regarding strikes: they were allowed as long as they were peaceful, but the parliament would decide whether they were so.[43] The constitution they drafted also retained the illegal status of the new independent unions and reproduced the dependence of the official workers' union, as instituted by Nasser. However, al-Sisi also projected himself as an inheritor of Nasser the populist as well, promising many benefits to workers and the poor in the future. In sum, the restoration is still in the making and its economic ingredients are far from clear.

Islam and the Aftermath of the Coup

Will the coup further fragment Islamic political society or lead to the emergence of something like the Turkish AKP (which could undermine the restoration in the middle run). The difficulties facing the Brotherhood in this regard are many, and in the first months following the coup religious forces became even more divided than before.

Al-Azhar came heavily on the side of the despicable massacres of Brotherhood members. ʿAli Gumʿa (the former Mufti of Egypt), and many other official figures, spoke favourably of the post-July 2013

43 'Workers' Rights under Attack', *Al-Ahram Weekly*, 8 October 2013.

repression. Qaradawi and other pro-Brotherhood clerics shouted against them on television screens.[44] Both sides used not only religious vocabulary, but also solid references to the Qur'an and the Hadith. Using mainstream, orthodox Sunni language, both accused each other of being '*Khawarij*', that is, those who have left the correct path, and both based this accusation on the grounds that the other side did not obey a righteous, legitimate leader (for some Morsi, for the others Sisi). Qaradawi also used 'Sufi' as a curse against ʿAli Gumʿa.

It should be recalled that the Turkish Diyanet (Directorate of Religious Affairs, the Turkish guardian of official Islam) was not so heavily deployed during the military's repression of Islamists in 1997. Even if it had been used in this way, it is unlikely that it would have had the same influence. Turkish official Islam has not been as divisive of (Islamic) political society.

Al-Azhar is arguably the most prestigious and oldest Islamic institution of education, scholarship and training in the world. Even though some have interpreted its reduction to an official organ as an old regime success (or, depending on the perspective, curse),[45] al-Azhar has actually backed stability and preached obedience throughout its history.[46] This position, moreover, is theologically in line with a key precept of 'traditional Islam': obedience to legitimate authority in order to preserve the unity of the Ummah. Legitimacy is defined here in a minimalist way, as the authority's ability to preserve an Islamic lifestyle throughout the land.[47] Based on this precedent

---

44 'Bi al-Fidyo .. "al-Inqilabiyyum" hum "al-Khawarij" .. wa 'ali Jum'a "'abd al-Sulta" ', almasyalyoum.com, 26 August 2013.

45 Al-Azhar's (and therefore official Islam's) subordination to the old regime should not be interpreted as a complete abdication of its will, since the institution has pursued its own agenda under the wings of the regime, for example, by attacking secularist intellectuals, Islamizing education and the media, and intervening in debates about population control, especially during Mubarak's reign. Steven Barraclough, 'Al-Azhar: Between the Government and the Islamists', *Middle East Journal* 52:2 (1998): 236–49. As a result, the institution's fervent anti-Islamism and pro-Mubarakism has not cost all of its legitimacy. The institution will probably play a similar role in the new Egypt and therefore it shouldn't be too quickly assumed that it will lose its legitimacy only because it has supported the coup.

46 Hatem Bazian, 'Religious Authority, State Power and Revolutions', aljazeera.com, 15 September 2013.

47 Nazih N. M. Ayubi, *Political Islam: Religion and Politics in the Arab World*, London: Routledge, 1991.

(and a huge bureaucracy and tradition of training, which attracts people from all over the world to pursue their education), al-Azhar holds an authority not easily comparable to the Turkish Diyanet.

The extensive links of al-Azhar with civil society built (and continues to build) further consent for the old regime. Al-Azhar figures sit on the boards of many charitable and philanthropic associations. They write columns for newspapers. There is no tight separation between civil society and official Islam.

Moreover, when the Brotherhood dared to mobilize the people against the generals, it not only faced stark opposition from official Islam but raised stirrings among the Salafis as well. The latter are motivated not only by their own take on Islam (more literalist and more obedience-oriented than even official Islam), but influenced by their solid ties to the Gulf as well. The most visible bifurcation in the Salafi field in the recent years has been its division into pro-military and pro-Brotherhood factions. However, if this were all, we could perhaps safely predict the marginalization of the pro-military factions and Turkish-style unification behind a single organization in the long run. In reality, the picture is much more complex. Two of the major Salafi organizations (Ansar wa al-Sunna and al-Gamaʿiyya al-Sharaʿiyya) have tried to sever themselves from the whole process and keep a distance from *both* the Brotherhood and the military regime in order to stick to their *daʿwa* and charity operations. Other major organizations are thoroughly dispersed and disorganized, and it is not clear which of the poles of attraction they will drift towards.[48] This leads to the further fragmentation of Islamic political society.

Labour and Islam in the Tunisian Process

The Tunisian uprising led to a more complete demise of the old regime, which precipitated the formation of an Islamist-led government. This coalition government, which included liberal elements, perpetuated the old regime's economic policies and links with the West. Unlike the Ben Ali regime, however, it faced both an Islamist insurgency and mobilized labour. Both became fatal for its chances of following the Turkish model.

---

48 Khalil al-Anani, 'Salafis Try Their Hand at Religious Politics', *Washington Post* (blog), 5 November 2013.

Labour mobilization was more than a thorn in the side of the Tunisian passive revolution. Sidi Bouzid became the centre of calls for a general strike starting in April 2012.[49] Serious unrest erupted here in the summer of the same year.[50] Calls for social justice were now directed against the Islamist-led government, and the general strike in this provincial town, which had kicked off the Arab Spring, called for a second revolution.[51]

More protests all over Tunisia followed in December 2012.[52] In January 2013, militant protests against unemployment were staged in a provincial town, which prompted the military to intervene to suppress dissent.[53] Other demonstrations and strikes shook the whole country during the second anniversary of Ben Ali's escape. The Islamist leaders admitted that they had been unable to address social problems such as poverty and unemployment.[54] It was in this atmosphere that two prominent leftist leaders were assassinated.

One of these leaders was Chokri Belaid. Belaid had been involved in labour and in socialist politics from his youth onwards, and he had been committed to uniting the Tunisian left. The international press, following its routine of reducing the tensions in the Arab uprisings to the secular–religious divide, presented him as a 'secular' politician. However, neither the new regime nor its opponents were characterized primarily by their religious or anti-religious sensibilities. Unlike the Brotherhood government in Egypt, the coalition government in Tunisia had a strong secular contingent. The street opposition also contained secular elements, but these assassinated leaders were first and foremost leftist leaders.

49 'Tunisia: General Strike Called in Sidi Bou Zid', opendemocracy.net, 11 April 2012.

50 'Tunisia: General Strike Staged in Sidi Bouzid', allafrica.com, 14 August 2012.

51 'Tunis: idrab ʿam fi Sidi Bouzid . . . wa al-hukuma taʿtabirhu ghayr-mubarrir', *al-Sharq al-Awsat*, 15 August 2012.

52 See, e.g., 'Sidi Bouzid to Go on General Strike Tomorrow', tunisia-live.net, accessed 24 March 2014.

53 'Tunis: intishar quwwa al-jaysh fi Bin Kurdan istijaba li matlab sukkanha', *al-Sharq al-Awsat*, 14 January 2013.

54 'Tunis: ansar al-hukuma yahtafilun bi al-dhikri al-thaniya li al-thawra . . . wa al-muʿarada tahtaj', *al-Sharq al-Awsat*, 15 January 2013.

The fragility of Tunisia's Islamic neoliberalism is demonstrated by the factors surrounding these assassinations. Organized and mobilized labour was no longer content with neoliberal policies, so in the regime's view labour leaders needed to be killed to clear the way. Islamists of various stripes were willing to assassinate prominent public personalities (or at least, they were unable to thwart conspiracies by old regime elements in this direction).[55] In short, a Turkish-style passive revolution became very unlikely in Tunisia.

The assassinations did not help the new regime much. More instability followed. For several months, both the government and the opposition parties called for national dialogue. Steps were taken to form a more stable government, but with no immediate results. A sector of the left refused to take part in these attempts at dialogue (while the UGTT and old regime forces joined in discussions). These leftists argued that 'dialogue' would be a cover for nontransparent elections.[56]

Meanwhile, labour protest continued, with 2013 experiencing a 14 per cent increase in strike activity according to government sources. The new regime remained steadfast in ignoring labour. It not only declared strikes illegal but pointed out that employment and wages would go up only if people 'worked harder'; strikes wouldn't help.[57] In other words, the new Tunisian regime was neoliberal not only in its policies, but also in its discourse and orientations: it staunchly subscribed to the creed that unemployment, poverty and low wages were due to individual shortcomings, most of all laziness.

Under these pressures, Rachid el-Ghannouchi, who has the reputation of being the world's top Islamist democrat, posted a comment on the *Guardian*'s webpage.[58] He rightly pointed out that his party had avoided monopolizing power and consistently shared ministries with certain secular forces and figures. Even though Egypt was not

---

55 Speculations abounded in regards to who actually murdered these leaders. Was it the governing Islamist party or the Salafis? Or perhaps it was old-regime elements trying to create the conditions for a coup, just like in Egypt?

56 'Bad' jalsat al-hiwar al-watani al-Tunusi fi zil ghiyab ahzab al-yasar', *al-Sharq al-Awsat*,16 April 2013.

57 'Ra'is hukuma Tunis fi ʿeed al-ʿummal: la li al-idrabat al-ashwa'iyya', *Al-Masry al-Yawm*, 1 May 2013.

58 Rachid Gannouchi, 'Tunisians Must Choose Ballots over Bullets if We Are to Secure the Revolution', theguardian.com, 28 October 2013.

mentioned, the negative reference was obvious. The Islamist democrat implied that his party was not the Brotherhood. However, he also avoided the real challenges they faced by attributing all of the violence to old regime conspiracies and implicitly denying that the religious situation in his country had become unmanageable. Recognizing them would be admitting the similarity to Egypt. But el-Ghannouchi actually shared a central tendency with the Egyptian Brotherhood in his characterization of the Arab revolt. He reduced the Arab Spring to a revolt for 'freedom and dignity', thereby marginalizing the other two core slogans of 2011–13: social justice and bread. These demands were what the assassinated leader Belaid advocated. Like the Egyptian Guidance Bureau, the top Islamist leaders in Tunisia decided to fight a now open, now covert fight against one face of the revolution.

As regards the 'Turkish model', Ghannouchi gave somewhat similar signals to those of the Egyptian Islamists. When speaking to a Turkish newspaper, he emphasized that he regarded the Turkish economic path as the most desirable one. However, in other contexts he also alluded to Swedish social democracy as his primary economic model, attesting to an even more confused state of mind than that of the Egyptian Islamists. But when it came to issues of religion and state, he was very clear: the AKP's neo-secularism was not the way to go. The Tunisian state would be based on a democratic form of Islamic law, not secular law as in Turkey.[59]

In line with this perspective, the governing party flirted with the Salafi currents, some of which remained inside the party. By March 2012, official sources estimated that Salafis had gained control over 400 mosques across Tunisia, in some places by ousting the former imam from office.[60] This Islamist offensive didn't look anything like the Turkish model.

In this confused atmosphere, it was not clear where the alleged Salafi 'sabotage' against the new regime was coming from (religious actors from within the party? religious rejecters of the party? old-regime conspiracy?). In this sense, the fragmentation of Islamic political

59 'Tunisian Islamist in Favor of Mild Shariah', *Hürriyet Daily News*, 7 October 2011; 'Ghannouchi: State Does Not Have Right to Monopolize Islam', *Today's Zaman*, 23 September 2011.

60 Teije Hidde Donker, 'Re-emerging Islamism in Tunisia: Repositioning Religion in Politics and Society', *Mediterranean Politics* 18:2 (2013): 207–24.

society in Tunisia was quite different from that in Egypt. Rather than organizationally and ideologically challenging the moderates' monopolization of religion, even Salafis gathered under a single roof institutionally, only to dynamite it from within.

Regardless of who predominated within Islamic political society, the overall context was also different from the Turkey of the 2000s. During the AKP's first ten years, Islamists had already been successfully demobilized (first by military intervention, then by the ruling Islamic party itself). By contrast, the ruling party in Tunisia was operating in a context of sustained mobilization. Unlike the AKP's glory years, even the first few months of the Tunisian Islamists' tenure in government were marked by intensive street mobilization that called for the Islamization of various institutions. These included the state television, the universities, and the ministries.[61] Al-Nahda walked a tightrope: it had to give the message that it shared Islamic mobilization's demands while simultaneously convincing everyone else that it was not building an Islamic state. We can't know at this point how much al-Nahda was able to convince its own base, but the perceived threat of an aggressively Islamizing ruling party led to a consolidation and counter-mobilization of the secularists.

As a result, a coalition of secularists, old regime elements, some leftist forces and labour defeated the Islamists in the October 2014 elections. It is too early to declare the end of Islamic liberalism in Tunisia, but the cards are currently stacked against it. In response to al-Nahda's willingness to relinquish power following democratic elections, there was loose talk of a 'Tunisian model' in the international press. It is, however, premature to celebrate establishment of a settled democracy since the paths of labour, the Salafis and al-Nahda still remain unpredictable.

The Interactive Making of Institutional Failure: An Explanatory Framework for Post-Revolt Processes

What can the partial failures and successes of Egyptian and Tunisian revolt teach us about revolutions in general? Most scholars of revolutions and mobilization want to come up with a few basic factors that would allow us to gauge the likelihood of mobilization. Humanities

61 Ibid., 216–8, 220

scholars, but some social scientists as well, argue against them: revolutions are by definition irregular events, they point out. Therefore, they can't really be explained, let alone predicted. These two extremes are dead ends. Actually, social sciences provide us with tools to study how the revolutionary process unfolds, even if they might not be able to predict when and where revolutions happen.

Research in the sociology and political science of the 1970s to the 1990s resulted in a broad (but not unchallenged) consensus on a few variables regarding the likelihood of not just revolution but also of revolt. The list of variables were as follows: divisions among elites, the emergence of a sympathetic elite, financial collapse of the government, decreasing willingness or capacity of the military and police to repress, and resources and networks at the disposal of oppositional forces. Especially for weaker states, a permissive world context also appears to be important. These state-centred variables were meant to be alternatives against the social-psychological and political-economic variables that dominated the explanation of revolutions before the late 1970s.

Plato's ancient observation seems to sum up the major emphasis on *opportunity* in the literature: 'All political changes *originate* in divisions of the actual governing power; a government which is united cannot be moved' (emphasis mine). As Jack Goldstone notes: 'This observation is no less true today.'[62] In other words, the social science mainstream takes state-based divisions not only as independent of but far more important than any other factor (as captured by the word *originate*).[63]

---

62 Jack A. Goldstone, *Revolutions: A Very Short Introduction*, Oxford: Oxford University Press, 2014.

63 Here I am inevitably simplifying a vast body of literature stretching from the works of Tilly, McAdam, Tarrow, and Skocpol to Goodwin and Goldfrank. And I am certainly glossing over some of the differences of emphases in these works such as Goldstone's combination of state collapse and elite divisions with rising grievances and increasing numbers of young people in the population (which could speak to some Arab cases); or John Foran's synthesis of the dependency, political culture and political process schools. Finally, I am not even touching on the works on revolution which do not fit this *consensus*, ranging from Jeff Paige's landholding-centred account, Sewell's eventful analysis, Abrahamian's political economy and many analyses of especially Third World revolutions that have focused on nonorthodox indicators. So what the Egyptian and Tunisian revolutionary mobilizations problematize is not social science as a whole, but a particular consensus around institutionalist accounts.

In the case of the recent uprisings, however, all the state-based changes were the results of the movements themselves, rather than factors preceding the revolts. Both in Tunisia and Egypt, the elite tried to stick to together to the degree that they could. People kept going out on the streets and forced more concessions (such as more resignations from the cabinet). Most tellingly in Tunisia, the ruling elite attempted to remain intact by getting rid of the dictator. Yet the people persisted until many more 'old regime' elements resigned in the few weeks that followed Ben Ali's ouster.

There were no international openings either. The French foreign minister offered military help to squash the Tunisian uprising. Hillary Clinton announced that the Egyptian regime, unlike the Tunisian, was stable. In both cases, the Western powers switched their positions only a couple of days before the ouster of the presidents. Nor did the Tunisian or Egyptian regimes seem to be cracking under financial collapse. IMF and World Bank numbers and estimates indicated steadily increasing GDP per capita and revenues for both countries. In Egypt, unemployment seemed to be declining, though it was rising in Tunisia.

Could there be a way of walking around these difficulties by focusing on the most crucial state-centred variables? What is the best that the extant scholarship on revolutions has to offer? Goodwin's book *No Other Way Out* sought to narrow down the state-centred variables by broadly studying all revolutions that happened after 1945 rather than basing its argument on a few cases. Goodwin's basic argument was that people carry out revolutions not when they are frustrated or when they have impeccable revolutionary organizations, but when they have no other choice, hence the title of the book (a phrase he borrowed from Trotsky). Taking the state-centred turn to its logical extreme, Goodwin denied the centrality of resources, network and ideology (the other favourite factors of mainstream scholarship). States which encourage revolutionary movements are repressive states, but infrastructurally weak ones, Goodwin argued. States that are prone to being overthrown, however, are not only repressive and infrastructurally weak, but also patrimonial (rather than bureaucratic) states.[64]

64 Goodwin has also posited other conditions: state support of unpopular economic policies and structures; political exclusion; indiscriminate violence; weak policing; corrupt elites and personalistic rule.

Egypt fit neither the general patterns observed by social scientists nor those singled out by Goodwin. In Egypt, there was a well-organized nonrevolutionary opposition (the Brotherhood). There was actually room to breathe (for instance, an increasingly independent press under Mubarak). There was international support for Mubarak up until the last days. There was no military collapse. And the state had high repressive capacity. For the same reason, the networks or resource mobilization explanations do not work very well either. The main organization that had networks or resources (the Muslim Brotherhood) put them in the service of the revolutionary forces only after 25 January (only *after* it had become clear that revolutionary mobilization was going to transform Egypt, not before).

The Tunisian uprising, too, problematizes most of the existing generalizations. It is true that the Tunisian state was highly repressive, but it is questionable whether it was patrimonial (or 'sultanistic').[65] Economists and social scientists discovered much evidence for the patrimonialism (or 'sultanism') thesis after the revolt, but before 2011 they had held up Tunisia as the exemplar of bureaucratization and low levels of corruption in the Arab (and especially Maghreb) context.[66] Moreover, there is no question that the state had the capacity to crush the urban and provincial mass protests that led to the downfall of the old regime (even if it did not have the capacity or willingness to repress more irregular insurgency, such as that organized by Salafi militia, after 2011). Goodwin's two key variables fail to account for Tunisian revolt.

---

65 Goldstone ('Understanding the Revolutions of 2011: Weakness and Resilience in Middle Eastern Autocracies', *Foreign Affairs* 90:3 [May/June 2011].) has written the most cogent mainstream social science piece on the Arab Spring and sought to demonstrate that mainstream scholarship can actually account for the revolts. However, Kurzman ('The Arab Spring Uncoiled', *Mobilization* 17:4 [2012]: 377–90) has demonstrated that neither 'sultanism' nor the other variables that Goldstone promotes (disgust with the regime's corruption; unemployment and inequality; a cross-class coalition of opposition; elite defection, especially among military officers; and international pressure) can explain why the revolt started in Tunisia and Egypt rather than other countries (and then spread to Syria, Yemen, Libya and Bahrain more than to the others).

66 Mounira Charrad, *States and Women's Rights: The Making of Postcolonial Tunisia, Algeria, and Morocco*, Berkeley: University of California Press, 2001.

Going back to Goodwin's title, it would not be accurate to say Egyptians had 'no other way out': they had plenty, including not only the Brotherhood and the increasingly independent press, but secular, Christian and Islamic charity organizations, which also worked as political channels. Nevertheless, the protests on 25 January did create an atmosphere that made people *think* (temporarily) that there was no other way out than revolution. The fact that the revolutionaries could not sustain this atmosphere (that is, the fact that first the ballot box and then the coup could come to be perceived as 'ways out') demonstrates that we have to focus as much on *the process of the revolt* as on the initial revolt itself. To put it differently, as chapter 1 demonstrates for the post-1980 Middle East, Islamist mobilization had succeeded in creating the impression that there was no *secular* way out. Islamists' activities increased the belief in the inevitably corrupt nature of secularism and in an imminent Islamist takeover. By contrast, the revolutionaries of 2011 failed to turn *their* version of 'the illusion of inevitability' into reality.

This observation also allows us to revisit the author behind Goodwin's striking title. When Trotsky argued that people resort to a revolution *only when* there is 'no other way out', it is unclear whether he was referring to an exclusively objective and measurable situation. Trotsky (implicitly) broke with Lenin's definition of a revolutionary situation.[67] Lenin's formula downplayed how the upper classes' inability to rule and the lower classes' unwillingness to be ruled were *partially produced* by the activities of the Bolsheviks themselves.[68]

---

67 'It is usually insufficient for "the lower classes not to want" to live in the old way; it is also necessary that "the upper classes should be unable" to live in the old way . . . Without these objective changes, which are independent of the will, not only of individual groups and parties but even of individual classes, a revolution, as a general rule, is impossible'. V. I. Lenin, 'The Collapse of the Second International', May/June 1915, available at marxists.org.

68 'The expression, revolutionary situation, is a political term, not alone sociological. This explanation includes the subjective factor . . . the Kerenskiade is not obliged to be in every situation, in every country, as weak as the Russian Kerenskiade. The weakness of the Kerenskiade there was a result of the great power of the Bolshevik Party'. Leon Trotsky, 'What Is a Revolutionary Situation?: The Decisive Importance of the Communist Party', 19 December 1931, available at marxists.org. Trotsky's essay also undermines any tight distinction between necessary and sufficient causes of a revolution (or between revolutionary situations and actual revolutions). Interestingly, the essay also resonates with

The generation of a revolutionary situation is not completely independent of human will (a key point that distinguishes Trotsky's definition from Lenin's). Goodwin has done a great service by reminding us of a long-forgotten formulation ('no other way out'), but we need to keep in mind that revolts and revolutionary activity are among the crucial factors that render nonrevolutionary 'ways out' impossible.

The 2011 uprisings seem to accord with anarchists' and autonomists' predictions and hopes, as well as with the insights of interpretive scholars. The revolt appeared to be 'leaderless' (though it wasn't really). A 'multitude' (a network of rhizomic groupings, combating fear through symbolic action) was central to the success, they held. No wonder, then, that the names and ideas of Deleuze and Negri were in wide circulation during 2011.

Even though Slavoj Žižek emerged as a critic as much as a proponent of the global wave, some of his approach was appropriated by those who reproduced the spontaneous ideology of this wave. Here is an image Žižek has invoked throughout his writings and speeches: 'In Tom and Jerry cartoons, the cat . . . walks over the precipice . . . but it doesn't yet fall down. When it looks down and sees that there is no ground under its feet, it falls down. Those in power must find themselves in such a situation in order to fall down.'[69] I will shortly come to what this philosophically rather than sociologically oriented interpretation of revolution actually means, but let me first start off with a more sociological nonexplanation.

There is only one major social science book in the last decades we might group together with these names from the humanities: Charles Kurzman's *Unthinkable Revolution*. This book sought to refute one by one state-centred, resource mobilization, political economic and

---

aspects of Kurzman's nonexplanation: 'It cannot be foreseen or indicated mathematically at what point in these processes that the revolutionary situation is totally ripe'. But Trotsky's next sentence moves us in another direction: 'The revolutionary party can only establish that fact by its struggles, by the growth of its forces through its influence on the masses, on the peasants, and the petty bourgeoisie of the towns, etc., and by the weakening of the resistance of the ruling classes'.

69 'Slavoj Zizek, Tom and Jerry, and Mubarak', youtube.com.

cultural explanations of the Iranian Revolution, arguing instead that the mobilization itself created the necessary opportunities, resources and culture. Kurzman did not, however, develop an alternative explanatory framework to show how the mobilization was able to do this. Such a framework would allow us to compare and contrast factors in the Iranian context to other cases, and maybe to the present cases. Instead, he argued that revolutionary processes necessarily *undermine* attempts at explanation. We can only interpret revolutions, he suggested, but cannot explain them.[70]

What, then, might an interpretation of Arab revolt look like? Now we can turn to Žižek, or rather one maverick sociologist's interpretation of the revolution's cartoon-image version. Here is Armando Salvatore's take on what started the revolutionary uprising:

> A glimpse of the terrible, beautiful, and impossible realm of the pure affirmation of people's needs . . . triggered by grievances ultimately sublimated into a hard politics of presence, of something that can get trivialized into the universal terms of 'popular will' for the sake of self-identification, comment, and press coverage, but is ultimately impossible to grasp . . . Not just collective effervescence or charismatic leadership . . . but almost its opposite, a reckoning with illusion and delusion as the Real-ization of the bottom line. No longer floating in the air, but touching, even if just for a blessed moment, the Real ground of suffering, solidarity, and joy.[71]

Behind the colourful language, what Salvatore actually suggests is that people always crave self-organization and solidarity, but cannot act upon these desires because of an imaginary attribution of near omnipotence to those holding power. Once that illusion is gone, people embrace the suffering and joys of revolution. Yet interpretive scholars do not tell us when and where the illusion of omnipotence is more likely to be shattered, and why, and how. History is quite messy, it seems, and the pinnacle of this mess is the revolution.

---

70 See Kurzman, 'The Arab Spring Uncoiled', for the application of this logic to the Arab revolt.

71 Armando Salvatore, 'The elusive subject of revolution', blogs.ssrc.com.

But there is an alternative path to looking for isolatable causes and reverting to non-explanatory interpretation: studying the process.[72] Both this chapter and the previous one sought to demonstrate the usefulness of social scientific concepts, first by looking at how the power bloc, the revolutionaries and the emerging elites have striven to manage the process; and then by bringing class into the study of this drama.

The tools of analytical social science come in handy when we focus on the revolutionary process rather than the moment of eruption. The autonomists' 'multitudes' might do well to undermine social science, but they are not very good in preventing power blocs (and sometimes reshuffled power blocs) from managing uprisings. In both Tunisia and Egypt, the revolutionaries failed to produce programmes and leaders to guide the revolutionary process, and certain actors from within the power bloc (and from some rising strata who sought to join or even lead the power bloc) quickly stepped in to fill the gap. The glorification of bottom-up solidarity is gratifying in the first weeks of revolt, but neither accounts for much nor alerts activists to dangers in the months ahead, as powerful groups reorganize to contain, absorb and repress revolt.

In the light of social science's troubles with the eruptive event, and of revolutionaries' troubles with the process, we need to ask whether analytical frameworks have anything to offer in explanation of revolts' *aftermath*. Even if we cannot explain the exact place and timing of revolt, can we analytically account for the process through which the revolutionaries (in interaction with institutions and other actors) create (or fail to create) a situation where there is 'no other way out'? Here I discuss this question by contrasting mainstream institutionalist insights with Gramscian ones.

---

72 Among other works centred on process, Doug McAdam's book on black insurgency demonstrates the fruitfulness of a process approach that brings together the study of political economy, popular organization, the international balance of forces, conjuncture and ideology. I leave it to the sociologist of knowledge to resolve how scholars who focused on process in their early work got canonized in variable-seeking institutionalist frameworks. Douglas McAdam, *Political Process and the Development of Black Insurgency*, Chicago: University of Chicago Press, 1982.

A Sociological Alternative to the Institutionalist Study of Crisis

A state-centred analysis of revolutionary failure, which is based on institutions and legitimacy, further highlights the distinctiveness of the political society approach developed in this book.[73] In a brilliant analysis of the two years that followed the toppling of Mubarak, Ellis Goldberg emphasized institutional legitimacy (and the mass protests that undermined it) as the driving factors in Egyptian politics. The army and the courts seemed to be the only legitimate institutions (despite the many grievances against them), whereas the (elected and Brotherhood-controlled) parliament and the presidency could not acquire sufficient legitimacy.[74] The persisting legitimacy of two old regime institutions led to limited state collapse, and there was no democratic legitimacy to fill the partial void. While this argument captures some important elements of the Egyptian post-revolutionary situation, it begs the central question: why were the parliament and the presidency not legitimate even before July 2013? Why weren't they able to rule, even though they were backed by the most organized religious and political force in Egypt (the Muslim Brotherhood), which was perceived (and therefore supported, grudgingly and with reservation and caution) by Western elites as the only force that could bring stability to post-Mubarak Egypt?

The parliament's and presidency's failures to secure legitimacy cannot be understood without introducing Gramscian concepts. If the Brotherhood had been hegemonic enough, it could have articulated all of the mentioned institutions into a legitimate bloc, and then weeded out ones that were unnecessary or threatened its interests. But this would have been possible only if the Brotherhood were organized as a professional political party. The dynamics of Egyptian political society, as chapters 1 through 4 showed, made this next to impossible. To put it differently, legitimacy can be made and unmade through politics; the legitimacy or illegitimacy of an institution cannot be taken as a given. Institutional legitimacy, therefore, cannot be the beginning point of analysis.

73 Four of the six following paragraphs draw on Tuğal, 'Religious Politics, Hegemony, and the Market Economy: Parties In the Making of Turkey's Liberal-Conservative Bloc and Egypt's Diffuse Islamization'.

74 See jadaliyya.com; and 'Egypt's Political Crisis', Middle East Channel, *Foreign Policy*, 10 December 2012.

Goldberg's comparison of Egypt with the classical revolutionary cases (France, Russia and China) resonates with the prominent sociologist Theda Skocpol's understanding of the central factors in these cases (state collapse and initially uncontainable mass mobilization).[75] Egypt presented a revolutionary situation (the old elites could no longer rule and the masses were persistently mobilized), but one in which two institutions of the old regime, the army and courts, had not collapsed. The contrast I want to point out with these classical cases is the fragmented and semi-professional structure of Islamic political society in Egypt, rather than limited state collapse. Certainly, the extent of state collapse is a central factor. This much had already been established as early as Lenin's and Trotsky's writings on the issue (as Tilly noted in his classical study of revolutions, and as Skocpol chose to neglect in hers).[76]

We could even say that the social science mainstream is stuck in a (depoliticized and neutralized) 'Leninist' phase: it overemphasizes the Machiavellian play of forces under conditions of state collapse, but does not theorize the historical preconditions (and does not analyse the making) of Machiavellian actors. Moreover, the analysis of the power bloc, as developed in the earlier chapters of this book, tells us much more than the concept of 'state collapse': what interests us here is not simply the crisis of institutions, but how the coordination of institutions with global and national dominant class interests (that is, their articulation around a 'power bloc') fails. We also need to study carefully what brings about the constitution of Machiavellian actors who can both *precipitate* and *intervene in* that failure. The diffuse hegemony set up as a result of the decades-old interaction between the power bloc and the Brotherhood allowed a revolutionary uprising, but not a revolution. 'State collapse' was 'limited' partly because of these hegemonic balances. Due to its underdeveloped hegemonic capacity, the Brotherhood could not further precipitate state collapse and instead invested its hopes in the resuscitation of the old regime's institutions.

---

75 Theda Skocpol, *States and Social Revolutions*, Cambridge: Cambridge University Press, 1979.

76 Charles Tilly, *From Mobilization to Revolution*, Reading, MA: Addison-Wesley, 1978.

In France, the Jacobins played the hegemonic role – though, as Gramsci emphasized, politics did not become thoroughly hegemonic before the late nineteenth century, even in Western Europe. In that sense, the hegemonic capacity and the party-ness of the Jacobins do not match the political orientations of modern actors, though they were harbingers of what was to come. The Bolsheviks initially acted as a hegemonic party and were therefore able to carry out a social revolution, though in time the Russian Communist Party degenerated into a nonhegemonic institution. The Chinese Communist Party was forged through the Long March and (despite destructive experiences such as the Cultural Revolution and the Gang of Four's policies) remained a relatively more hegemonic party, with sustained links to the masses and ongoing cultural and political work that articulated their demands with a 'sinified Marxism'.[77]

In other words, it might be true, as Ellis Goldberg has pointed out, that one factor differentiating Egypt from these classical revolutionary cases was the survival of two old regime institutions; but he neglected to say that a hegemonic political force could further undermine the surviving institutions of the old regime through successful management of mass mobilization. Brotherhood leaders were very much aware of this possibility and did their best to deploy the streets in their endeavours to infiltrate and subordinate the judiciary. Yet their capacity in this regard paled in comparison to the Turkish AKP's mixture of mobilization (not only of hard-core Islamists, as in the Brotherhood's attempts, but of liberals and even *some leftists*) and international public relations (where even the liberal Anglophone press was summoned). This incredible mobilization-manipulation ultimately subordinated and contained the Turkish military and judiciary (through the famous Ergenekon process). The pre-2013 AKP, I argue, was the true heir to the Jacobins (and Machiavelli) in the Islamic context, despite the Kemalists' and other secularists' deep-rooted (and misleading) self-designation as Jacobins. The contrast with the Egyptian case suggests that hegemonic parties are central to

77 Perry Anderson, 'Two Revolutions: Rough Notes', *New Left Review* 2:61 (January/February 2010): 59–96; Ho-fung Hung, *Protest with Chinese Characteristics: Demonstrations, Riots, and Petitions in the Mid-Qing Dynasty*, Columbia University Press, 2011.

the realization and consolidation of revolutions (and passive revolutions), though this insight will have to be further elaborated elsewhere in the light of a discussion of other cases.

In sum, revolts open up possibilities for many strata: the excluded and the oppressed, but also the subordinate wings of the power bloc, and ambitious strata on the verge of joining the power bloc. The structure of political society has a huge influence on whether a revolt leads to a major (and systematic) reshuffling and expansion of the power bloc (its contents in terms of groups, and its capacity for effective force and consent).

The professionalized and united Turkish political society ushered in a passive revolution, even though the old power bloc was not shaken by millions-strong street revolts (the Islamist revolt was a patchwork of resistance and consent; the Kurdish revolt was regionally confined; worker and youth revolt were weak). Fragmented and semi-professional Egyptian political society failed to absorb the most massive revolt in Egyptian history, and both the revolution and the passive revolution were smashed by restoration. The mountain of tasks before a potentially solid bloc (absorb the revolutionaries, marginalize or absorb the counter-revolutionaries as well, and so on) proved too much for a fragmented political society. All political forces sympathetic to the revolution were in worse condition when compared to the passive revolutionaries: they were mobilized, yes – but also weak, inexperienced, disorganized and unprogrammatic.

Rather than expanding the power bloc (as happened in Turkey), the revolt, the failed passive revolution and the counter-revolution ended up contracting the bloc and diminishing its capacity to generate pro-system hope and consent. Not that there is *no consent* in Egypt. Rather, the consent is so diffuse and shapeless that the nation cannot flex its muscles to embark on a well-defined path. In short, it might be extremely difficult to *explain* the timing and place of a revolt; but we do have the tools to analyse whether and how a revolt turns into a revolution.

Bringing Class Back In

The other potential contribution of the social sciences to the study of revolt is a thoroughly revised class analysis. Political economy and capitalism have been excluded from the political sociology of revolt during the last three decades, and this neglect has resulted in serious blind spots. This argument will be opened up further in the last two chapters of the book.

The pattern of the 1848 uprisings had repeated itself in 1905: the intellectuals and the business class initially mobilized the working class, but retreated to a more moderate position and gave in to the conservatives afterwards.[78] Do we see this (or at least a similar) pattern again in the revolt wave of 2011–13? The following chapters will discuss this comparative question through the theorization of the new middle class.

78 See Eric J. Hobsbawm, *The Age of Capital, 1848–1875*, New York: Vintage Books, 1996 [1975]; Charles Kurzman, *Democracy Denied, 1905–1915: Intellectuals and the Fate of Democracy*, Cambridge, MA: Harvard University Press, 2008; Jonathan Sperber, *The European Revolutions, 1848–1851*, New York: Cambridge University Press, 2005 [1994].

CHAPTER 6

Gezi: The End of the Turkish Model or the Beginning of the Left?

Secular corporatism is all but dead in the Middle East. The revolutionized and Islamized corporatism of Iran and the Islamic liberalism of Turkey are both in deep crisis. What lies ahead for the region? We know that there are no solid, fully formed alternatives, but are there potential ones?

This chapter will suggest that the left has the potential to offer alternatives, but that its potential to do so is latent. To understand the deep-rooted weaknesses as well as the possible strengths of the left, I first seek to shed some light on why the left has so far been unable to present working platforms, coalitions and strategies.[1] I then turn to how the recent wave of revolt might counterbalance some of the left's historical weaknesses. If the social history of the region renders the centrality of the working class–business conflict of the Western mould a lesser possibility, can developments in late capitalism, which are unevenly experienced throughout the region, generate new possibilities for postcapitalist transition, which might even turn out to parallel new potentials in the Western world itself? I first address these questions through an analysis of middle-class revolt in Turkey, which has opened unexpected venues. The next chapter puts the Turkish revolt in both regional and global perspective to discuss these novel horizons.

Sketches for a Long-Term History of the Middle Eastern Left

A prehistory of today's possible left alternatives is paramount: we need to understand these forces in historical context to gauge what they could contribute and how. Why did Islamic politics come to be the main source of opposition by the end of the twentieth century?

1 A thorough review certainly would require a much deeper history, and only a sketch can be provided here.

Why have left-wing movements been the lesser alternative in the long history of the modern Middle East?[2]

The most prevalent answers to these questions have drawn attention to the economic moment. A nonfeudal version of the tributary mode of production, characterized by an extremely strong centre and the centrality of conquest, has led to a fragility of ownership,[3] with devastating consequences for left-wing alternatives. First, the feebleness of private ownership has resulted in gigantic states, in which the ruling strata and the dominant class have merged (in contrast to feudalism, where they remained relatively distinct). Throughout the demise of the tributary mode of production in Europe, the absolutist monarchies mobilized the merchant class against the feudal landlords.[4] By contrast, class mobilization never became as central in the demise of Middle Eastern tributary production.[5] Struggles within the elite were relatively more decisive, which left a political legacy unconducive to class struggles of the capitalist kind as well.

---

2 Even though this question cannot be fully answered without also developing an understanding of the late transition to capitalism in the Middle East, there is no space to engage that debate here. The answers provided so far have ranged from the simple (Asiatic mode of production, Oriental despotism or simply Islam as impediments to development) to the complex (an articulation of various factors, including an uneven persistence of tribal rule and surplus extraction; Islamic law; extremely advanced tributary economic, cultural and political systems, again unevenly appearing and disappearing ever since post-Rashidite Islam; and military invasions and colonialisms, which have reinforced the first three factors). See Samir Amin, *Eurocentrism*, New York: Monthly Review Press, 1989; Nazih N. M. Ayubi, 1995. *Over-Stating the Arab State: Politics and Society in the Middle East*. London: I. B. Tauris, 1995; Fawzy Mansour, *The Arab World: Nation, State, and Democracy*, London: Zed Books, 1992. A reformulation of this debate will have to draw on similar ongoing debates about late capitalist transitions in other parts of the world. See especially Giovanni Arrighi, *Adam Smith in Beijing: Lineages of the Twenty-First Century*, London: Verso, 2007; and Ho-fung Hung, 'Agricultural Revolution and Elite Reproduction in Qing China: The Transition to Capitalism Debate Revisited', *American Sociological Review* 73:4 (2008); and Hung, *Protest with Chinese Characteristics: Demonstrations, Riots, and Petitions in the Mid-Qing Dynasty*, New York: Columbia University Press, 2011.

3 Amin, *Eurocentrism*.

4 Charles Tilly, *Coercion, Capital, and European States, AD 990–1990*, Cambridge, MA: Blackwell, 1990.

5 Fawzy Mansour, *The Arab World: Nation, State, and Democracy*, London: Zed Books, 1992.

Moreover, these specific structures of the state and the economy have also resulted in the underdevelopment of large-scale private production (further reinforced but not caused, according to some political economists, by Islamic law's interdictions against usury and *secure* private property in land,[6] and its tendency to divide up property among offspring).[7] Massive peasantry or working-class concentration and organization have been as a result less intense when compared to Latin America and Europe.

Marxist and other explanations also emphasize the political moment. The analysis of the interaction between local and international politics is condensed in three points in the literature: the history of nationalist struggles; the influence of the Soviet collapse; and American involvement.

Ever since the late eighteenth century, Middle Eastern peoples have been obsessed with the question of how to catch up with the West. Depending on the country, this obsession has also been tangled with the issue of political and military independence. The left contributed important organizational and intellectual resources to this struggle, a contribution which increased its popularity and political viability for a while, but which backfired in the long run.

Anticolonial struggle based on nationalist, Sufi and/or Islamist themes and organization led to the marginalization or subordination of socio-economic questions. Socialism subsequently became window dressing for nationalist movements and developmentalist regimes. While this problem has tormented the left elsewhere (for example, in Mexico and Argentina), the availability of Islamic politics after the

6 It should be emphasized that Islamic law and the Middle Eastern tributary production did not prevent the accumulation of private property as such (as there was proto-feudal concentration, as well as mercantile capital accumulation, under the Umayyads, Abbasids and Ottomans, and even post-mercantile accumulation under the Fatimids), but rather rendered it precarious and retransferrable to the centre (Karen Barkey, *Bandits and Bureaucrats: The Ottoman Route to State Centralization*, Ithaca, NY: Cornell University Press, 1994; Mansour, *The Arab World*, 59, 62–3, 73–4). It is therefore quite misleading to construct medieval Islam as *the* impediment to the birth of capitalism, as some neoclassical economists do (see, e.g., Timur Kuran, *The Long Divergence: How Islamic Law Held Back the Middle East*, Princeton, NJ: Princeton University Press, 2011).

7 Mansour, *The Arab World*, 51–2, 66–7 and passim.

failure of left nationalism and the collapse of the Soviet bloc further added to the impasse of the Middle Eastern left. The post-1970s US policy of reproducing the dominance of Islam, especially against left-wing nationalism, served its immediate purpose as well, even if it proved problematic to US interests in the long run.

Nevertheless, the specific challenges the religious question poses in the Middle East cannot be reduced to these political, diplomatic and military dynamics. Not even the most pressing and novel issue – the rise of Islamic politics and its replacement of the left among impoverished strata – has been adequately understood and strategically considered. And the complications go much deeper than that.

The following question has to be asked and explored, especially through comparisons with Latin America and Asia: why was there a popular, sustainable and distinctively nonsocialist, religion-based political and ideological line ('Islamism') in the Middle Eastern context (in contrast to the relatively transient nature of Buddhist-, Confucian-, Catholic-, and Hinduism-based hegemonic projects on these two continents)? Among many other implications of a deep-rooted Islamist (and not just 'Islamic') tradition, which took shape primarily in the late nineteenth and twentieth centuries, was the inhibited and curtailed formation of an interpretation of Islam comparable to Latin American liberation theology.

At first glance, the main historical difference with Latin America seems to be the institutionalized insecurity of private property, whereas the main difference from India and China was a well-established monotheistic tradition (with its vast political resources). Possibly, it is the combination of these two factors, rather than Islam's essential difference from Christianity, that explains the differences with Latin America. Whereas nonproletarianized and disorganized subordinate strata came together around radical leftist parties in other nonfeudal tributary societies, they had the alternative of uniting around Islam in the modern Middle East. For instance, a dispersed peasantry was forged into a strong, collectivistic weapon through the Communist Party in the Chinese case, while class dispersion could not be overcome in a similar manner in Middle Eastern cases. In Latin America, there was sufficient proletarianization and ability to self-organize, which allowed the left to influence Christianity and transform it in a leftist direction.

In other words, the resolution of the religious question gained additional importance for the left in the Middle Eastern context, and not simply because of the way Islam is more deeply woven into economic and political structures when compared to other religions. In places such as Latin America, and even in early modern Europe, the resolution of the religious question was essential *first* to the establishment of capitalism (as Weberians emphasize), and *then* to producing and popularizing alternatives to capitalism. The centrality of religion to radical societal transformation, then, isn't exclusively Middle Eastern or Islamic. Middle Eastern liberalism and conservatism are now going through a similar stage of religious development in so far as capitalism is concerned: the further spread of capitalism in the Middle East is drawing on more and more (refashioned) Islamic resources. The monopolization of wealth analysed in chapter 3 is sanctified by religion. However, neither the left nor the religious fields in the Middle East have yet discovered how to resolve the religious question in a way that would be conducive to a postcapitalist transformation.

The Arab Socialist Twist and the (Partial) Autonomy of the Turkish Left

If modes of production,[8] the history of national struggles and broader politics and the specific role of Islam are some reasons behind the left's entrenched weakness, another is intellectual history. The region's intellectuals were no doubt aware of many of the problems noted above (if not exactly along the lines presented here) and they discovered in left-wing, corporatist and statist nationalism a possible path to overcome these hurdles (a move occasionally supported by the Western left and by the Soviets). Apparently

8 Further research is needed to explore how and why the capitalist concentration of the last three–four decades have not engendered proletarian concentration, thereby reproducing the residues of Middle Eastern specificities quite *unevenly*. Although one obvious answer is the coincidence of the biggest capitalist leap in regional history with global neoliberalization (which deproletarianizes in most of the world), Chinese proletarianization during the same era is enough of a cause to go under the surface. Beverly J. Silver and Lu Zhang, 'China as an Emerging Epicenter of World Labor Unrest' in Ho-fung Hung, ed., *China and the Transformation of Global Capitalism*, Baltimore: Johns Hopkins University Press, 2009.

plausible, this pseudo-way out of the quagmire intensified the left's marginality.

Arab socialism was the expression of a search for what would be today called an 'alternative modernity': a desire to be a central actor in the contemporary world without imitating American/European or Soviet models. This emphasis on having one's own path had partially developed under the impact of the German romantic notion of authenticity. Just as some of today's academics embrace the Islamic version of modernity as an alternative to entrenched paradigms, Western scholars hailed the Arab socialist officers and intellectuals as makers of their own destiny, as the authors of 'creative modernization' – a fact conveniently ignored by most intellectuals today, who mistakenly attribute the authoritarianism and stalled modernization of Middle Eastern societies (mostly) to military tutelage.[9] Romanticism, with partial roots in Western thought, had a significant role to play in this drama. We should not forget that today's 'alternative' movements also have strong authoritarian tendencies, and that they were not the first movements to claim 'authenticity'. Also note that Arab socialists were committed to democracy on paper (it was one of Nasser's six principles!) and used it as a rallying cry against monarchies, much as today's Islamists and conservatives use it against secular nationalists.

The development of leftist ideas, especially of the Arab socialist variety, started under the shadow of the solidarism of the 1930s. Partly due to the heavy influence of interwar solidarism, self-organization was de-emphasized from the beginnings of Arab socialism onwards.[10] This influenced the left's approach to class. Class conflict was in fact looked down upon, not only because it was harmful to economic development and political stability, but also because it disturbed the romantic notion of the undivided people. And it was also deemed unnecessary, since the state would take care of the people's needs anyway. The 'Islamic socialism' of the early Syrian Muslim Brotherhood, which the Islamist movement later dropped in favour of a more compromising attitude with respect to capitalism,

9 Sami A. Hanna and George H. Gardner , eds, *Arab Socialism: A Documentary Survey*, Leiden: Brill, 1969, 8–10.

10 Ibid.

inherited these tendencies from Arab socialism and the overall intellectual climate of the 1920s through the 1950s.[11]

When the military officers who took power in the 1950s looked for a legitimizing rhetoric, this intellectual tendency came in handy. Except in a few places, left-wing solidarist intellectuals did not have enough power to control the way in which the officers deployed their ideas: they were disorganized and had no organic and democratic ties with the officers. Nasser, with his pragmatic recourse to (and scorn for) Arab socialist 'theory' is a prime example of this military trivialization of socialism.[12]

Arab socialist regimes, particularly Nasser's,[13] paid lip service to popular participation, but never developed it in practice. Nasser's socialism promised popular control over the means of production. When the promise did not materialize, he attributed the failure to the multiplicity of forces within the new regime, using this as a further excuse to purge opposition within the regime.

The independence-seeking ruling elites of the 1950s and 1960s were actually *pushed* to the Arab variant of socialism. The hostility of the West, the oil-rich Arab states and the local merchants and landowning classes to 'national development' intensified the anti-imperialist and anti-capitalist rhetoric and policies of the regimes regardless of their initial intentions, which were in fact not socialist. However, their official discovery of socialism created a hollow ideology without any real mass base, even if some elites started to believe in the necessity of mass mobilization after a certain point.[14]

Turkey was a partial exception to these regional tendencies. Kemalism was only roughly comparable to Nasserism, for though it also had its 'socialist' interpreters (the Kadro movement, the Yön circle, and others), as an official ideology it was hostile to socialism. Despite that, the most prominent left-wing intellectuals remained

---

11 Ibid., 72–6.

12 Fayez Sayegh, 'The Theoretical Structure of Nasser's Socialism' in Hanna and Gardner, eds, *Arab Socialism*, 103.

13 Ibid., 121–3, 133–4.

14 Mansour, *The Arab World*, 101–2. The discursive depletion of socialism analysed in this subsection was no doubt reinforced by the long-term structural legacies discussed earlier in terms of the relative marginality of private property and class struggle.

loyal to socialist interpretations of Kemalism, thereby reproducing the dominant regional intellectual pattern.[15]

This pattern was broken in the 1960s and 1970s. The weakness of Turkish socialism (and the marginalization of socialist intellectuals) from the 1920s to the mid-1960s became a strength for self-governmental, autonomy-oriented, less statist and class conflict–prone understandings of socialism: militant youth made a relatively easy break with more top-down visions of socialism towards the end of the 1960s. They had (relatively speaking) no major communist party or union tradition that could challenge them, unlike the situation in Arab countries. Though the first step in the break was towards an even more vanguardist vision of social change (as in the case of organizations such as THKP-C, THKO and TİKKO), the followers of the first wave learned from the pioneers' mistakes and shifted to a relatively more bottom-up variety of their left-wing populism. This led to organizations that had a mass base for the first time in Turkish history (Devrimci Yol, Kurtuluş, Halkın Yolu and their offshoots), even if their mass ties could not be sustained beyond short stretches of time. Most notably, the Kurdistan Worker's Party (PKK) adjusted the THKP-C's founder's teaching and strategy to the Kurdish context, which enabled it to wage one of the most sustained guerrilla campaigns in history.[16]

By the 1960s, when revolutionary currents throughout the world were shaking American and Soviet hegemony (and the Stalinist hold over the definition of the correct left), Arab youth did not experience similar breakthroughs. A solidaristic and top-down version of socialist nationalism had become *official ideology*, as the next section further underlines. Revolutionaries could only define themselves

---

15 Such similarity, to be sure, does not entail identical stances with respect to statism, Islam, authenticity, class struggle, self-organization and popular participation. A comparative history of radical intellectuals in the region is yet to be written. Such an analytical history would also enable us to appreciate how and why a few intellectuals (such as Hikmet Kıvılcımlı) diverged from the patterns discussed here even before the 1960s.

16 On the PKK's debt to the THKP-C leader Mahir Çayan, see 'Öcalan'dan,' Mahir Çayan mesaji', radikal.com.tr, 18 October 2013. Whether Kurdistan's socio-economic and political uniqueness throughout history explain more of this success than its neo-Çayanist (and more clearly neo-Maoist) strategy should be seriously explored.

against this official ideology. They either fell back into the Soviet fold or (sticking to the theme of authenticity) switched to radical Islamism.

The Great Irony

The strengths of the Arab left, then, prepared the route to its absorption, while the weak Turkish left was pushed to find its own independent voice in the 1970s. Many layers of irony are embedded within this greater irony.

The relative strength of the Arab left and the less repressive interwar regimes (when compared to the initial CHP regime) set the stage for nominally 'socialist' countries, whose populations were unperturbed by the world revolution of 1968. Another irony preceded this: Turkey's independence in 1923 had set the stage for its joining NATO in 1946, while Arab countries and Iran witnessed left-wing popular-national movements in the 1940s and 1950s as a response to ongoing foreign control. Turkey did not.

Alongside the left-wing nationalist movements, particularly decisive for the regional left was the fate of communist movements throughout the Arab world. Egyptian communists, though only intellectually influential in the 1920s and 1930s (except for a restricted base in the urban working class), came to control strikes and also to have an impact on the anti-imperialist struggle in the 1940s and 1950s.[17] The first communist advances in trade unions occurred in the late 1930s, especially in Egypt and Syria.[18] In Jordan, the peak of communist power came in 1956–57, when the Jordanian Communist Party briefly had one seat in the cabinet.

Iraqi communists were even more influential. They went beyond having a hand in strikes to partially controlling the countryside and even influencing the Kurdish national movement as well as religious preachers across Iraq. Eventually, they played a large role in the military's overthrow of the colonial regime. In Iraq, there was even a short period, in 1958–63, when communists came close to claiming the leadership of the national movement. The Iraqi communists were quite exceptional due to more solid organization (with 7,000 active

17 For example, the Port Sa'id armed resistance; see M. S. Agwani, *Communism in the Arab East*, London: Asia Publishing House, 1969, 44–51, 80.

18 Ibid., 181–2.

members); Chinese backing; and self-protective reaction to the dissolution of Syrian and Egyptian communists.[19] After 1963, however, most communists, including those in Iraq, were content with subordinate roles in nation-building.

International balances of force were decisive here. The Soviet Union supported the Egyptian, Syrian and Iraqi regimes even during times of harsh anticommunist repression, and dictated cooperation with the regimes to the local communists as well. Only the Iraqis did not completely conform to this policy, even though they also ultimately sided with the Soviets against the Chinese.[20]

With the advent of nationalist regimes, communists focused on securing good relations with and maintaining influence on them (rather than organizing the working class or the peasantry). In the case of Egypt, this tendency found its most extreme expression: the communist party disbanded itself in order to join Nasser's Arab Socialist Union.[21] Nasserism fluctuated between merciless repression of the left (especially between 1959 and 1964) and the appropriation of its cadres and ideas (in fluctuating waves throughout the 1960s). The price was not only lack of independent organization, but also sharing the humiliation of Nasserism's defeat and even partaking in Sadat's restoration,[22] after which a good part of the left joined the ranks of the loyal opposition to the old regime.

Nevertheless, the overall result of socialist and communist mobilization in these decades should be read as the institutionalization of a politics of absorption rather than a complete 'caving in' of leftist forces (in comparable fashion to the aftermath of the Islamist mobilization in the region from the 1970s to the 1990s). What characterized the region was the absorption of communist ideas into noncommunist regimes: even though communists did not wield much formal (governmental or other) power, they shaped the scene through their influence on Baath and Nasser, who borrowed many ideas and practices from them.

Adding to the irony, the post-Stalinist Soviet rhetoric of peaceful coexistence further pacified the Arab left, whereas the Turkish left

19 Agwani, *Communism in the Arab East*, 207.
20 Ibid., 214–5.
21 Ibid., 86, 165–76.
22 Mansour, *The Arab World*, 103.

(less and less controlled by the Soviets) continued to wage revolutionary struggle. In the 1960s and 1970s, the Soviets did not want much disturbance along their borders and promoted 'peaceful' change in most of the nonsocialist world, hoping to secure the lessening of Western support of anti-regime activity in state 'socialist' countries (a horrible calculation, it turned out). Arab communists mostly toed the Soviet line, while the Turkish left had the luxury of going its own way. In a matter of ten years, around a dozen non-pro-Soviet or anti-Soviet left-revolutionary organizations came into existence. They borrowed from Mao, the French left, Che Guevara and the Arab left in highly original ways. Iran witnessed a similar proliferation, due at least partly to similar dynamics (for example, the regime did not call itself socialist, and therefore this word was not as tainted).

Despite all this activity, the Arab and the Turkish left both stagnated after the 1980s. When the global wave of 2011 arrived, neither was ready to take the lead. The Tunisian left, as chapter 4 demonstrated, was only a partial exception. If a combination of repression and absorption brought about the stagnation of the Arab left, the decline was much more directly attributable to merciless repression in the Turkish case. The military intervention of 1980 devastated the left through executions, life-altering torture and exile. Nevertheless, we should not forget that more brutal repression in Latin America and elsewhere never terminated the left's popularity. The success of the 1980 coup makes sense only in light of the socio-economic, political and religious dynamics noted above.

Leftist Opposition in Turkey and Egypt after the 1980s

In the depressing post-coup scene, the secular opposition to Turkey's religious neoliberalization had two major components: Kemalist foot-dragging and the worker–civil servant opposition. Kemalists mostly focused on fighting the religious component of this package and only infrequently protested against the erosion of corporatism (rather than developing a novel, working alternative to neoliberalism). Once the CHP reopened in the mid-1990s, it relied mostly on its pre-1960s mission of authoritarian secular nationalism (at the expense of Kemalists' flirtations with left-populism and then Third Way politics from the 1960s to the early 1990s). The CHP thus became the political leader against Islamism. However, due to the liquidation of its prominent social democratic leaders, it alienated even secularized sectors. In the 1990s and 2000s, some secular (and also Alevi) groups still voted for the CHP because of its emphasis on anti-Islamism, thanks to which it claimed the position of the second party in parliament. But the party lacked the moral authority of the AKP, the leaders of which were perceived to be true believers with popular origins, while most of the CHP's voters deeply distrusted their leaders.

Meanwhile, any political force to the left of the CHP line was violently suppressed not only by the recurrent coups, but also through ongoing torture and other forms of repression. The offshoots of the radical organizations of the 1970s did not disappear, but they became more dispersed, less mass-based and ever more factional. Still, some retained their intellectual dynamism, impact on the (occasionally massive) student movement and organization in Kurdish-Alevi neighbourhoods. Yet none of them accomplished all three at the same time: no faction combined rigorous campus and neighbourhood organization with intellectual and institutional dynamism.

Turkish labour, the second major impediment to Islamic neoliberalization, had its post-liberalization spring between 1989 and 1995. First a workers' movement, then a movement of proletarianized civil servants shook the system. Neoliberalization stumbled (as attested by a slowing down of privatization in the 1990s and at least some initial wage gains). However, these movements not only lacked a political leader, but even a political interlocutor within the system. The new CHP was not deeply interested in labour issues. Not only its turn to the right but institutional and structural factors account for this lack of interest. The coups had cracked down on labour and made unionization quite difficult; direct links between parties and unions were banned; and, last but not least, the financial turn of the economy and the expansion of the service sector had slowed classical proletarianization and expanded the informal working class, with its notorious (if not insurmountable) difficulties of organization.

With its only interlocutors now outside the system, the discourse of activist labour (especially of civil servants) soon became socialist, pro-Kurdish and democratic. But the (still deeply nationalist) Turkish masses gradually deserted the militant unions and joined right-wing ones. The labour movement's abrupt and radical politicization was also completely out of synch with the depoliticization (and sharp right turn) that characterized society after the 1980 coup. The street protests had stopped attracting big numbers by the mid-1990s. And by the end of the 2000s, the leftist unions (which had *started* unionization among civil servants in the 1990s) became the least influential among civil servants.[23]

The secular left had a different fate in Egypt. Most leftist organizations and leaders were either repressed or willingly co-opted by the Nasserist regime, seeing in that regime an authentic voice of socialism. As Sadat and Mubarak abandoned corporatism, Nasserism became one of the rallying points of the opposition, akin to the Kemalist left in Turkey. However, socialists and communists did not have a voice as independent as the Nasserists. For instance, Tagammuʿ, the main leftist party, had shady relations with the regime. Yet despite a seemingly strong footing within the system, these two parties combined (Nasserists and leftists) could never advance beyond winning a few seats in parliament. The Brotherhood was the only major (quasi-) party alongside Mubarak's official party (the National Democratic Party).

The counterpoint to the weakness of secular non-neoliberal forces in parliament was their vibrancy on the street, as we have seen in chapter 4. But wasn't there any organization in political society that could potentially lead the rambunctious street? Only a year before the 2011 revolt the Egyptian left seemed alive and well. During the 2010 elections, many leftist parties fielded candidates. They were a natural part of political life, though they remained in a pro-regime meld. Tagammuʿ (the inheritors of Marxism and syndicalism) and the Nasserists were quite shy in embracing even the 25 January revolt (though some of their leaders weighed in without official backing). This spilled over into 2011–13: Tagammuʿ became an appendage of a liberal and old regime coalition, and the Nasserists remained

23 Together with repression, an ever-rising Turkish nationalism was the reason of this defeat. That nationalism, in turn, was fuelled by the Kurdish guerrilla struggle in eastern Turkey.

completely unimaginative. This can be contrasted with the independent and more effective (but still very limited) role the Turkish left was able to play in the 2013 Gezi revolt.

If different organizational, intellectual and strategic choices had been made in the past, the Middle Eastern left could have intervened in the revolts of 2011–13 in more hegemonic ways. Yet the street went beyond anybody's imagination, putting into doubt how much the left could have been 'ready' for this wave.

The recent explosions in the Middle East brought to the fore dynamics quite different to those the twentieth century left dealt with. Desires for autonomy, individual as well as collective freedoms, and common urban space have moved to the centre of the agenda. These desires are partially novel,[24] and they do not fit neatly into the left's (or anybody else's) agenda in the region. Interestingly, demands that seemed to be ruled out by the specificities of Middle Eastern societies and states (for example, collective struggles for autonomy) now promise to become the order of the day.

The new demands also signal massive participation by well-paid professionals in mass revolt, another novel feature for the region. Class conflict has re-entered the scene in an unexpected way. We need to evaluate whether the left can expand its natural(ized) base through careful engagement with the new middle class. The ongoing Marxist insistence that Gezi was a proletarian revolt obscures the political need to intervene imaginatively in the moment.

One distinguishing feature of the recent revolt wave is how it both challenged and reproduced elements of neoliberalism. By drawing on classical liberal themes such as the leverage of individual freedoms against governmental excess, and by reproducing the neoliberal theme of the end of ideology (and of revolutionary organization), the revolt wave stood on the same ground with neoliberalism. Yet the revolt wave at the same time attacked commodification. This contradiction at the heart of the revolt cannot be understood without analysing its class character.

24 In Turkey and elsewhere, there were intellectual circles and social movement organizations that grappled with these issues in the 2000s, but they were extremely dispersed and quite un-institutionalized.

In the light of these concerns, the Gezi uprising has a twofold significance. First, it signals not only the end of the Turkish model (which even the mainstream has recognized), but also the crisis of liberalism (which had invested all of its hopes in the success of that model and its export to the rest of the Muslim world). Second, it dramatizes the contradictory potentials of the new middle strata in much starker fashion than the Arab and Iranian revolts, pointing out that the new middle class has a love/hate relationship with free market capitalism even in the most successful neoliberal cases. It thereby provides fertile empirical ground on which to discuss how the left can refashion itself to address twenty-first-century dynamics.

The Gezi Explosion: The Dagger in the Front

One of the AKP's more nationalist figures had described an academic conference on the Armenian genocide as a 'dagger in the back of the nation' (see chapter 2). Let's rephrase this characterization. This conference, organized by scholars and intellectuals some of whom were sympathetic to the AKP's democratization project, was a dagger in the back of the passive revolution. It disturbed the smooth coalition between the liberals, conservatives, Islamists and right-wing nationalists through a left-liberal war of position. The intent was not to kill the passive revolution, though, but to democratize it. In the coming years, the conservative manoeuvrings after such destabilizations successfully reduced such stabbings to mosquito bites.

Against this background, the Gezi revolt came as a dagger in the front of the passive revolution. This time, neoliberal hegemony's outsiders (rather than the semi-insiders) dealt the blow, and they attracted many semi-insiders as well. The spark of the Gezi uprising was ignited by urban issues. The AKP's urban policies had met dispersed resistance for a decade (see chapter 3). The protests in and around Taksim seemed to be part of a chain of isolated resistances. The AKP had been tearing down buildings here to open up space for shopping malls. When intellectuals and artists mobilized against the demolition of first a café (İnci Pastanesi) and then a historic movie theatre (Emek Sineması) on İstiklal Caddesi in early 2013, they appeared to be fighting a rearguard elite battle, focusing on sites that were of little interest to the popular classes. But when police brutally cracked down on several dozen protesters who wanted to protect the last green area (Gezi Parkı) near Taksim, popular determination to save this park initiated the biggest spontaneous revolt in Turkish history.

It turned out that people referred to as 'tree-huggers' in Anglophone parlance were not that isolated after all. In fact, it was the dragging away of several activist bodies from the trees (which were subsequently cut down) that initiated the revolt. And this in a country where most people had remained silent as millions of minorities were dragged away from their villages and tens of thousands were butchered during a civil war in the 1990s. How could this be? Why was this 'environmental' imagery so strong?

The answers to these questions will allow us to better understand both the strength and the limits of the Turkish model. Throughout the first few days of the revolt, the emphasis on urban, environmental and anti-commodification issues was gradually decentred (but not eliminated). Initially, thousands flocked to the square in solidarity with those attacked. As a result, police brutality moved to the top of the agenda. Still, during the first day of popularization talk about 'urban transformation' (the official name for the AKP's project of accumulation by dispossession) was prominent. In a couple of days, however, the focus on police violence, the increasing authoritarianism of the AKP, and the persistent lack of democracy in Turkey marginalized the focus on urban issues. Many tweets and other information circulating on the web emphasized that the protests were 'not about a couple of trees', but about democracy.

Nevertheless, there were still banners that insisted on emphasizing the trees, not only as a symbol of nature, but also of the popular democratic uprising. This was much truer to the initial spirit of the protests. One banner in Taksim read: 'Capitalism will cut down the tree if it cannot sell its shadow' (a sentence accurately or inaccurately attributed to Karl Marx). This was also translated into other languages and carried as a banner throughout the world in pro-Gezi demonstrations. In the second week of the revolt, a handwritten sign in a pro-Gezi demonstration in Berkeley, California, captured the whole spirit: 'We are the seeds of the saplings you hanged and the trees you cut down.'[25] This sentence condensed the anti-authoritarian

25 The word *sapling* referred in general to all young martyrs of state violence, but in particular to the leaders of a revolutionary groupuscule who were

and the anti-commodification feelings of the revolt. It was this *temporary condensation* that gave the environmental image a resonance beyond solely environmental issues.

The Gezi uprising started as a resistance to the commodification of urban space. This brought the protestors into confrontation with the government and the police force, who overreacted to anti-neoliberal protest. However, stronger dynamics decentred the focus on urban transformation and commodification.

From Anti-commodification to Anti-authoritarianism

The Gezi revolt erupted in a moment when struggles over a number of issues swiftly condensed. Unlike single-issue mobilizations, major historical revolts come about when several contradictions conjuncturally overlap.[26] It is therefore meaningless to look for the major cause(s) behind such earth-shattering events.[27] The process that leads to them, however, can give us insights into their major dynamics, and as important, why some issues outweigh others at different stages of the revolt.

Some elements within the AKP government made a very risky calculation during the months that led to the Gezi revolt.[28] The government had been preparing Turkey for a regional war (which has so far not arrived) and needed a unified country with no threatening opposition. This was why after a decade of persistent marginalization it reached out to the Kurds. The Turkish rulers (quite reasonably, it would seem) saw the PKK (and its affiliates) as the only force that could stop the government in its tracks. With the Kurds on their side, the calculation went, they could divide, marginalize and repress the

---

hanged by a military junta in 1972, whose stories are captured in a poetic biography from the era that has become a classic, *Three Saplings on the Gallows* by Erdal Öz.

26 The analysis below owes its logic to Althusser's handling of the Russian Revolution, see 'Contradiction and Overdetermination' in *For Marx*, trans. Ben Brewster, London: Verso, 2006 [1962], marxists.org.

27 This point is along the lines of Kurzman's criticism of the literature on revolutions. See Charles Kurzman, *The Unthinkable Revolution in Iran*, Cambridge, MA: Harvard University Press, 2004.

28 The next two paragraphs were previously published as a part of my essay: 'Occupy Gezi: The Limits of Turkey's Neoliberal Success', jadaliyya.com, 4 June 2103.4

rest of the population, which was already much more disorganized than were the Kurds. The peace process with the Kurds also gave the government the chance to win back many liberals, who had been disillusioned with it since 2010. With its renewed hegemonic bloc, elements in the new regime felt that they could easily silence everybody else. The governing party thus intensified police brutality and some other conservative measures (such as tightened regulations on alcohol). People outside of this renewed bloc (whether elite, middle class or lower class; secular or Alevi; male or female; right-wing nationalist or socialist) had been feeling a sense of threat for the previous ten years, but in the first months of 2013 they felt as though their very survival was at risk. When the Gezi resistance turned into an anti-police protest, hundreds of thousands therefore joined in to voice their frustration with increasing authoritarianism.

This naturally brought into the picture a lot of people who had been benefiting from urban commodification as well. Some of these people did not have any problem with police brutality and authoritarianism – as long as it was channelled against striking workers, Kurds, socialists or Alevis. Some of them chanted extreme nationalist slogans throughout Istanbul and across the country. Despite government propaganda, they constituted a minority around Taksim Square, but were certainly the majority in better-off parts of metropolitan areas (that is, the chic neighbourhoods of Istanbul, Izmir and Ankara). There were more organized nationalists among them who wanted to hijack the protests. Yet most of these disjointed masses did not even understand the issues that initiated the protests. They were in it mostly as a way to defend their own interests and lifestyles. These people did not define the Gezi uprising, but they did muddy the waters. The Gezi uprising became strong partly due to their participation, but its national and international message became less clear.

The revolt also spread to other points in the country. A look at a few places will allow us to appreciate how (and whether) the two defining features of the (anti-commodification and anti-authoritarian) Gezi revolt were reproduced (and refracted) throughout Turkey. In İzmir, known for its westernized lifestyle, the message from the street was loudly and clearly secularist. In Hatay, an Alevi town on the border of Syria, masses reacted to the governing party's warmongering, and repression was heaviest in this medium-sized town. In Tuzluçayır, an Alevi neighbourhood of the capital city Ankara, one of the main targets was the Gülen community's creative projects of assimilation (through the establishment of a religious centre that would combine the Sunni mosque and the Alevi place of worship, *cemevi*). Sunni Kurdish towns throughout eastern Turkey were mostly silent, though many Kurds in urban Turkey participated (without their organizations' public endorsement). Kurdish-Alevi neighbourhoods in metropolitan areas (such as 1 Mayıs mahallesi) and provincial towns (such as Tunceli) joined in with clearly socialist slogans. All of the revolt's martyrs were Alevi, which both pointed out to the sectarian makeup of the new Turkish regime *and* the Alevis' engagement in more militant fights when compared to the new middle-class participants of the revolt (who were mostly from secularized Sunni backgrounds). Such swift politicization of multiple issues could indeed topple an ordinary Middle Eastern regime, but not one based on consent. The dilution of the revolt's initial anti-commodification message also helped the regime's consent-based reconstruction.

In what sense was the regime still hegemonic? Major revolts in history politicize multiple issues. A hegemonic actor is defined by its capacity to link these issues in a single chain. This, the Turkish regime was able to do; its mirror image (the secularist opposition) sheepishly reinforced the AKP's reduction of Gezi to an anti-Islamist revolt. Islamist media and politicians highlighted (or fabricated) acts that could be interpreted as impious during the revolt (such as drinking alcohol, the alleged attacks against a veiled woman, the apparent occupation of a mosque, and the perceived deterioration in public hygiene). Despite regime setback after the revolt, then, Islamic politics was successful in one very important regard: the hegemonic parameters it had naturalized over the decades had circumscribed Gezi's anti-commodification message. In the popular imaginary, Gezi was anti-AKP and therefore anti-Islamist. This perception simply played into the hands of the regime. Had a leftist hegemonic organization successfully intervened, Gezi would be interpreted as 'anti-regime, and therefore anti-neoliberal, as much as anti-authoritarian'. Marginalizing all alternative perceptions was the success of hegemony at the moment of its failure.

As important as the uprising's multiclass and multi-issue character was its style. Social movements in Turkey had been becoming more colourful and festive ever since the mid-1990s. But this was the first time that a mass uprising was marked by fully carnivalesque tendencies. The contrast with the sombre tone of other major revolts in Turkish history (the working-class revolt of 15–16 June 1970, and the small merchant and artisan-led austerity protests in 2001, for instance) was striking. As surprising as this turn was the composite nature of the actors who circulated the carnivalesque repertoires.

Gezi as Confrontational Carnival

Throughout the June revolt, men and women in business clothes were present all across Taksim Square, along with the usual suspects (the soccer fans and activists). Finance, management, insurance, advertising and real estate professionals participated in the tens of thousands in the most violent protests. They would simply leave their workplaces (which are concentrated around the square) at 6 p.m. and go to Gezi Park to fight the police. The protests became massive only after they left work and dined, around 7 p.m. or so. Ironically, this was a convenient revolt that (for the most part) did not disrupt their career routines.

The barricade-building activity throughout the revolt was emblematic of its nature. Occasionally, young men and women in fashionable clothing started to build barricades before the most militant leftist groups could reach a decision about the relevance of barricades in this specific revolt. In one incident, the leading activists of a Maoist party (which the police reports declared to be the main organizer of the violent clashes)[29] were discussing among themselves whether to turn the uprising into a revolt with barricades. (Taksim was not their turf, after all. If the revolt had started in one of the subaltern, Kurdish-Alevi neighbourhoods in which they are heavily organized, they would probably have started building the barricades without even thinking about it.) As they were wrapped up in their internal debate, a young man with an earring approached them and asked whether they could give him a hand by pulling the stones out of the sidewalk and handing

29 'Gezi olaylarında yasadışı örgütler koalisyon yaptı', *Star Gazetesi*, September 2013.

them over. The militants turned around in amazement and realized that the barricade-building process had already started.[30]

This interaction was cognitively challenging. While a male militant with earrings is a common sight in the West, it is a novelty in Turkey. Parties such as the one referred to above usually looked down upon such male paraphernalia and interpreted them as 'petty bourgeois tendencies' (while less 'orthodox' socialist parties had opened to some such men during the early 1990s). What was disorienting was not necessarily men with earrings participating in a demonstration, but their taking the lead in a militant revolt and showing the way to (rather than being led by) the Maoists in barricade building.

What was as surprising as seeing these young people chant combative slogans (and building barricades) was their body language. Unlike the leftists and the soccer fans with their serious faces, they were smiling and almost dancing as they chanted. Despite the gas and the rubber bullets flying in the air, the mood was festive.

Such young men and women built barricades all over the city. Women with high heels and high-quality make-up participated extensively in the process, as did soccer fans. The soccer fans had gained a lot of experience in fighting the police over the previous years and that experience came in handy. At many critical junctures, they either slowed down or prevented the police from taking or retaking certain areas in and around Taksim. However, neither they nor the middle-class professionals had ever built *barricades*. The only ones who had that experience were again the relatively more militant leftist groups (whose base of organization was not Taksim, but the subproletarian Alevi neighbourhoods miles away from the area, and barricades were built in these neighbourhoods as well during June 2013); and PKK-connected Kurds who worked in the service sector around Taksim. They haphazardly educated the newcomers. However, two weeks were not enough for a thorough education. Tens of thousands of people unprofessionally built barricades around the square as the police attacked to take it back on June 16. They were easily dismantled by the police due to their poor construction.[31]

---

30 An eyewitness account, collected in late June 2013.

31 On one main artery that led to Taksim, young and mostly unaffiliated men and women had built five to ten barricades and the police passed through

June 16 was one of the decisive days of the revolt. Several thousands gathered in a number of assemblies held in the square. Fearing a massacre, virtually all the leftist organizations wanted the people to leave Taksim. They had pushed far enough, and now it was time to reap the benefits through (institutional) politics. Unorganized teenagers and young men and women screamed, cried and protested as the socialist groups pressed for an end to the occupation of Taksim and Gezi. After hours of back and forth between the articulate, aged and relatively more cautious 'big brothers' (*abiler*, as they are called in Turkish) and the angry youth, the former understood that they would be unable to convince the latter. Exhausted and demoralized, their faces turned pale.[32] The leaders hoped a middle-way settlement would appease the youth: they suggested that everybody leave, but whoever chose to do so could remain in the square. Many young people protested angrily again (some cried 'treason'), in vain. The occupation had ended despite the militancy of the unorganized youth,[33] which was barely kept in its place by the (predominantly male) professional revolutionaries (even though the government and the police insisted on picturing the latter as the motivators and organizers of clashes with the police).[34]

The street battles went on for another couple of weeks, gradually

them in fifteen minutes. The organized socialists, enmeshed in their debates in the square during most of the police attack, were shocked to hear this and could not understand how it was possible. Had the police developed new techniques or acquired new technology they weren't aware of, they wondered. It turned out that the young people had left small openings between the buildings and the barricades. The police did not even deal with the barricades, but simply shot their way through the gaps with rubber bullets. Based on several eyewitness accounts, collected in late June and early July 2013. Information on what percentage of the barricades was built by unorganized youth on this decisive day is not available at this point.

32 Based on several eyewitness accounts, collected in late June 2013.

33 These debates took place during the mass participatory assemblies organized during the last days of the occupation. It is possible, as one of my informal interviewees suggested, that at least some of the youth who appeared to be inexperienced, unorganized men and women were actually undercover members of the more militant leftist organizations.

34 It is true that a couple of socialist organizations insisted on remaining in the square, but it is too early to provide a cool-headed, non-partisan analysis of whether their position was more sensible.

subsiding by mid July.[35] The clashes lasted several hours each night. Some protesters would take breaks from tear gas and visit the chic bars and cafés around the square, have drinks, and then go back to fight; others would rather take their breaks at the rundown left-wing teahouses in the back streets. People could not always choose the localities where they ended up, as things partly depended on the pace of police action and the reach of the tear gas bombs. On several occasions, people were penned up in bars or stores where they were perceivably out of place: chic men and women in rundown left-wing teahouses; carelessly dressed people (most likely members of socialist organizations who did not reside or work around Taksim) in highbrow women's underwear stores on the main street. Though many people tried to keep the mood festive ('We hope to see you again', said the young sales clerk with a smile on her face, as several people left her high-end store), some of the locations were certainly more sombre than others. Entertainment, a carnivalesque aesthetics and politics were innovatively linked, but the linkage was full of frictions.

This atmosphere of quasi-entertainment was not due to the lack of risks. Several people died, even more people lost their eyes, and dozens suffered serious, sometimes permanent injuries during the protests. While the leftists and soccer fans were used to taking such risks in Turkey, this was the first time that huge numbers of comfortable professionals fought the police. Even though scholars and journalists have noted heavy middle-class participation in the protests of the last few years across the globe, some of the contradictions here have gone unnoticed.

The Class Content of the Confrontational Carnival

The Gezi uprising was a multiclass revolt, but one on which the new middle class put its stamp culturally and politically.[36] From 28 to 31 May, as the numbers of protesters climbed from hundreds to thousands, professionals (and relatively privileged students, most likely on their way to becoming professionals) outweighed others (in

35 The analytical narrative provided below is based on my participant observation between June 17 and mid August, unless otherwise noted.

36 Some of the following paragraphs draw on my essay 'Resistance Everywhere: The Gezi Revolt in Global Perspective', *New Perspectives on Turkey* 49 (2013): 157–72.

comparison to their overall ratio in the population). Then the masses that flooded Taksim became much more heterogeneous (for example, informal proletarians from Gaziosmanpaşa and Ümraniye came in big numbers). For the following two weeks, this class heterogeneity persisted and even became more complex with massive protests in informal proletarian (1 Mayıs Mahallesi, Gazi, Okmeydanı, Alibeyköy) as well as established elite (Etiler, Nişantaşı, Bağdad Caddesi) areas.[37] After the security forces emptied Gezi Park and Taksim Square in mid June, the only formal *proletarian* demonstration within the June revolt (on 17 June, organized by DİSK and KESK) attracted very small numbers, and protests stopped in most informal proletarian regions. At this point, the resistance changed tack and focused on organizing popular assemblies (*forums* in Turkish). Despite low expectations, thousands of people in two key middle-class district centres (Beşiktaş and Kadıköy) participated in the assemblies, while only dozens regularly attended them in elite and informal proletarian neighbourhoods.

Statistical findings support these ethnographic observations. The extensive survey conducted by the polling institution SAMER demonstrates that the class structure of those who participated at any one of the events in İzmir and İstanbul closely resembled the class structure of these cities. This survey confirms the overall multiclass nature of the revolt. However, the survey conducted by another institution (KONDA) shows that those occupying the Gezi Park itself on 6–7 June were extremely educated,[38] with 13 per cent of them holding post-graduate degrees (compared to less than 1 per cent of Turkey's overall population). Moreover, a good proportion of them hailed from relatively better-off parts of Istanbul (such as Kadıköy, Şişli, Beşiktaş and Üsküdar). Those who occupied Gezi had a profile different to those who participated in the June revolt throughout Turkey.

---

37 These observations of events before 17 June are based on several eyewitness accounts, as well as frequent web reports by journalistic and political sources. Among these, the most informative was sendika.org, which renewed its estimation of the numbers of protestors by neighbourhood, district and square, sometimes as often as every five to ten minutes during the first two weeks of June.

38 KONDA, 'Gezi Raporu: Toplumun 'Gezi Parkı Olayları' algısı; Gezi Parkındakiler kimlerdi?' (Report on Gezi: The Public Perception of 'Gezi Park Incidents' / Who Were the Gezi Occupiers?), available at http://konda.com/tr/tr/raporlar/KONDA_GeziRaporu2014.pdf.

The SAMER research also indicates that Istanbul and Izmir residents who found the Gezi protests positive tended to be slightly more middle and upper class than those who opposed the uprising. KONDA's second representative survey, conducted throughout Turkey, indicates that farmers, workers, the retired, housewives and *esnaf* (shopkeepers and tradesmen) – and the lower income brackets overall – were more likely to think that 'the protesters were wrong from the beginning' and that 'the police made no mistakes'. In short, the heart of the revolt was much more privileged than its peripheries, and the popular classes felt less invested in this revolt.

The accounts that downplay the middle-class nature of Gezi tend to neglect three factors.[39] First, while it is true that multiple strata participated in the revolt, only the middle class participated with a discernible *class belonging*. The point is not simply that working-class *unions were near-absent* and *professional associations* (of engineers, architects, lawyers and other middle strata) *weighed in heavily* (which is also true). What is as important is that proletarian and subproletarian participation was heaviest in Alevi regions. That is, these strata seem to have participated based on sectarian (or rather, anti-'sectarian regime') as much as *class* dynamics. This is not to deny that class had a role in their participation, as many working-class Alevis have remained class conscious. What is significant here is that there was no sustained revolt in non-Alevi proletarian and subproletarian cities and districts. Second, the *organizational style* the Gezi occupation developed in its last days *consistently spread only to middle-class districts*. There were no massive and recurrent assemblies in popular districts. In other words, *Gezi as Gezi* resonated with select strata. When revolt spread to other parts of Istanbul and Turkey, it became an amorphous 'June Revolt': secularist in İzmir, anti-sectarian in Tuzluçayır and anti-war in Hatay. Last but not least, the *innovative aspects of the revolt* (especially its aesthetics) were heavily new petty bourgeois. The creativity and the dynamism came from this class, although others also participated. Even if the AKP and the Kemalists ultimately succeeded in reinforcing the Islamic–secular divide, only the new petty bourgeois style and spirit (rather than solidly

39 Erdem Yörük and Murat Yüksel, 'Class and Politics in Turkey's Gezi Protests', *New Left Review* 2:89 (September/October 2014): 102–23.

proletarian or socialist demands and slogans) unsettled this divide for a few weeks. What exactly was this unsettling, new petty bourgeois structure of feeling?

We can get a sense of it by looking at the reasons behind the professionals' intense participation in such a risky revolt. Exploitation, (socio-economic) marginalization, impoverishment and other categories that emphasize the process of production and/or the redistribution of resources cannot tell us all. A good proportion of today's Turkish professionals have experienced upward mobility throughout their lives (though we certainly need more research on these groups' weight in the new petty bourgeoisie as a whole). Their living standards are (or promise to be) incomparably higher than those of their parents. As important, it is doubtful whether they would benefit from or be harmed by an egalitarian redistribution of resources throughout the country. In that sense, they do not resemble the 'fearless' Spanish youth who portray themselves as 'without a house, without work, without pension'. The occasional fearlessness of the protesters in Turkey is an intellectual challenge in this regard.[40]

What really hurts this class is not exploitation and impoverishment in absolute economic terms, but their impoverishment of social life. Free market capitalism has actually delivered (to many of) them its promises: lucrative jobs, luxurious vacations, fancy cars, (at least the prospect of) comfortable homes and many other forms of conspicuous consumption. Yet none of this has resulted in fulfilling lives.

The Gezi revolt provided a noncommodified space (the barricades, the public park, shared meals) where this class momentarily tasted the fruits of a collectivistic life. Whatever social ties existed in the life of these professionals was transparently 'social capital': these social ties were not only convertible to economic capital and upward mobility in their professions, they were established with the semi-explicit goal of being converted to such 'cash' at some point. What the revolt provided was the pleasure of social ties for the sake of social ties – that is, the revolt starkly demonstrated to these sectors that a different

40 We do have to be very careful here, as the most fearless within the revolt were proletarian/subproletarian, revolutionary and Alevi actors, as the death toll clearly demonstrates. It is not their fearlessness, apparently much sharper and more fatal than that in Spain, which constitutes the intellectual challenge.

world was possible, one in which pleasure was not based on commodities but interpersonal ties. That is why tens of thousands of people stuck to 'their' park (which was not heavily used before it was attacked) for twenty days and then thousands attended the assemblies for another month.

The common talk of the virtues and pleasures of sharing and solidarity among the Gezi occupiers did not (and at this point, could not) find any parallels in the shape of a common talk about the virtues of nationwide equality. To the contrary, the nonsocialist participants frequently voiced their contempt for the 'ignorant' lower classes who kept on voting for the AKP. I encountered either class contempt or class blindness among the participants at the assemblies (most heavily engineers, lawyers, doctors, media and social media experts, real estate experts and finance professionals). Those without any social science and/or socialist training looked down on the lower classes. They talked about the need to 'go to' the lower classes and enlighten them about the evils of the governing regime (that had allegedly 'bought' their votes with coal and food, a folk analysis often repeated on the stage of the assemblies and in the working groups and committees). Those with more sociological or socialist training avoided such reductionism, but instead insisted that they (as 'white-collar workers') also were a part of the working class and hence there was no real distinction between them and the workers (the people the nonsocialist participants talked of as 'they').

This (misrecognized, denied) new middle-class character of the revolt certainly constituted a strength in a country where the lower classes were reduced to silence through force and engineered consent. However, this also rendered the revolt a quite restricted one that, by its very nature, was bound to have limited effects on the macrostructures of the country. There were solid structural-class elements that prevented this revolt from *institutionally* spreading from the middle-class neighbourhoods to proletarian strata and areas (and becoming a *sustained* nationwide movement with a common platform and leaders).

A careful analysis of middle-class dispositions can constitute a basis for deepening the general theory of the new petty bourgeoisie (and the movements and revolts in which it predominates). We first need to realize that commodification (of labour, everyday life and nature) has produced a quite monotonous life for this class, a monotony which it has broken thanks to the Gezi revolt. Yet at the same time many factions of this class directly or indirectly have benefited from the commodification of the last three decades; they can easily renew their coalitions with the current order, even in the sphere of the commodification of urban space (which incited the revolt to begin with). The middle-class opposition to commodification is thus full of self-contradictions.

Another difficulty the revolt faced has to do with the cultural (rather than economic) dispositions of this class. The new petty bourgeoisie of our day (perhaps unlike the same class as analysed by Poulantzas in the context of the twentieth century) has strongly participatory and anti-authoritarian tendencies (though its anti-authoritarianism can go in individualist as well as collectivist directions). This fosters a political culture where discussion for the pleasure of discussion can trump the formation of programmatic goals. This, added to other linguistic and cultural differences between this class and proletarian and subproletarian sections of society, rendered the post–16 June institutionalization attempts less attractive among broader popular sectors (hence the low level of participation in the assemblies in subaltern neighbourhoods that had participated in the uprising, as well as the more heavily new middle-class character of the well-populated assemblies).

Other examples of (*potentially* exclusive) new petty bourgeois tendencies included the aestheticization of politics and the innovative melding of entertainment and revolt. Potential distinction through entertainment (for example, status competition based on clothing, alcohol consumption, bars frequented, and so on) risked the exclusion of subordinate sectors. This is not to say that entertainment *in itself* is an exclusive tendency: Bakhtin has pointed out that (especially premodern) popular revolt frequently had carnivalesque characteristics. However, it *can* become exclusive in modern multi-class revolt as groups with conflicting tendencies repel each other (not only due to different ideologies, but because of alien dispositions).[41]

---

41 Nevertheless, the Turkish new petty bourgeoisie also displayed signs of political maturity. Examples of 'self-restricting' entertainment abounded, as when habitual drinkers avoided alcohol on a hot evening in order not to offend

Ignoring the class nature of the Gezi revolt automatically shut off a discussion about the lack of massive and sustainable proletarian and subproletarian participation. Hence, by sticking to the illusion that Gezi was a 'white-collar' working-class uprising (or, in the more refined versions, a multiclass uprising that did not have a predominantly petty bourgeois character), those organized actors who had the potential to institutionalize the uprising and create a movement out of it remained oblivious of the reasons why there was no organized class alliance in the body of this specific revolt. The fallacy of treating all salaried employees as segments of the working class therefore locked them up in a theoretical cage. This was specifically the danger that Nikos Poulantzas had pointed out in the aftermath of the 1960s.[42]

The restricted and restrictive class character of the revolt brings us to a deeper problem: the inability (at least, at this point) to offer alternatives to the current order, and to sustain societal coalitions that will realize those alternatives. The new middle-class stamp on the revolt reinforced (but did not singlehandedly create) the disorganized (not 'leaderless') and unfocused tendencies of post-1979 worldwide revolt.

The umbrella organization that attempted to give some direction to the revolt, Taksim Dayanışması (Taksim Solidarity), distinguished the Gezi revolt from those in Spain ('Indignados') and the United States ('Occupy'), which remained 'leaderless' throughout (at least on paper, if not in actual practice). Taksim Solidarity was a coalition of professional associations, social movement (environmental, urban, feminist, LGBT and others) organizations and socialist groups with at times conflicting agendas. The most important contribution of this umbrella organization (and therefore of the accumulated experience

the pious revolters in and around Gezi-Taksim (simply because it was Mawlid, the night when Prophet Muhammad's birth is celebrated). Adapting and popularizing masculinist soccer fan chants is another example of the new petty bourgeoisie's (*potentially*) flexible aesthetics.

42 Nikos Poulantzas, 'The New Petty Bourgeoisie', *Critical Sociology* 9 (1979): 56–60. Should these strata be articulated to the proletarian party or do the circumstances of the twenty-first century require a radical overhaul of political society, with new organizational forms that could unite the middle and subordinate strata against capitalism? We can't even start to discuss this question without acknowledging the centrality of middle strata to today's revolt.

of the Turkish left) becomes obvious in comparison to the June 2013 revolt in Egypt. Despite aggressive and organized movements on the part of the forces of the old regime, the Gezi revolt did not play into the hands of an old regime conspiracy, in opposition to its Egyptian counterpart.

Moreover, despite the confusingly multi-issue character of the revolt, Taksim Solidarity formulated demands and crafted documents throughout the summer of 2013 that solidly focused on the core anti-commodification and anti-authoritarian spirit of the revolt. The organization's demands and its overall discourse revolved around the governing party's urban renewal projects and its policing practices. That is, due to the accumulated organizational experience and ideological maturity of the Turkish left, Taksim Solidarity did not go on tangents (quite possible when a coalition organization harbours dozens of mutually suspicious partners). Nevertheless, even this organization was unable to formulate a roadmap towards a more democratic and decommodified country. Mature as it was in comparison to its counterparts in many corners of the Western and non-Western world, it was far from ready to intervene decisively in such a massive revolt.

Eventually, the revolt subsided and the various attempts to turn it into a sustained movement could not reach the broader masses. The prime minister had mocked the revolt by saying that all these (privileged, he implied) youth would soon go on their usual vacations and the revolt would end. It did indeed. The new petty bourgeoisie did not return from its summer vacation. The left in Turkey retracted to its pre-2013 base. After mid July 2013, clashes and protests persisted throughout the country, but mass attendance dramatically dropped. Even the protests around Taksim became much less colourful. A solidly 'socialist' spirit replaced the new petty bourgeois spirit. The slogans, faces and clothes started to resemble those from pre-2013 Turkish protests. Humour, entertainment and laughter took a back seat.

This doesn't mean that the left could not make any advances after June. To take one example, the students at one major college, Middle East Technical University (ODTÜ), combined forces with squatters around campus to fight further accumulation by dispossession in the fall of 2013, protesting urban renewal projects and road construction that would destroy squatter housing and certain areas of campus. Nevertheless, such geographically restricted acts of resistance paled in significance when compared to the June 2013 explosion. The left could not pull together the forces that had momentarily coalesced during that phase of the protests.[43]

The extant hegemony in Turkey and the extremely factional character of the Turkish left are not the only reasons behind the failure, even though they played a role. The practical task ahead is not only to go beyond the left's factionalism and nurturing working leaderships, programmes and practical agendas (all of which are important and pose formidable challenges), but also to develop an organizational and ideological framework that could sustain long-term coalitions between various subordinate strata, including the fickle (but now decisive) new middle class.

Gülen's Assault: The Dagger from Within

Following Gezi, the power bloc seemed to implode. The bickering in Islamic circles would not put an end to the passive revolution but did permanently destabilize it. Whereas consent outweighed force before the revolt, now the importance of force in this balance increased. This shift occurred mostly in response to the revolt, but also in interaction with dynamics in the make-up of the regime. Since I have written a long essay on the Erdoğan-Gülen fallout elsewhere, I will summarize only the aspects of this drama relevant to the arguments developed in this book.[44]

For a while, the Gülen community had wanted an AKP without Erdoğan. This was not surprising, since that had become the line of Western powers as well. The Gülen community, as the AKP's Westernist wing, simply endorsed this line. Tension had escalated between Gülen and Erdoğan in the months that led to Gezi. Both sides saw Gezi as an opportunity to liquidate the other. In December 2013, Gülen-connected prosecutors rained down thousands of pages of corruption accusations on Erdoğan and his coterie. The Gülenist

43 None of this rules out the possibility that the working groups and committees that have emerged out of the June revolt could plant the seeds of the model revolutionary organization of the twenty-first century.

44 'Towards the End of a Dream? The Erdogan-Gulen Fallout and Islamic Liberalism's Descent', jadaliyya.com, 22 December 2013.

press astutely used the revolt's language to characterize the prime minister and his entourage as pillagers of nature for profit. The Gülenists wanted to hit two birds with one stone: they would both get rid of their internal enemy and absorb the Gezi resistance into the passive revolution.

However, the assault backfired. Contrary to Gülenist expectations, all the other Islamic communities and circles within the power bloc united behind the prime minister. This was actually the logical thing to do, given the balance of forces within the Islamic field (even if it was not completely logical in terms of regime sanity). The Gülen community had succeeded in reducing all other communities to insignificance, and for them it was payback time. Erdoğan attacked with vengeance, and the purges of Gülenists from the police, the judiciary, public television, ministries and other official institutions were still going on unabated as I completed this book in early 2015.

The Islamic press interpreted Gezi and the Gülenist assault as a combined neocon-Israeli conspiracy planned in advance. This interpretation consoled the AKP's base. Its supporters have become much more committed ever since Gezi, since they now see the regime as under Israeli threat. However, this conspiratorial turn came with a cost. The regime not only lost many of its qualified cadres (since Gülenists were arguably the most educated and refined of the bureaucrats), but its sectarian policies took on self-destructive characteristics. It is speculated that Turkey has become one of the major supporters of sectarian-jihadi forces in the Middle East (temporarily including ISIS), a move that cannot but further sectarianize, militarize and destabilize Turkey. This would be unthinkable if the Gülen community had remained a solid part of the power bloc. Indeed, the Gülen community dealt one last blow by not only stopping but also publicly exhibiting a Turkish truck full of weapons allegedly destined for al-Qaeda or perhaps ISIS.

Some of the consequences of 'the dagger from within' are now clear and some are still unfolding. The AKP regime is now much more based on coercion than it was during its first eleven years in power. In that sense, it is less hegemonic. It has further consolidated its base and power bloc, but it has done so at the expense of the ongoing purges of secular and Islamic liberals. The AKP's professionalism has also declined after the assault on Gezi and the Gülenists. However, the assault has not (yet?) resulted in a fragmented Islamic field. Islamic civil society and political society are still quite unified, if much less professionalized. In fact, the AKP is destroying that professionalism to hang on to its monopoly of power. Hence, a new combination has emerged. Whereas monopolization and professionalization of Islamism went hand in hand in the cases traced throughout this book, monopolization is now linked to deprofessionalization.

The Three Eras of Post-war Hegemony and the Way Ahead

For non-Western peoples, a good chunk of the twentieth century was an era of national developmentalism. The end of the twentieth century marked the end of that project as non-Western leaders embraced liberalism, authenticity and/or religion. As we get deeper into the twenty-first century, however, the non-Western world seems to be waking up to a new spring of collectivism and extended participation (or hopes thereof). Since similar desires are being expressed strongly in the West, the distinction between the West and the non-Western world may further erode.

Three distinct set of themes have shaped politics in the Middle East since World War II. From the 1950s to the 1970s, nationalism and development were the leading themes (themes already at the centre of Turkish politics from the 1920s onwards). National independence required economic independence and development, the Middle Eastern progressives asserted. The left supported the new regimes wherever nationalist goals prevailed (especially in the Arab republics). The classical European leftist goals (equality, freedom, class-based solidarity) were therefore subordinated to nationalism and economic advancement (and postponed until the ever-receding dawn of full national progress). The left got hegemonized rather than becoming hegemonic, absorbed because the proclaimed goals of progressive nationalisms seemed close to its own goals. It was led astray.

The authoritarian hell that resulted from nationalism pushed even progressives, leftists and Marxists to rediscover the virtues of liberalism (especially its emphasis on pluralism and individual liberty). Frequently wedded to this was a concern with authenticity: even though nationalism had promised independence from the West, it had enslaved the non-Westerners' souls and minds by measuring their progress based on Western criteria. Islam (and occasionally, other aspects of local culture) was now perceived to be the antidote. From the 1980s to the 2000s, liberalism and Islam gradually became the distinguishing markers of the hegemonic intellectuals. But rather than delivering on its promises of freedom and authenticity, Islamic liberalism (with help from its leftist and secular-liberal allies) built a soft totalitarian democracy in the only country where the new path to modernity was fully tried out: Turkey.

In this process, the left 'suffered' in two distinct ways. Its smaller organizations and mid-level intellectuals were thoroughly marginalized in political, academic and intellectual fields (while also facing serious repression stretching over three decades). Its top intellectuals and their political circles, by contrast, became the core organizers of Islamic liberal hegemony.

The 2011–13 revolt wave is the last leap of faith in this drama. The dreams of previous generations have not been systematically rejected, but they have been called into question. This revolt to preserve and extend the commons (and for extended participation in the political arena) does not simply render the dreams of those generations meaningless, but it does tend to marginalize them (even though the new era will not bear any fruit if it does not answer some of the issues raised by the earlier eras: the national, developmental and religious questions).

In this new era, then, the left has a real chance to lead. Yet it is weak, disorganized and demoralized. And the opening revolt of the new era was predominantly petty bourgeois, rather than proletarian, which unsettles the intellectual baggage of the left and points to the need for a theoretical overhaul. Still, the goals of the revolt pose major challenges to capitalism as well. It is not clear whether and how the current world order will be able to reorganize itself in response to the growing revolt – and this opening gives the left ample room for manoeuvre.

CONCLUSION

The Counterpoint to Capital

Soon after the storming of the Bastille, Istanbul and other Ottoman cities were decorated with French flags. Not only French communities in those cities, but the local Muslim and non-Muslim populations took to the streets to celebrate or denounce the French revolution. In the following years, the Greek Orthodox Church and the Ottoman elites joined forces as they attacked the spread of egalitarian and anti-clerical ideas.[1] Selective recollections of 1789 continued to divide and unite the Ottomans along unexpected lines of cleavage in the decades to come. More than a century later, the Kemalists perceived a kinship between their 1923 and the French 1789 in terms of anti-clericalism, but they chose to marginalize the mass-mobilizing dimension of Jacobinism.

Ever since 1789, fascination with (and fear of) revolution has propelled social change in Turkey. The last decades of the Republic have been marked by attempts to absorb the shock waves of global and local 1968 and the Iranian revolution of 1979. Following 2011, Turkish rulers also flexed their neocolonial muscles as they sought to shape the revolts breaking out across the region; manipulation was added to fear and fascination. Seen from this angle, the Turkish model was a contradictory ensemble: a potentially explosive effort to regulate, absorb, control and contain revolt at home and abroad. In this sense, the primary contribution of Turkey to world history has not been the smooth marriage of Islam and liberalism (or democracy), but a renewed confidence in passive revolution.

The Arab Spring of 2011 marks the beginning of the end of that contribution. In light of post-2011 developments, this chapter calls for

1 Ali Yaycıoğlu, 'Révolutions de Constantinople: The French and the Ottoman Worlds in the Age of Revolutions' in Patricia M. E. Lorcin and Todd Shepard, eds, *French Mediterraneans: Transnational and Imperial Histories*, Lincoln, NE: Nebraska University Press, forthcoming.

a discussion of whether the Turkish, Iranian, Tunisian and Egyptian experiences can inform world history in some other distinct way.

Reconnecting the Dots in Middle Eastern History

History has no prime mover, but this fascination plus fear of revolution (among both the rulers and the ruled) was one of the main dynamics behind much of the liberalization, democratization and Islamization in Turkey after 1980. Moreover, this contradictory relation to revolution also connects the dots between disparate events, social groups and institutions both at home and abroad: what unites and divides Turkey is its relation to 1789, 1968, 1979 and 2011 (more than the military-paternalistic state tradition and the struggle between the centre and periphery, as in liberal accounts). The socio-political blocs in Turkey are partially shaped by how they situate themselves in reference to these upheavals.

Marxist accounts of Turkish and Middle Eastern history (as a history of integration into capitalism) can be refined through the incorporation of this counterpoint.[2] The role of explosive events in world history cannot be reduced to socio-economic developments (or even class struggle). This book has only initiated the work of rewriting regional history from the standpoint of revolution–restoration by focusing on the post-war era. What needs to be done next is not only the deepening of our appreciation of these crucial decades, but also rewriting the history of modern social and political formations as contradictory responses to the events of 1789, 1848, 1905, 1917, 1949, 1968, 1979 and 2011.[3]

Turkey and Iran were not only receivers but makers of the 1905–11 revolutionary wave. In Iran, the revolutionary uprising was completely crushed, but its cultural and political traces set off what John Foran has called 'a century of revolution'. In Turkey, by contrast, some of the revolutionaries of 1908 came to power, but in less than a year they

2 This chapter's emphasis on counterpoints and transculturation is inspired by the anthropologist Fernando Ortiz, particularly his *Cuban Counterpoint: Tobacco and Sugar*, Durham, NC: Duke University Press 1995 [1940].

3 These comments are loosely based on a non-loyal reading of Giovanni Arrighi's (heterodox and Gramscian) version of world systems theory. I hope to extend on my debt to and differences from Arrighi elsewhere.

distorted, twisted, contained and absorbed what remained of the initially democratic uprising of 1908.

Revolutions from above were concocted on the ruins of the Iranian and Turkish revolts of 1905–08. The Pahlavi regime (built by a general who had fought the Bolsheviks) and the Kemalist regime not only repressed home-grown 1917s, but also absorbed the energy, hopes and institutions of global 1917–19. Mustafa Kemal, inspired first and foremost by the centralizing vision of French Jacobinism (but an opponent of its socio-economic radicalism and mass mobilizing dimension), took the concept of central planning from the Soviets, only to build a national bourgeoisie. The first Pahlavi Shah retained a mostly negative relationship with 1917, and his revolution from above resulted in a grotesque version of Turkish modernism.

Nasser's revolution from above was again both a receiver and producer of the Third Worldist revolutionary wave that stretched from 1949 to 1968. It not only replicated Kemalist (national-capitalist) absorption of the Soviet economic model, but put a further radical and subaltern spin on it. Nasserism emphasized socio-economic equality much more than its Turkish counterpart and deployed local culture more thoroughly to 'transculturate' modernity.

The student and worker mobilizations intersected with and hybridized this Third Worldism in the wake of 1968. In Turkey, the local version of the New Left drew on both Third Worldist and Parisian themes, leading to quite innovative (Turkish and Kurdish) versions of Maoism and post-Maoism. The Kurdish guerrilla struggle, a stretched-out people's war, both strengthened and destabilized the post-2002 Turkish passive revolution. In Iran, Marxism was married to Islam through a re-reading of Sartre, Fanon, Mao and the Shiite tradition.

The year 1979 saw the crowning (and demise) of Third Worldism: it further emphasized the vigour of local traditions (now deployed to deny Western modernity in total, if only on paper) to build a more egalitarian world (but this time, as Foucault noticed, a world with a spirit too). If the victories of 1979 put Iran on the map as a major player in global politics (and Islamic revolution as a credible threat in the hearts of the regimes), its restrictions became more striking in the following years: the Islamic revolution failed to usher in a more just (and 'spirited') world.

Though 1979 could not bring about more equality, it did put *equality* and *revolution* in the centre of Islamic discourse – for a while. *The accomplishment of the Turkish model*, seen from this angle, *was the Islamic decentring of both themes*. By reducing social justice to a technocratic management of absolute poverty, by ignoring relative poverty and inequality, by disorganizing labour with the support of disadvantaged strata, it managed to couple Islam with democracy, while reducing both to technique and appearance (the Turkish model = alcohol regulation + voluntary veiling + plebiscitary voting). This reduction seemed to be proceeding well until a new wave of revolt in 2011 destabilized the passive revolution, which had remained (relatively) unshaken even by the global financial crisis of 2008. The Gezi revolt was another twist in the counterpoint. Turkey's ultimate contribution to world history might indeed come not from its passive revolutionary genius, but (unexpectedly) its late revolutionary awakening. This is the lesser possibility, but it is worth exploring.

The Global 2011

A peculiarity of the June revolt in Turkey was its simultaneity to other revolts. Egypt's and Brazil's June 2013 revolts come first to mind, but the Turkish revolt was also a part of a broader wave that stretched from 2009 to 2013. A wave of revolt had started with Iran, Greece, Iceland and other Western countries in 2009 and then spread to Tunisia and Egypt, and then back to the West in 2011, with the United States, Greece and Spain at the centre. As the wave seemed to subside, Turkey and Brazil erupted in 2013. Ukraine and Venezuela joined the revolt in late 2013 and early 2014, taking it in a right-wing direction.

The Middle-Class Defence of the Commons

The most spectacular revolts of this wave were anti-commodification, but not anti-capitalist. They were anti-commodification in form: they sought to reclaim public services and public goods such as main squares ('the Commons') against the onslaught of the market. The partially common content was based on global marketization and its malaises (real estate bubbles, soaring housing prices and the overall privatization-alienation of common urban goods).

These were mostly multiclass revolts with new petty bourgeois characteristics. With a few exceptions such as Greece and Tunisia, the middle class was the heart and mind of the revolt. The other classes followed their lead. Occupations of workplaces, factories, poor neighbourhoods and industrial towns remained secondary to the emphasis on the main square; when they were carried out (as they were frequently in the case of Egypt's Mahalla and Tanta), they were quite disconnected from the heart of the revolt (for example, from Tahrir). Most crucially, the revolts were vociferously pro-autonomy, rejected hierarchy and sought to build solidarity without resort to authoritarian measures. Nevertheless, the creative forms of popular empowerment and direct democracy on occupied territory (assemblies in Greece, Spain and Turkey; the 'people's mic' in the US) empowered the articulate, hyper-educated new middle classes more than anybody else. Hierarchy and authority were denied in principle, but not avoided in practice. The contributions and contradictions of this revolt wave will remain intellectual and political challenges for the decades to come.

Like other revolutionary waves, that of 2009–13 expressed discontent with broad global affairs and structures despite its focus on national conditions. Unlike almost all previous revolutionary waves, however, 2009–13 did not have a unifying ideology or programme. In that, it was closest to the Eastern European rebellions of 1989. Yet 2009–13 was also quite distinct from 1989, in that it expressed the crisis of the hegemonic world order, rather than reinforcing it.

The Crisis of the Hegemons

This book has focused on the study of hegemonies at national and regional scales. Yet national and regional hegemonies are situated within global hegemonic orders, even if they are not always perfectly aligned.[4] We can call a global capitalist order hegemonic when there is cross-national consent (backed by force) for a core *economic* model. There might be national and regional variations on this core model. Its political and cultural implications are also likely to be contested. But if the order is truly hegemonic, the variation and the contestation will remain within the boundaries of the model. This consent is

4 Some of this section draws on a previously published piece, 'Resistance Everywhere: The Gezi Revolt in Global Perspective', *New Perspectives on Turkey* 49 (2013): 157–72.

contingently articulated to global and regional *territorial* balances. Despite the increasing significance of nongovernmental institutions, states have been the main (but by no means the only significant) actors of this articulation.[5] Ever since World War II, the United States has been at the centre of this game.[6]

The United States itself has been turning away from consent to coercion in its external as well as internal affairs. The number of wars, victims of war, and the intensity of war-related torture, have been on the rise. Internally, too, the government has been increasing repression of its own citizens, even over non-war-related issues. The techniques of repression and excessive surveillance travel from one sphere to the other. Telephone tapping, collection of personal data on the Internet, extra-legal IRS audits, and other methods are becoming routine measures (not only against Occupy activists, but even against conservatives and Tea Party figures). The US is also having a difficult time lining up its Western allies behind its projects for war and repression, though most of them participate willy-nilly in these efforts, as well as in the 'war on terrorism'. Consent is even weaker outside the Western world, where wars and torture breed more than distrust.

The ever fluctuating Middle Eastern policy of the United States is both a sign and maker of its hegemonic crisis. That is, the United States is not able to show a clear way forward for the Middle East: it is not able to *lead*, even if it succeeds occasionally in repressing unwanted movements and trends. The American invasions of Afghanistan and Iraq, taken by some as signs of US power, have actually undermined its hegemonic capabilities. They led to the unintended, quick and deceptive rise of Iranian influence. The United States then bolstered the Saudi-Gulf counterattack to fight its greatest enemy in the region, Iran. However, this move produced more

---

5 The leading actors of articulation might be different on different scales. For the national scale, see Cedric de Leon, Manali Desai and Cihan Tuğal, eds, *Building Blocs: How Parties Organize Society*, Stanford, CA: Stanford University Press, 2015. In that book, we emphasized the centrality of political parties as actors of articulation, but did not extend our arguments to regional and global scales. As we have seen here, political parties might also attempt to become the relay points between regional and global hegemony. The AKP indeed embarked on such a project, but failed.

6 Giovanni Arrighi, *The Long Twentieth Century: Money, Power, and the Origins of Our Times*, London: Verso, 1994.

unintended results, primarily the sectarianization of politics across the region and the resulting demise of the Turkish model. In early 2015, the US once again attempted to normalize its relations with Iran in order to counterbalance the murderous ISIS, further attesting to the profound confusion of the world hegemon. The processes studied throughout this book (the interactions between Turkey's economy, politics and religion with regional dynamics) evolved in the context of these failed American interventions.

These political-military ('territorial') problems have their economic counterparts. As in other hegemonic crises, the leading power has been turning away from productive growth to financially driven growth. Production and technological innovation are shifting to non-Western regions of the world in an uneven fashion. The processes alluded to in the pages above (real estate bubbles, especially in the United States and other Western countries, privatization and accumulation by dispossession, particularly in non-Western regions) unfold against this background of financialization (which is, again, unevenly distributed throughout the world order). The American economy has started to count disproportionately on either financial or real estate bubbles, or a combination of the two.[7] As seen in the 2008 crisis, while this speculative model of growth lends dynamism to the economy for a while, it then leads to shock waves throughout the world's economies. As a result, the United States and other Western powers are no longer the world's unquestionable leaders of economic growth. In short, the political-military crisis of the hegemon is articulated to its economic crisis.

The so-called 'Turkish model' was a lifesaver in these troubled times. Global hegemonic powers hoped that the new regime in Turkey would spread the belief in (an Islamized version of) the American way in military, diplomatic, economic and cultural venues throughout its region and the Muslim world. With its (perceived) economic miracle, marriage of religion and liberal-authoritarian democracy and participation in the Greater Middle East Project, Turkey served all of these purposes.

The Arab uprisings further fuelled the hope that the new democracies in the Middle East would rush to imitate Turkey's path (and

7 Robert Brenner, 'New Boom or New Bubble? The Trajectory of the US Economy', *New Left Review* 2:25 (January/February 2004): 57–100.

thereby serve American efforts at consent-building). However, the realities on the ground turned out to be much more complex. Rather than quietly following Turkey, the Islamic movements and organizations in the region learned selectively from Turkey's success, engaging in multiple and shifting coalitions with regional powers – not all of them in line with global hegemonic interests, let alone with Turkey's specific interests. In sum, despite Turkey's insistent projection of itself as a hegemon (and its leaders' and intellectuals' deep and sincere belief in their historic mission in this regard), Muslim/Arab allegiance to Turkish military-political leadership became weaker and consent for the Turkish model shakier as the Arab uprisings unfolded.

Just as in the case of the United States, Turkey's imperial overreach intensified coercion at home. This became all the more obvious in early 2013. As the new regime's imperial project reached its limits, it ratcheted up police repression. Police violence, one of the main catalysers of the Gezi protests, reached its peak right after the Turkish prime minister's trip to the United States, where he attempted one last time, in vain, to push the Western powers to take a more bellicose role in Syria.

As the hegemons turn from consent to coercion, anti-authoritarian and antiwar protests have spread, and might spread further. Depending on the national context and the timing, anti-commodification protests still have the potential to be articulated to anti-authoritarian protests. However, as the cases of Venezuela and Ukraine demonstrate, the – so far – weak articulation of these issues open the way to pro-'world order' appropriations of the revolt wave (and aspects of its style). Even worse, the wave of revolt that deepened the crisis of secular authoritarianism throughout the region led not to Islamic liberalism (as the West hoped) or to Islamic revolution (as the Iranian regime desired), but to the spread of murderous sectarian paramilitaries.

The sectarian apparatus that calls itself 'the Islamic State in Iraq and al-Sham' (ISIS) is not just a temporary accident, but a culmination of various processes: the crisis of American hegemony at the global level and Turkish hegemony at the regional level; the rise of Saudi Arabia and the Gulf states (and their increasing ideological, if not always diplomatic, influence on Turkey); the decline of both

Islamic liberalism and revolutionary Islam, a void that Salafism now fills; the slowing of economic growth regionally, as a result of which the youth turn to non-economic adventures (in the absence of well-formulated liberal or leftist ideologies). During the optimistic days of 2011–13, it seemed that any such right turn could be met with even bigger antiwar feeling. At the end of 2014, we were rather witnessing the potential of these bloody paramilitaries to consolidate their hold on territory into full-blown states. The immediate aftermath of global 2011 might be one of the darkest waves of reaction in world history.

Given these strong tendencies in incompatible directions, the ultimate impact of the revolt wave remains unpredictable. We can tentatively conclude that the uprisings that stretched from 2011 to 2013 have rendered the Turkish model meaningless. Hence, we can say what 2011 *won't* lead to, but we cannot yet spell out what it *will* lead to.

2011 and the World History of Revolt

Yet, what if we discuss 2011 in terms of what it *might* lead to? Placing 2011 within the world history of revolt as such could be a thought-provoking exercise. The first sections of this chapter pointed out that there is something to gain analytically from such a perspective inasmuch the Middle East is concerned. But now the task becomes not only re-writing the history of Middle Eastern revolution, but of world revolution as a whole. Where do the recent revolts fit into this overall history? And as important, can we find new clues about the strengths, potentials and limits of the 2011 revolt if we see it as one major step within the unfolding of the global history of revolt?

One problem the Egyptian revolutionaries faced was coming up with clear formulations and demands based on their overall slogan of social justice. The next difficulty was the attainment of even the most modest social justice demands within national boundaries. Setting generous minimum wages as well as restrictive maximum wages in both the public and private sectors (a push which led to only small gains) would most probably lead to capital flight, had it succeeded fully – as not only economists but all non-leftists underlined. Does this mean that the push was meaningless? And should we frame its lack of realization exclusively as a failure?

The picture looks a little different (though still not rosy) when we realize that the insistence on social justice demands (when coupled with other demands elsewhere) broadened the horizon of activists inside and outside Egypt and put social justice questions squarely back in the centre of global activist discourse. We need to go back to Marx's metaphor of the old mole and take it quite seriously.[8] Demands such as this go underground like a mole, but then resurface elsewhere more effectively (if, that is, the tunnel has been prepared professionally). The Egyptian demands could come closer to realization under more favourable circumstances (say, in a country surrounded by regions with much higher minimum wages and/or regions with more sustained social justice revolts). This is possible as the whole world gets drawn into more intense protests.

However, such world-historicization of revolt also invites the protesters to occasionally push much bolder demands. The question is not simply opting for the 'maximum' (or the 'transitional'[9]) rather than the 'minimum programme', but thinking contextually about 'demand' itself: pushing for aspects of the so-called maximum rather than the minimum programme might make more sense at one specific juncture and in one specific location, but not in another place and time. While this or that specific demand might come to the fore of popular struggle partly independent of conscious leadership, the task of the leadership would be putting each demand and/or action within the context of a broader historical and interconnected struggle (and based on this, deciding what kinds of resources to pour into sustaining certain demands and actions).

The concepts at our disposal (democratic revolution, socialist revolution, national-democratic revolution or even permanent revolution) would not be able to capture such a strategy, for they neglect the

8 As Marx stated in 1852, when the revolution concentrates its destructive forces against executive power, 'Europe will leap from its seat and exult: Well burrowed, old mole!', 'The Eighteenth Brumaire of Louis Bonaparte', available at marxists.org. My comments on revolutionary failure and the old mole are inspired by Alain Badiou, as well as my discussions with Aynur Sadet.

9 This term was coined to talk about the possibility of pushing for certain popularly desirable but immediately unviable demands in a way that would corner the current system and lead it to collapse, so as to prepare the ground for organs of popular power and revolutionary leadership of those organs. See Leon Trotsky, 'The Transitional Program', available at marxists.org.

intermittent nature of revolt waves. The path of global revolution is neither smoothly integrated nor divided up into stages. Rather, the world revolution *comes in jolts*. It does not arrive as a global event, but through uneven combinations of the most modest and the boldest demands and actions in sometimes the least-expected corners of the globe.

Moreover, most revolutionary uprisings are either defeated, thwarted or absorbed, yet still leave deep cultural and organizational marks, locally and globally. And some uprisings lead to structures and institutions that are at odds with the initial plan of the leadership, even when these structures and institutions are labelled socialist or revolutionary. Hence, the climate of revolt, while conducive to path breaking institutional innovation, cannot be counted on as the *sole* source of postcapitalist institutional novelty. A focus on institution-building in relatively quiet times is therefore necessary, not only to prepare the way for the next uprising, but also to prevent popular and revolutionary forces from developing nondemocratic and counter-revolutionary structures and institutions.

This new understanding of demand, defeat, interconnectedness and leadership takes us to the concept of 'intermittent' (though certainly not 'interrupted') revolution.

Intermittent Revolution

What are the most prominent examples of such cultural and organizational marks of failed revolt in world history?[10] The revolutionary wave of 1848, for instance, did not lead to any lasting democracies, but it convinced the European working and middle classes that a more democratic world was possible. It put socialization on the agenda. Furthermore, the defeats of that massive revolt taught militants that they needed much more resilient leadership and organization to realize their aims. A bunch of dispersed working-class and republican political fields had been replaced by solid national and continental organizations by the end of the century.

The wave of 1905, another potential parallel, is known for its defeats more than its victories. Yet those defeats not only provided the

10 Some of the following thoughts were previously published as 'Turkey: A Second 1848 . . . or 1905?', Counterpunch, 11 June 2013, counterpunch.org.

groundwork for further political experience, education and organization, but also created the most massive directly democratic organizations of autonomy that world history had ever seen (the workers', peasants' and soldiers' councils). Without the defeats, semi-victories, and lessons of 1905–11, there would neither be a Russian revolution, nor a Chinese one (nor, for that matter, persistent oppositional cultures in Mexico, Turkey and Iran).

In short, even though the immediate aftermath of the global revolt was much more demoralizing in 1905, its ripple effects were arguably more revolutionary. The question, then, is whether 2011 will be a second 1848 or 1905. Will we have to wait decades for the fruits of these struggles, or is 2011 the harbinger of something to come sooner, perhaps a second 1917?

Some might ask: Why would we want a second 1917, given that the hopes invested in the first one were overblown? The council revolution of that year had spread quickly to parts of Europe, to be defeated and crushed completely in a few years. It was perhaps politically and economically immature to strive for socialism in an isolated Russia, as the resulting one-party dictatorship demonstrates. Nevertheless, the few years following 1917 showed that popular classes could organize themselves and take decisions that influence the fate of their countries and the whole world. Moreover, the capitalist West had to reorganize its political and economic structures to incorporate popular voices and demands out of fear of total annihilation by direct democracy (and then by 'communism'). Still, the leaders of the Russian councils could have served themselves and the world better if they had set more realistic goals and persistently pushed for them in the rest of the world, rather than attempting, in vain, to build socialism in an isolated and impoverished semi-capitalist country.

The first time around, the postcapitalist revolution was a tragedy. Since people are rightfully averse to farce nowadays, no mass movement will want to learn from 1917 unless we find the concepts with which to draw the proper lessons from that pivotal event.

What would it take today to build up to a second 1917 without the illusions, defeats and horrors of the first one? Neither the economic structures nor the political and ideological levels of activists and ordinary people are ready for a postcapitalist world today. The Russian leaders knew that none of this preparation was in place in 1917, either. Their solution, as one of them formulated it, was a 'permanent revolution' (or, in the words of another leader, 'uninterrupted revolution') that combined the tasks of the preparation with the revolution, of capitalist and democratic transformation with postcapitalist transformation. There was a valid insight in this endeavour: If capitalism is left on its own path, it will destroy itself and the earth, rather than preparing the world for a postcapitalist civilization. We are aware of that reality much more starkly today. For that reason, any postcapitalist transformation has to be immature. But the next logical step they took was flawed: they trusted that the process of revolution (of which the councils were the spine) and their own leadership would be sufficient to successfully combine the preparation for socialism and the revolution. This overconfidence in popular will and misleading optimism about revolutionary leadership was the kernel of the illusions of 1917. In an isolated Russia, the revolutionaries were pushed to silence first those who disagreed, then the councils and ultimately each other. The structures that weighed on them cannot be simplified into a quick formula that emphasizes the bad intentions and authoritarianism of a few bad apples. If the illusion repeats itself under favourable circumstances, so will the horrors.

But if any postcapitalist transformation has to start immaturely, what can sustain it, if not a permanent revolution? Popular energy (of the kind expressed in the Russian councils, or in the 2011 global wave's direct democratic assemblies, and the anarchistic innovations of Occupy Wall Street) and revolutionary leadership are indispensable, but not sufficient. If left to their own devices, either of these two are bound to destroy the other, and the revolutionary process along with it. A slow process of political maturation and ideological co-education (an interactive education, where intellectuals and masses are simultaneously transformed) has to accompany these. People dissatisfied with capitalism also need to build their own postcapitalist institutions (such as cooperatives and other collectivist enterprises), though never forgetting that these are not sustainable (as popular and democratic) in the long run without revolutionary interventions (and massive revolts).

Such a process – where activists and people focus on building alternative institutions, on co-education and on accumulating political experience during calmer periods, but then recursively focus on revolt against barriers that block the flowering of these institutions – could be called an intermittent or recursive revolution.

The intermittent revolution is not a permanent revolution: it is based on the realization that periods of calm are necessary for institution-building and co-education in civil society. But intermittent revolutionaries would also acknowledge, unlike reformists, the necessity of mass revolts to create and sustain organs of popular power and cultures of solidarity, and to remove the impediments that undermine alternative institutions.

Despite some family resemblances, the intermittent revolution should not be confused with an 'interstitial' strategy. This strategy is built on the idea of bringing down capitalism through building noncapitalist civil society. The interstitial strategy would not work if applied exclusively, since late capitalism has become an expert of taming noncapitalist associations. For instance, environmental protection ends up working more to the benefit of rich constituencies; enterprises that start with postcapitalist principles slide into capitalism. Erik Olin Wright,[11] though a primary proponent of interstitial transformation, points out that the workers' cooperatives of Mondragon and Brazil's participatory budget have the potential of degenerating into capitalist ventures. The Mondragon is an important case Wright discusses, as in contrast to the usually small workers' cooperatives, it is quite vast, and, as Mondragon expanded, especially overseas, it started to function like a capitalist firm. As Wright reminds, this was one of Marx's predictions about cooperatives.

The only way of sustaining these institutions as anti-capitalist would be to situate them in a wide sociopolitical network. Parts of this network would work on the 'interstitial' civil society aspect (the central nervous system of the network); parts of it would negotiate with the state and the capitalists to implement solid victories for the subordinate strata within the boundaries of capitalism (the 'reformist' right hand of the network); but other parts of it would actually struggle for revolutionary transformations (the left hand of the network). In other words, an interstitial strategy can work only if it is embedded in a revolutionary strategy.

---

11 Erik Olin Wright, *Envisioning Real Utopias*, London: Verso, 2010.

In this sense, an intermittent revolutionary path would be based on an *uneven* combination of revolutionary, interstitial and reformist strategies: although the core of the actual activities would be interstitial, the heart and mind of the combination as a whole would be revolutionary to prevent the interstitial and 'reformist' work from turning into adjustments within capitalism. To put it differently, the actual revolutionary organization against capitalism would play a secondary part in comparison to the *work* of organizing an egalitarian civil society (except during days of revolt); but it would still *lead* the core activities.

Nevertheless, we should be aware that many people who participated in the recent revolt wave are quite averse to thinking along such strategic lines or supporting movements that have such visions. Apparently, then, the self-destructive tendencies of the current Middle Eastern powerholders are likely to shape the future unless citizens break from their post-1980 (disorganized and disorganizing) habits and intervene decisively in the drama.

Developing New Hegemonic Potentials

The Turkish model, as we know it, is on its way out. The Iranian model has become a weak shadow of itself and does not promise much to the region. The fate of Tunisia is uncertain. We are heading towards a void. The role of coercion is likely to increase as the Saudi authorities start to speak more assertively, encourage sectarian paramilitary activity across the region and beyond, and Turkish leaders follow their lead.

We can no longer look at these established forces (and their local liberal and mainstream Western benefactors) as sources of consent. They are losing their potential to form a solid power bloc. The region's only true hope is the millions who have participated in the recent wave of revolt. Yet those millions can trace a new path only if they go beyond some of their current inclinations and formulations. This is easier said than done.

Citizens of the Middle East are today thinking, day in and day out, about the earthquake that shook their world. Some are engaging in new collectivist experiments on the ruins of the subsiding revolt. Others are reading about these developments, as well as about past experiences with bottom-up democracy, and trying to connect what they have witnessed with other attempts to build a better world. If the rise and fall of hegemonies in the last several decades is any guide, such localized action is necessary but not sufficient to go beyond the way things are.

How could the solidarity and freedom experienced in Tahrir, Taksim, Kasbah and Mahalla capture the imagination of broader strata in sustained ways? How could that imagination also guide the everyday conduct of ordinary citizens from different walks of life and with different levels of education? How could the seeds of Tahrir-Gezi-Mahalla grow into a full-fledged 'model' with distinct economic, political, cultural and religious dimensions? These are the questions that await answers as the region is drawn into authoritarianism and sectarian warfare.

Index

Headnote: Page numbers followed by t indicate tables.